WALT WHITMAN

Walt Whitman in carpenter's garb: an engraving used as the frontispiece of the first edition of *Leaves of Grass* in 1855.

WALT WHITMAN

Here and Now

Edited by
JOANN P. KRIEG

Prepared under the auspices of Hofstra University

Greenwood Press
Westport, Connecticut • London, England

Library of Congress Cataloging in Publication Data

Main entry under title:

Walt Whitman : here and now.

    Proceedings of a scholarly conference held at
Hofstra University.
    "Prepared under the auspices of Hofstra University."
Bibliography: p.
Includes index.
    1. Whitman, Walt, 1819-1892—Criticism and inter-
pretation—Congresses. I. Krieg, Joann P. II. Hofstra
University.
PS3238.W355   1985   811 '.3   85-922
ISBN 0-313-24895-8 (lib. bdg.)

Library of Congress Catalog Card Number: 85-922
ISBN: 0-313-24895-8

First published in 1985

Greenwood Press
A division of Congressional Information Service, Inc.
88 Post Road West, Westport, Connecticut 06881

Printed in the United States of America

The paper used in this book complies with the
Permanent Paper Standard issued by the National
Information Standards Organization (Z39.48-1984).

10 9 8 7 6 5 4 3 2 1

Contents

Preface

When Hofstra University decided to commemorate the 125th anniversary of the publication of <u>Leaves of Grass</u> with a scholarly conference it was not difficult to choose a focus. Walt Whitman has always been a contemporary, part of the "here and now" of succeeding generations of readers whom he addresses directly, assuring them, "I stop somewhere waiting for you."

America has been catching up with the Whitman who waits. Sometimes the pace slows, but at other times we seem to double our stride in the effort to more quickly close the gap between ourselves and the great figure who, like us, once set out along the nation's open road. In the century-plus that has elapsed since the first <u>Leaves of Grass</u> in 1855, America has made a passage "to more than India" that has taken us to realms of outer space Whitman knew by intuition alone. Closer to home, we find that the "forbidden voices" who once spoke only through him are forbidden no more.

Yet we still have a long way to go; for Whitman would have us know that the doing is not enough, and the achievements of here and now are not sufficient in themselves unless we are at the same time mindful that "a kelson of the creation is love." Hofstra is proud that the conference of scholars who gathered here in April 1980 seemed to hold this fact uppermost, so that in this instance fine scholarship was enhanced by faithfulness to the spirit of its subject.

A deliberate effort has been made, in compiling this volume, to retain as much as possible of the flavor of the conference; therefore, if, in some instances, the contents seem somewhat informal it is for this reason.

The proceedings as they appear here do not follow their original order of presentation. After a word of greeting from Charles Feinberg, whose generosity and graciousness have marked Whitman scholarship for many years, and a brief review of the state of Whitman scholarship in 1980 by William White, editor of the _Walt Whitman Quarterly Review_, there are two addresses. The papers are then presented in accordance with the section headings, whose devising was an editorial decision. All quotations from Whitman's poetry, unless otherwise indicated, are from the Comprehensive Reader's Edition of _Leaves of Grass_ edited by Harold W. Blodgett and Sculley Bradley (New York: New York University Press, 1965). Two papers presented at the conference, "Walt Whitman and New York," by Paul A. Marx, and "America Always Pictorial!, Whitman and Landscape Painting," by Philip Herzbrun, are not reproduced here for technical reasons. Two other papers were withdrawn by their authors.

Walt Whitman has a special significance for our university because of shared Long Island roots. Here, on his beloved Paumonok, Hofstra maintains a close relationship with the Walt Whitman Birthplace Association, and the University Center for Cultural and Intercultural Studies is extremely grateful to the Association's Board of Trustees for their cooperation in the conference. Special thanks go, too, to Marcia E. O'Brien, Director of the Nassau County Office of Cultural Development, and to the staff of the Hempstead Public Library, the Huntington Historical Society, and the Smithtown Historical Society.

The extraordinary kindness of William White must not go unmentioned. Not only did Professor White grace our conference with his presence and his introductory remarks, he came forward once again to make this volume timely by providing an updated bibliographic essay. For this and for all his endeavors within the Whitman "industry" we are most grateful.

1.
Greetings
CHARLES FEINBERG

Thank you for inviting me to say a few words to your
Walt Whitman Conference at Hofstra University. Whitman
would have enjoyed the fact that his poetry was being
discussed in Hempstead, a town that was well known to
him in his early years on Long Island. About a hundred
years ago Whitman said:

> I am destined to have an audience. There is
> very little sign of it now -- my friends are
> only a few at best, scattered here and there
> across the globe: that does not disprove me,
> does not make me doubtful: I still see the
> audience beyond: maybe in the to-morrow or
> the to-morrow of to-morrow.;1

In gathering my collection of Whitman, which
started seriously with my buying my first Whitman letter
over 65 years ago, I was helped by many who shared with
me their knowledge and interest in Walt Whitman. I am
most grateful to Anne Montgomerie Traubel, who honored
me with her friendship and bridged Whitman's generation
and mine, and told me of her reminiscences of Walt
Whitman. I am grateful, too, to the others who helped
me locate and acquire, whether one item or many, the
collection of Whitman that is now one of the treasures
of the Library of Congress.
Today this conference is a continuation of the
prophecy that Whitman's audience will never be
exhausted.
Thank you.

1. The source of this quotation remains
unidentified. [Editor's Note.]

2.
The Whitman "Industry": Introductory Remarks

WILLIAM WHITE

To say that 1979 was a boom year for the Whitman "industry" -- the production of books and articles by and about Walt Whitman -- and that there will be just as much noise in 1980 is meaningless; every year is a banner year for America's poet.

This year not only celebrates the 125th anniversary of the first (1855) edition of Leaves of Grass, which we are remembering with a supplement to the Walt Whitman Review to be called 1980: Leaves of Grass at 125, but it is also the 25th birthday of the Review itself, a remarkable record for a one-man scholarly journal. In addition, it is the 80th birthday of the Review's "angel" Charles E. Feinberg, who had so many other fine things in Whitman scholarship finer by his generosity.

To begin our overview of the current state of Whitman activities, we need to look little further than this very meeting here at Hofstra University: Walt Whitman Here and Now. Then there are the Whitman periodicals in addition to the Walt Whitman Review, which if they do not make money at least thrive in other ways: The West Hills Review: A Walt Whitman Journal, published by the Walt Whitman Birthplace Association in nearby Huntington (Vol. 1, No. 1 came out in Fall 1979); The Mickle Street Review, published by the Walt Whitman House Association, Camden, New Jersey (Vol. 1 was issued in 1979); Calamus: Walt Whitman Quarterly, International, edited by William L. Moore and published by Taibundo Ltd. of Tokyo, Japan in English (Nos. 17 and 18 were published in 1979); and the annual Walt Whitman Supplement of The Long-Islander, appearing on or about Whitman's birthday, May 31, which will consist of 1855 reviews of Leaves of Grass.

Another indication of how Whitman is doing in the marketplace may be seen in Books in Print 1979-1980, which lists no less than 71 Whitman titles, many of them reprints issued by Folcroft, Norwood, Richard West, Arden, and other such houses. Even more important than reprints are the volumes in The Collected Writings of Walt Whitman that the New York University Press has been publishing since 1961 under the general editorship of Gay Wilson Allen and Sculley Bradley. Completed are five volumes of The Correspondence, two of Prose Works 1882, the Comprehensive Reader's Edition of Leaves, and a volume of The Early Poems and the Fiction; and now we have Volume 6 of The Correspondence: A Supplement with a Composite Index, edited by Edwin Haviland Miller (1977), and three volumes of the Daybooks and Notebooks, approved by the Center for Editions of American Authors, Modern Language Association, which I have edited (1978, copyright 1977).

This year will finally see the publication in three volumes of Leaves of Grass: A Textual Variorum of the Printed Poems, edited by Sculley Bradley, Harold W. Blodgett, Arthur Golden, and myself. Further volumes in this project listed as "in preparation" are Edward F. Grier's edition of Notebooks and Unpublished Prose Manuscripts, in three volumes, and Herbert Bergman's five volumes of Journalism, in which I have had a hand. The final volume is expected to be a descriptive, full-length bibliography of just about everything Walt Whitman wrote.

As for doctoral dissertations on Whitman, about ten or a dozen a year seems the average, if we may judge by those that appear in Dissertation Abstracts International. Comparisons of Whitman with other poets are among the topics, such as Whitman, Wallace Stevens, and W. S. Merwin (Thomas Beall Byers, Iowa); Whitman and Emily Dickinson (Charlotte Josephine Downey, Brown); Jalal al-Din Rumi and Whitman (Ghulam Muhammad Fayez, Arizona); and Whitman, Hart Crane, and Denise Levertov (Joan Frances Hallisey, Brown).

Among recent books about Whitman, by far the most interesting and valuable is by the always reliable and thought-provoking James E. Miller, Jr., who wrote The American Quest for a Supreme Fiction: Whitman's Legacy in the Personal Epic (Chicago: University of Chicago Press, 1979). Two other books are not entirely devoted to Whitman but include chapters about him: Robert K. Martin's The Homosexual Tradition in American Poetry (Austin: University of Texas Press, 1979); and Karl Keller's The Only Kangaroo among the Beauty: Emily Dickinson and America (Baltimore: The Johns Hopkins University Press, 1979), "The Sweet Wolf Within: Emily Dickinson and Walt Whitman," pages 251-93.

Pulitzer Prize winner Justin Kaplan (for his book on Mark Twain) is writing a biography of Whitman expected later this year. Mr. Kaplan writes about his problems in biography in Marc Pachter's Telling Lives: The Biographer's Art (Washington, D.C.: New Republic Book/National Portrait Gallery, 1979), pages 17-55, and in Daniel Aaron's Studies in Biography (Cambridge, Mass.: Harvard University Press, 1978), pages 1-8. The University of Illinois Press has announced that it will be publishing Harold Aspiz's Walt Whitman and the Body Beautiful, and Betsy Erkilla, who has written articles on the subject in the Walt Whitman Review, has had her book, Walt Whitman among the French, accepted by the Princeton University Press.

Last year, when I was a visiting professor at the University of Southern California, I read in manuscript the dissertation of Scott Giantvalley. It has been accepted for publication by G. K. Hall of Boston and is certain to be an extremely useful work. Entitled Walt Whitman, 1838-1939: A Reference Guide, it is an annotated list of 4,886 books, chapters in books, and articles in periodicals about Whitman for 102 years. In addition, the author tells me that it is expected that Donald D. Kummings' supplement to his list, which will cover the period from 1940 to 1975, will also be published by G. K. Hall. Anyone doing research on Whitman will be deeply indebted to Mr. Giantvalley and Mr. Kummings for these long-awaited compilations.

Let us now turn to statistics, for whatever such facts and figures are worth in scholarly areas of endeavor. By this I mean, what does the 1979 MLA International Bibliography tell us about Walt Whitman in comparison with other nineteenth-century American authors? Well, Whitman has 68 entries -- articles, chapters, dissertations, and books. More "popular" than Whitman are Nathaniel Hawthorne (112 entries), Herman Melville (110), and Henry James (107), while Mark Twain (65), Henry David Thoreau (61), Edgar Allan Poe (58), Emily Dickinson (54), and Ralph Waldo Emerson (43) have fewer. For the same period, the Modern Humanities Research Association's Annual Bibliography of English Language and Literature for 1979 has these statistics for nineteenth-century American writers: James, 102; Melville, 75; Whitman, 62; Thoreau, 57; Hawthorne, 52; Twain, 51; Poe, 41; Emily Dickinson, 38; and Emerson, 34. Because it has a wider scope than either the MLA or the MHRA lists, the "Walt Whitman: A Current Bibliography" compilation in the Walt Whitman Review has 100 items dated 1979. So, no matter whose figures you look at, Whitman is certainly alive and well, and living in the hearts of scholars and researchers in America and abroad, for the articles and books are from Japan,

India, China, Canada, Germany, the Soviet Union,
England, and Spain, as well as America.

I'd like to end this introduction to the Hofstra
Walt Whitman Conference on an offbeat note. Charles
Hamilton of the Hamilton Galleries, an authority on
autographs and handwriting, has written a fascinating
book, Great Forgers and Famous Fakes: The Manuscript
Forgers of America and How They Duped the Experts (New
York: Crown Publishers, 1980). Among the forgers is
"The Dapper Baron of Fakedom: Charles Weisberg" (pp.
62-65), whose fake Whitman letter, dated "Camden, New
Jersey, April 3, 1891," is reproduced on page 65; and
another chapter, "Wizard of the Pen: Joseph Cosey" (pp.
88-120), deals with a forger, of whom Charles Feinberg
has had much to say, who manufactured a "Comanche"
document signed by "Indian agent" Walt Whitman (see p.
113, where it is reproduced). It is described as a
bizarre fake that was bought from Cosey by Alfred F.
Goldsmith, a rare book dealer who also was the
co-author, with Carolyn Wells, of A Concise Bibliography
of the Works of Walt Whitman (Boston and New York:
Houghton Mifflin, 1922). Even the best sometimes get
snookered.

Part I

Biographers and Critics

3.
Whitman and the Biographers
JUSTIN KAPLAN

"And so will some one when I am dead and gone write my
life?" Walt Whitman asked in a poem of 1867, "When I
Read the Book,"

> As if any man really knew aught of my life,
> As if you, O cunning Soul, did not keep your
>   secret well!

(el. 4-5)

In these and in his other reflections on the problems of
biography Whitman appears to be suggesting that no
ultimately true or authoritative version of a life is
possible. Conscious resistances, evasions, and
ambiguities aside, by invoking his "cunning Soul" he
also suggests that only a tiny part of even our own
internal lives and psychological continua is available
to us. Given such challenges, it is not surprising that
Whitman biography, like the literature about any figure
of comparable magnitude and achievement, remains an open
road.

Nominally at least, Whitman biography goes back
even farther in time than Whitman's emergence as a
poet. The 125th anniversary of Leaves of Grass is also
the 130th anniversary of this note from James Brenton's
collection of prose and poetry by "practical printers,"
Voices from the Press.

Delivered as an address at the opening of the conference
not as a scholarly paper. The author has not identified
his sources, though some have been editorial additions.

Whitman, Walter, was born at West Hills, in
the town of Huntington, L.I. At the age of
thirteen he was placed an apprentice to the
printing business in the office of the
'Patriot,' a weekly newspaper then published
in Brooklyn. The establishment passing into
other hands, he found himself, at the age of
sixteen, teaching school on Long Island. He
continued in this occupation three or four
years, intermitted only by establishing the
'Long Islander,' at Huntington, L.I., which he
sold out at the end of the first year. While
teaching a school near Jamaica, he wrote a
sketch entitled 'Death in a School Room,' for
the purpose of making odious the use of the
rod in the school. It was published
originally in the 'Democratic Review,' and was
very popular. Mr. W.'s literary career
commenced with sketches of that character.
. . . Mr. W. is an ardent politician of the
radical democratic school, and lately
established the 'Daily Freeman,' in Brooklyn,
to promulgate his favorite 'Free Soil' and
other reformatory doctrines.;1

The picture changed, of course, when Whitman in
1855 introduced into world literature

. . . an American, one of the roughs, a
kosmos, Disorderly, fleshy and sensual . . .
eating drinking and breeding.
("Song of Myself," 497-98 of the original version.)

He had set out to express, in appropriately
open-frontiered verse, the personality of his nation and
his century, but it was easier for readers to believe
that Leaves of Grass was personal, specific, and
truth-bound testimony. The tender, visionary, and
always unrequited poet was confounded with the sexual
braggart and priapic mystagogue of his poetry, and in
the ensuing furor Whitman biography was launched on a
polemic course.

The Whitman of William Douglas O'Connor's The Good
Gray Poet was larger than life size, a sage, martyr, and
redeemer fit to stand with Aeschylus, Socrates, and
Christ. A master of fleshcreeping invective and verbal
overkill, O'Connor, in Whitman's description, was "a
born artillerist," "a battleship firing both sides fore
and aft" and, it might be added, often suffering
frightful explosions in its own powder magazines.
Although he shied away from O'Connor's excesses of zeal,
John Burroughs, in his Notes on Walt Whitman as Poet and
Person (1867), was guided by the same partisan spirit.

His book contained perceptive discussions of Whitman's
work, but it was also a campaign biography of a man
nominated and vigorously running for the office of
American bard. Whitman, as we know, was not altogether
passive in sitting for these two portraits, and his role
in Dr. Richard Maurice Bucke's biographical study,
published in 1883, was that of an active although
unacknowledged collaborator. Bucke's biography depicted
Whitman as a Titan whose work provided "a picture of the
world from the standpoint of the highest moral elevation
yet reached."

With mingled pleasure and resignation, during the
decade before his death Whitman accepted the role of
guru, founder of an apostolic church whose communicants
celebrated his birthdays with eucharistic banquets.
Some cultists believed that in years to come his
grotesquely expensive granite burial house in Harleigh
Cemetery would be a holy place like the Kaaba at Mecca.
Unlovely Camden, "the refuge of those who were in doubt,
debt, or despair," as Bliss Perry wrote, "was now to
have its _vates sacer_, with the band of disciples, the
travel-stained pilgrims, and ultimately the famous
tomb. A lucky town, therefore, however commonplace.";2

Perry's _Walt Whitman_, published in 1906, came along
at a turning point in the poet's official standing.
"American Men of Letters," the title of the notable
series for which Perry's book was commissioned, hardly
suggested the close company Whitman had kept during his
lifetime, and probably Whitman would not have wanted it
otherwise. "I do not value literature as a profession,"
he remarked to Horace Traubel. "I feel about literature
what Grant did about war. He hated war. I hate
literature. I am not a literary West Pointer.";3 Perry
was above all a literary West Pointer. In the course of
a full life -- he died in 1954 in his mid-nineties --
Perry wrote short stories, biography and memoirs,
novels, essays, and criticism; taught literature at
Williams, Princeton, and Harvard; and was an early
member of the American Academy of Arts and Letters. For
ten years he served as editor of the _Atlantic Monthly_
and, as such, was the apostolic successor of James
Russell Lowell, William Dean Howells, and Thomas Bailey
Aldrich, all of whom had taken a distinctly negative
view of Whitman. Perry, however, had long been a
passionate admirer of _Leaves of Grass_, and his book,
somewhat like the Englishman Henry Bryan Binns' study
(1905), was in itself a turning point in biographical
understanding and purpose. It introduced into Whitman
biography what Bible scholars used to call the Higher
Criticism. Perry applied to the gospel Whitman had
transmitted to O'Connor, Bucke, Traubel, and William
Sloane Kennedy the historical and scientific methods
found useful in the study of mere literary lives.

Perry did not do quite the amount of fieldwork and primary research that Binns did. On the other hand, he did not, like Binns, spin out an alluring but unlikely story about Whitman's New Orleans romance with a "woman of a higher social rank than his own" who became the mother of his children. Perry's book is evenhanded and reasonably historical and, for all its reservations about Whitman's character and conduct, both affectionate and enlightening. Perry places Whitman's work in the context of post-romanticism and "steady progress towards a greater freedom in the whole field of aesthetic sympathy"; he reminds the reader of 1906 that "a generation trained to the enjoyment of Monet's landscapes, Rodin's sculptures, and the music of Richard Strauss will not be repelled from Whitman because he wrote in an unfamiliar form." He rejects O'Connor's "Sir Galahad myth" and Bucke's "'Superman' myth" and, anticipating the approach of modern biographies of Whitman, concludes that we have in the place of these myths "something very much better; a man earthy, incoherent, arrogant, but elemental and alive.";4

Perry's book marks the end of discipular biography. He enjoyed the confidence of members of Whitman's intimate circle, especially John Burroughs, and he drew on their recollections and their papers. The extent to which he nonetheless managed to preserve his independence and freedom of spirit is shown by the responses of Traubel and "other admirers of Whitman — idolaters all," as Perry said, "who resented as slander some statements in my biography." The disciples reacted like a collective widow to Perry's depiction of Whitman as a literary egotist who was on occasion petulant and self-pitying, whose "perception of American life as a whole" was relatively narrow, and who had "altogether too many shrines. . . . . he dropped on his knees anywhere, before stick or stone, flesh or spirit, and swore that each in turn was divine." In retrospect Perry relished the "vulgar comfort" he had derived from realizing that the more bitterly the "Whitmaniacs" (as he called them) attacked and abused his book, "the better it sold."

Perry had been straitlaced, even purblind, on the subject of what he regarded as "sins against chastity." By and large it has been the Europeans, following the aggressively inquiring lead of John Addington Symonds and Edward Carpenter, who have been forthright in their speculations in this area, specifically about Whitman's homosexuality. Until recently American writers have preferred not to acknowledge this even as a possibility. Says Robert K. Martin, "I can think of no parallel example of the willful distortion of meaning and the willful misreading of a poet in order to suit critics' own social or moral prejudices.";5 Whitman's biography,

like Whitman himself, who confessed that "maybe I do not
know all my meanings," testifies to the supreme power of
the faculty of denial.

The late Emory Holloway, a dedicated, vigorous, and
pioneering scholar victimized in the end by his own
preconceptions, presents us with a cautionary example of
denial in action. Holloway's discovery in 1920 of the
original version of "Once I Pass'd through a Populous
City" -- it referred to a man instead of a woman --
eliminated one of the foundations of Binns' New Orleans
romance. Since lyric poems are events in themselves and
not necessarily "evidence" of events, Binns' conjecture
was shaky enough to begin with. But in the face of what
should have been a terminal setback, as late as 1960,
like the bereft whaling ship Rachel at the end of Moby
Dick, Holloway was still deviously cruising in search of
Whitman's children and their Creole mothers.

Fortunately, the climate of discussion has
changed. The writing of Whitman biography is no longer
an exercise in moralism and forensics. One does not
have to "prove" that Whitman was straight or "defend"
him against the "charge" that he was not. The
biographer's job is to create a sensitive, candid, and
empathetic reliving of Whitman's life. He must give
Whitman the freedom Whitman may never have enjoyed while
alive to pursue his recognition that love, of whatever
sort, was the root of roots. At the same time the
biographer must admit that it is often difficult or
impossible to say for a certainty what, if anything,
particular people in less nakedly confessional times
than ours actually "did." Despite the famous amorous
achings and urges that reminded D. H. Lawrence of a
steam engine, the area of Whitman's sexual activities,
as opposed to his fantasies, remains closed to us. In
the absence of hard information what counts is the way
Whitman defined himself through his poetry; but if you
think of the Whitman of the Calamus cycle as a
homosexual liberator you must also consider this
possibility: he may have been like Moses, who also
announced a new dispensation but still did not cross
over into the promised land.

In the three-quarters of a century since Perry's
book, about three dozen biographies or biographical
interpretations of appreciable value have appeared.
Inevitably, they represent changing modes of
understanding and approach, different gestalts and
focusses of projection on the part of their authors, and
this, of course, is as it must be. Some of these
studies are highly romantic, some ideologically
tendentious in one way or another, as suggested by these
titles and subtitles: Poet of Democracy, Free and
Lonesome Heart, Builder for America, American Giant. In
general these books bring an increasing degree of

sophistication and respect to discussions of Whitman's originality and technique; he is characterized as a deliberate craftsman and a conscious artist with more complex antecedents, models, and backgrounds than he and the disciples had been willing to acknowledge. (Even so, as late as 1934, a scholar writing for the journal American Literature felt that he had to open with the defensive statement, "The average layman will laugh at the idea of accounting Whitman an artist.") Newton Arvin's Whitman, published in 1938, gave a superb account of the literary and intellectual backgrounds of Leaves of Grass; but, reflecting a decade of writers on the left, Arvin's book made Whitman out to be a sort of archetypal socialist, even though Whitman in later years was conspicuously skeptical about politics and across-the-board solutions of any sort. Henry Seidel Canby's Walt Whitman, An American, published two years after Pearl Harbor, depicted him as "the symbolic man of the nineteenth century" and also as a democratic spokesman who remained "intelligible and dynamic" for a generation fighting a war against totalitarianism.

Meanwhile, psychoanalytic contemporaries of Arvin and Canby were making a hash of Whitman. They read "Song of Myself" as if it were the transcript of several hours of free association from the couch; they also failed to understand that the theory of neurosis does not offer an adequate accounting of creativity or that creativity, as Whitman knew, was a miracle and a force in itself and had to be respected as such. One feels much more kindly disposed toward two recent psychoanalytically oriented studies by Edwin Haviland Miller and Stephen A. Black, both of whom are literary scholars.

With Gay Wilson Allen's The Solitary Singer, first published in 1955, the centennial of Leaves of Grass, we arrive at the full application of disciplined, systematic biographical scholarship and critical understanding to an extremely recalcitrant subject. Allen's book is indispensable, and the same may be said of Miller's edition of the correspondence; his notes and commentary are a biographical resource of the first order of importance. But after more than a century of biographical inquiry we still have only the most approximate notion of how and why Walter Whitman, printer, schoolteacher, editor, fiction writer, and building contractor, a shadowy figure in most accounts, untamed, untranslatable, projected his barbaric yawp over the roofs of the world. This, of course, is the heart of his mystery.

Unlike the novelist, who is in the habit of making up plots, the biographer (as Diane Johnson has suggested) must extract the plot of a life already lived from a shapeless mass of historical materials. The

internal and external plots the biographer extracts may
be different from one another, contrapuntal. This
exercise in plotting and the management of plot demands
from the biographer the same sustained imaginative
effort we expect from the novelist. The aim of literary
biography, as I understand it, is to create a sense of
the density and texture of another existence; to invest
facts, events, and conjectures with a dimension of
symbolic meaning and action -- all of this leading to a
narrative which, if it works, will have a life of its
own and also be "true to life." To do this one may have
to depart from chronology and make a distinction between
the shape of the life as lived and the shape of the life
as written. With Whitman it appeared to me that such a
wrenching is dictated by the balance of the historical
materials and the nature of his experience.

     Of the approximately 3,000 letters in Professor
Miller's edition of the correspondence, only 12 predate
the first publication of Leaves of Grass in 1855; to put
it another way, we have only 12 letters to show from the
entire first half of Whitman's life. A few of these
letters were written by or with the poet's brother Jeff;
almost all of the others are of a routine business or
editorial nature; with the exception of a remarkable
letter to Senator John Parker Hale, none of them
directly illuminates the crucial period between 1852 and
1855, when we may imagine Whitman's miracle was
happening. The other documentary evidence for this
period, including Whitman's manuscripts and notebooks,
is at best fragmentary.

     In contrast, Whitman's later years, especially his
last decade, which was relatively barren of achievement,
appear almost to be overdocumented in letters, daybooks,
interviews, public statements, notes kept by visitors
and members of the Camden circle, transcripts of
speeches and conversations. With apparent fidelity and
in fanatical detail Horace Traubel recorded the flow of
Whitman's talk, recollections, associations, bodily
complaints, and mental meanderings. The five volumes so
far published of Traubel's With Walt Whitman in Camden
cover only a brief period between March 1888 and
September 1889; for the remaining two and a half years
of Whitman's life there is at least as much Traubel
material still in manuscript. For the biographer
writing Whitman's life in the usual linear way, from
birth on, all this material can be dismaying in its
quantity, even an obstacle to the completion of a story
that has already run on too long. The writer smells the
stable and gallops through Whitman's last ten years.

     By its very nature the story of that decade tends
to be the story of a disappearing act, not a compelling
pattern for narrative. The man and the bones of his
life and personality go into the rendering vat and are

steamily absorbed into a sweet-smelling colloidal
suspension of disbelief and borax. The incomparable
poet gives way to the guru of Mickle Street, agent of
"cosmic consciousness" and "Brahmic splendor." "Do you
suppose," William Sloane Kennedy asked in all
seriousness, that "in a thousand years from now people
will be celebrating the birth of Walt Whitman as they
are now the birth of Christ?";6 The ultimate effect of
this sort of cultism, as James Huneker said, was that
its "slush, hash, obscurity, morbid eroticism,
vulgarity, and preposterous mouthings well-nigh spoil
one's taste for what is really great in Leaves of
Grass.";7

This over-plus of documentation, along with the
cult phenomenon in itself, can serve different purposes
altogether if one begins at the end instead of ending
with it. The record left by Traubel, for example,
brings us directly into Whitman's presence and renders
with enormous credibility the sound, rhythm, and style
of his informal discourse, which was earthier, funnier,
and more acerb than generally supposed. (John Burroughs
said that as he read With Walt Whitman in Camden he
could almost hear his old friend breathe.) The first
section of my Walt Whitman deals with the
well-documented last decade of the life. The famous
horse-and-buggy fund, although brought to a successful
conclusion in 1885, dramatizes Whitman's isolation as
well as the vagaries of literary fame. He is sometimes
depressed and despondent; these moods illuminate, by
contrast, the extraordinary spirit that had made him
willing in 1855 to gamble all on the proposition, "The
proof of a poet is that his country absorbs him as
affectionately as he has absorbed it." For the most
part the low moods of his final years give way to a
radiance, serenity, and generosity of spirit that set
Whitman apart from most of the other major American
writers as their careers drew to a close. By
indirections, random links, discriminated occasions
invoking "the costless average, divine, original
concrete," Whitman had suggested in Specimen Days how
immense creativity, perturbations, loneliness, the
bustle of the cities, and the suffering of the Civil War
had their own enclosing significance and were also paths
to stillness and health at Timber Creek.

With the onset of his final illness the members of
his inner circle drew themselves closely about him.
Protective, possessive, and a little stifling, a saving
remnant, they became his chief audience and he their
dependent and captive. He meditates on mysteries of
self and creation, on how Leaves of Grass came to be --
he likens his book to a great modern city, or an eldest
daughter, or something found in nature, a tree with many
growth rings. He churns through his archive and recalls

cities, rivers, people he has known, the turning points of his life. He teases Horace Traubel with the promise that someday soon, "not yet," he will unravel a great mystery. He examines photographs of himself, tirelessly seeking in them, and in painting and sculpture, physical and psychological correlatives for the poise, equanimity, and amplitude he has come to value in his work. He discourses on events and issues of the day and sees in the America of Grover Cleveland and Benjamin Harrison a falling off from the democratic hopes of the prewar period. But he still believes that "the crowning growth of the United States is to be spiritual and heroic," that "the strongest and sweetest songs yet remain to be sung." Hearing his songs and considering his life now, we must ask ourselves whether the United States is still believed to be the light of the world and to what extent Whitman's prophetic creed remains valid for us. But at the same time, and avoiding the distortions of "presentism" and its categories of "racist" and "imperialist," we must accept Whitman's own manifest destiny.

For the biographer the rendered voice, personality, and preoccupations of Whitman in old age can be a way of entering the remoter past. The old Whitman lends flesh and conviction to what, in the absence of a great deal of information, will have to be a partially speculative reconstruction of the young Whitman and the emerging poet, and perhaps the action or event in the main narrative of his life thereby acquires a richer texture of meaning and overtone. In this perspective Whitman's early literary prose, mainly fiction and didactic essays, takes on new significance. This is a sizable body of work which the biographers have scanted and which Whitman himself, in later years, dismissed as irrelevant. He said that it had come from the surface of his mind only and therefore had little or nothing to do with the unconscious "simmering" that preceded Leaves of Grass. But the early prose is part of the "long foreground" Emerson knew was there, and even the roughest inventory of theme and metaphor reveals a pattern of continuity, concern, and development pointing in the direction of Whitman's mature poetry. The young writer was preoccupied with the terror of death, the obliteration of identity, the sanctity of sepulture, the great natural cycle of growth, decay, and renewal. The grass is already "the long uncut hair of graves"; the "beautiful gigantic swimmer" of "The Sleepers" swims through the early prose, where we also meet the "dark mother" of the great elegy for Lincoln; the series title "Sun-Down Papers" foreshadows "Sun-Down Poem," as "Crossing Brooklyn Ferry" was originally called. And there are any number of other cues and rehearsals which allow the biographer to recount the "miracle" of Leaves of Grass with increased precision.

Phrenology and the other pseudosciences of
Whitman's day, hydropathy and animal magnetism among
them, also demand new understanding from the biographer,
who must suspend his historical hindsight in order to
experience them as Whitman did: as ways of permitting
him to become the man and the poet he wanted to be.
Existentially, it scarcely matters that he may have
arrived at the right conclusions by reasoning from the
wrong data. In the phrenological cabinet of Fowler &
Wells he entered a wonderland of funhouse mirrors, but
he saw reflected in them the lineaments of "Walt
Whitman, an American, one of the roughs, a kosmos," "a
man cohered out of tumult and chaos." "You see I am
very old fashioned," he told Horace Traubel. "I
probably have not got by the phrenology stage yet.";8
Again, the aged Whitman is saying something
revealing about the young poet when he remarks to
Traubel, "I think Swedenborg was right when he said
there was a close connection -- a very close connection
-- between the state we call religious ecstasy and the
desire to copulate. I find Swedenborg confirmed in all
my experience. It is a peculiar discovery.";9 He was
not a mystic, as Bucke sometimes tried to make him out
to be. He was the beneficiary or recipient of certain
experiences of illumination shared by countless numbers
of quite ordinary people, but he had learned how to
invite these experiences, to understand their rhythm of
tumescence and detumescence, and to prolong their
"afterglow." He said that the poet was to be the priest
of modern society; perhaps we should think of Whitman
the poet as a shaman, in Mircea Eliade's phrase a master
of "the techniques of ecstasy."
Whitman's preparations for his death recapitulate
many of the themes of his life. On a 20-by-30-foot
plot, gift of the Harleigh Cemetery Association, the
former housebuilder ordered the construction of his
tomb, "a plain massive stone temple" of unpolished
Quincy granite. He regularly had himself driven out to
Harleigh to oversee its progress and took pride in it as
a celebration of personality, like his book. He
encouraged reporters to write about the tomb, sent
photographs to his friends, and gave happy thought to
how it would look in the years to come, reclusive and
secure in its wooded hillside, half-hidden among vines,
shrubs, creepers, and mature trees. He enjoyed his
reviews. The cemetery superintendent told him that many
visitors had expressed their admiration for the burial
house and that a certain old army captain who had
travelled a great deal pronounced it the best he ever
saw.
"Whenever he gets a little flutter of hope that he
may live longer," Traubel complained, "he seems to start
in at once to husband what money he has so he may not

get stranded. His economies last a day or two. Then he lets himself go again.";10 Whitman let himself go in October 1890, a year and a half before he died, when he signed a contract that obligated him to pay $4,000 for his mausoleum, more than twice what his house and lot in Mickle Street had cost. "I do not complain," he told Bucke, who, like Traubel and some of the others, made no secret of the fact that they considered this expenditure outrageous, the contract a "swindle," and the tomb a "foolishness or freak," a "false step" of Whitman's declining years. Said his old friend John Townsend Trowbridge, "That such a man should have cared about his tomb, or have hoarded money for it, when he was living on the bounty of others, is something heart-sickening.";11

"My foothold is tenoned and mortised in granite," Whitman had declared in the 1855 Leaves. "I laugh at what you call dissolution." ("Song of Myself," pp. 108-09) Built according to his designs and specifications, the granite burial house -- "the rudest most undress'd structure . . . since Egypt, perhaps the cave dwellers" -- was also tenoned and mortised, and it was guarded by an iron gate with a massive bronze lock (the granite door he originally called for proved to be too heavy to hang). Some of the blocks weighed eight or ten tons; the roof was a foot and a half thick. The vault, built deep into the hillside, was faced with marble and tile and contained eight burial spaces. As he told his sister Hannah, he planned "to gather the remains of our dear father and mother and have them buried here in the tomb I have built for myself.";12 After his death his parents were moved there from graves in Brooklyn and Camden, and in time the burial house also held Hannah's coffin and those of his brothers Eddy and George, George's wife Louisa, and their infant son. In death Whitman reunited his scattered family under his granite roof and also, in a lasting assertion of self, merged their identities into his; the pediment of his mausoleum bears only one name, "Walt Whitman," carved in high relief. For a while, during construction, his name had a date below it, "May 31, 1890," the stonemasons having inserted it under the grotesque misapprehension that the tomb was a birthday present from Whitman's friends when he turned 71 (the masons might as well have added a cartouche of ribbons and candles). Whitman ordered the date chipped off -- "an improvement." The deletion left his name standing oddly high of visual center.

Something more fundamental than vanity in old age had led Whitman to build his extravagance, completed at just about the same time as the "Death-Bed" edition of Leaves of Grass. "Faulty as it is," he said of his book in an announcement he prepared for the New York Herald, it is "by far his special and entire self-chosen poetic utterance.";13

Whitman's tomb, too, was a special and self-chosen utterance. As a boy he had been enthralled by a knowledge of death that with time became more compelling even than the knowledge of sex. He grew up near the neglected burial grounds of his forebears on Long Island -- "depress'd mounds, crumbled and broken stones, cover'd with moss." In Brooklyn and Manhattan he saw the graves of soldiers of the Revolution, "the Sacred Army," dug up to make way for shops and dwellings. His heroes Thomas Paine and the Quaker preacher Elias Hicks had not remained safe in the earth; Swedenborg's skull was stolen from the grave; for 26 years after Poe's death his grave remained unmarked; the unburied dead of the Civil War, "the strayed dead," strewed the fields and valleys and woods of the South; in 1876, the Centennial year of the Republic, Abraham Lincoln's tomb at Springfield was violated -- the grave robbers were about to break into the inner lead casket when they were caught; two years later the body of Alexander T. Stewart, the New York merchant prince, was stolen and held for ransom. But even in Whitman's earliest work the violated or neglected grave had become a constitutive metaphor, and this was a decade before the poet of Leaves of Grass celebrated the earth as a vast compost heap and life as the rich leavings of many deaths.

> I bequeath myself to the dirt to grow from the
>   grass I love
> If you want me again look for me under your
>   boot-soles.
>
> ("Song of Myself," 1339-40)

The old Whitman demanded more pharaonic arrangements. He built himself a burial house that was stark, elemental, and secure, declaring, without inscriptions or symbols of any sort, that he had seen yesterday and knew tomorrow. Like his book, Whitman in the tomb was "a candidate for the future." It would require an earthquake and an angel of the Lord, and perhaps Whitman's biographers as well, in their way, to roll back the stone from his door.

NOTES

1. James Brenton, Voices from the Press, A Collection of Sketches, Essays, and Poems by Practical Printers (New York: C. B. Norton, 1850).
2. Bliss Perry, Walt Whitman, His Life and Work (Boston: Houghton Mifflin, 1906), p. 214.

3.   Horace Traubel, With Walt Whitman in Camden, vol. 1 (New York: Rowman and Littlefield, 1961), p. 58.
4.   Perry, pp. 282, 282-83, 291.
5.   Robert K. Martin, The Homosexual Tradition in American Poetry (Austin: University of Texas Press, 1979), p. 6.
6.   The Correspondence, The Collected Writings of Walt Whitman, vol. 5, ed. Edwin Haviland Miller (New York: New York University Press, 1969), p. 140n.
7.   Quoted in Larzer Ziff, The American 1890s (New York: Viking Press, 1966), p. 14.
8.   Traubel, With Walt Whitman in Camden, vol. 1, p. 385.
9.   Traubel, With Walt Whitman in Camden, vol. 5, p. 376.
10.   Traubel, With Walt Whitman in Camden, vol. 4, p. 30.
11.   Quoted in R. A. Coleman, "Trowbridge and Whitman," PMLA, 63 (March 1948): 269.
12.   The Correspondence, vol. 5, p. 240.
13.   Ibid., p. 275n.

4.

The Critical Heritage: "Hot Little Prophets" and Johnnies-Come-Lately

MILTON HINDUS

Some time ago a friend in London sent me a copy of Robert Ingersoll's <u>Address at the Funeral of Walt Whitman</u>, which had been printed in Berkeley on the occasion of our Bicentennial in 1976. Shortly afterwards someone else asked me how it had come about that Ingersoll was asked to speak at Whitman's funeral. This led me to refresh my memory of a passage in Gay Wilson Allen's <u>The Solitary Singer</u>:

> The Harneds gave a birthday party for Whitman in their home (in 1888), and he enjoyed it immensely. Two or three days later he was still feeling exhilarated and drove his horse later than usual. Before returning home he rode down to the river and sat for some time at the edge of the water, enjoying the sunset and late spring air. But the weather was cooler than he realized and that night he suffered another stroke. . . . Dr. Bucke and Thomas Harned were especially concerned for fear the poet had not made a will -- they were particularly anxious about his literary estate -- and on June 9, accompanied by Donaldson, they called on him to persuade him to attend to this matter. But Walt was in no hurry, and they mercifully desisted. However, Dr. Bucke telegraphed J. H. Johnston, on vacation in Saratoga Springs, that Walt was dying and asked him to see if Robert G. Ingersoll, the great freethinking orator, would speak at the funeral. Ingersoll happened to be at Saratoga

> Springs also, but he refused Dr. Bucke's
> request because at the time he had a low
> opinion of Leaves of Grass, though he admitted
> to Johnston that he had never carefully read
> the book. Johnston made him promise to do so,
> and the result was that Whitman soon afterward
> gained another enthusiastic friend.;1

Quite unexpectedly, Whitman survived for almost four
years, until March 1892, and these were harvest years so
far as reputation was concerned. They were the years
during which Horace Traubel was making one of the
greatest and most interesting records of a human being
in the language. In these records we come across many
expressions of esteem by Whitman for Ingersoll's talents
and for his courage in challenging conformist
religiosity in America and the assumptions of Christian
fundamentalism everywhere. The two men did not meet
until May 31, 1890, at the celebration of Whitman's 71st
birthday in Philadelphia. They were not of the same
opinion about immortality and said so frankly, but they
were not disappointed in each other, and there was an
unaffected cordiality and warmth of human feeling
between them. The following October, Ingersoll
delivered a benefit lecture on Whitman entitled "Liberty
in Literature" in the Horticultural Hall in
Philadelphia. More than 1,800 people attended, and $870
were collected and turned over to the poet. Whitman
himself sat on the platform and thanked Ingersoll when
he had done speaking. The latter, in turn, "handed him
the lecture neatly printed and bound.";2 It was the
last time Ingersoll was to see Whitman until the funeral
some 17 months later.
      According to a biographer of Ingersoll, Leaves of
Grass was his favorite American work, and he had gotten
to know it first in the 1860s. This does not
necessarily contradict Allen's statement that he had not
really studied it closely until the late 1880s.
"Liberty in Literature" is not all hyperbole or flattery
of the subject who was listening to it. Ingersoll
discovered "a touch of chaos" in Leaves of Grass. But
could it be otherwise in one who was breaking up old
forms and creating new ones? Besides, said Ingersoll,
in even the greatest books (Shakespeare as well as
Whitman) "there are many things that I neither approve
nor believe -- but in all books you find a mingling of
wisdom and foolishness, of prophecies and mistakes -- in
other words, among the excellences there will be
defects.";3 It is tolerably clear that Ingersoll was
nobody's man but his own, and it is equally clear that
Whitman, from his talks with Traubel, would not have had
it otherwise. He did not like stooges or yes-men. If
Ingersoll, as Allen indicates, came to love Whitman's

poetry "on second sight" rather than on first sight, I
for one should find that sympathetic, because my own
most durable enthusiasms (including my enthusiasm for
Whitman) came to me only "on second sight."

Ingersoll's appreciation of Whitman's poetry is
reflective and discriminating. That is shown by the
excellence of his choice of illustrative quotations. I
find it interesting that one of his most persuasive
exhibits in "Liberty in Literature" in 1890 should
coincide with a quotation chosen by Malcolm Cowley 65
years later when asked to speak in 1955 at Brandeis
University to celebrate the centenary of Leaves of
Grass. It is the beautiful section from "To Think of
Time," describing a stage-driver's funeral:

> Cold dash of waves at the ferry-wharf, posh
>   and ice in the river, half-frozen mud in
>   the streets,
> A gray discouraged sky overhead, the short
>   last daylight of December,
> A hearse and stages, the funeral of an old
>   Broadway stage-driver, the cortege mostly
>   drivers,
> Steady the trot to the cemetery, duly rattles
>   the death-bell,
> The gate is pass'd, the new-dug grave is
>   halted at, the living alight, the hearse
>   uncloses,
> The coffin is pass'd out, lower'd and settled,
>   the whip is laid on the coffin, the earth
>   is swiftly shovel'd in,
> The mound above is flatted with the spades --
>   silence,
> A minute -- no one moves or speaks -- it is
>   done,
> He is decently put away -- is there anything
>   more?
> He was a good fellow, free-mouthed,
>   quick-temper'd, not bad-looking,
> Ready with life or death for a friend, fond of
>   women, gambled, ate hearty, drank hearty,
> Had known what it was to be flush, grew
>   low-spirited toward the last, sicken'd,
>   was helped by a contribution,
> Died, aged forty-one years -- and that was his
>   funeral.

Only one who understood Whitman deeply would have chosen
these 13 lines. There were no anthologies to guide
Ingersoll in 1890. Besides, lines like these always
seem to escape anthologists, even later. One
understands, reading them, how literally he must have
meant his own moving farewell to Whitman in 1892: "Long

after we are dead the brave words he has spoken will
sound like trumpets to the living. . . . And so I lay
this little wreath upon this great man's tomb. I loved
him living, and I love him still.";4

I dwell on Ingersoll as a representative of a
generation that chose to honor Whitman while he was
still alive. Such early enthusiasts are often a source
of embarrassment to latecomers. Even in Whitman's time,
Algernon Charles Swinburne, who had recanted his early
recognition of Whitman, scorned them as "Whitmaniacs."
Afterwards, Bliss Perry spoke scathingly of "hot little
prophets." And Paul Elmer More assured readers of his
Shelburne Essays that Whitman might yet prove to be
acceptable, but one "must begin by forgetting his
disciples.";5 Even Gay Wilson Allen, while expressing
indebtedness to Traubel, also thought it necessary to
describe his "voluminous record" as (unintentionally)
"one of the cruelest in literary history.";6

Whitman himself had been quick to react and to
foresee. Swinburne he dismissed as a "simulacrum." As
for professors and critics, he told Traubel:

> No doubt the literary, professional fellows
> may take hold of us if we last, but I confess
> I shrink from it with horror. . . . Leaves of
> Grass might get benefit of clergy -- benefit
> of professors, critics -- by a liberal
> construction of the traditions: but I suppose
> it would have to be damned liberal. . . . I
> need toning down or up or something to get me
> in presentable form for the ceremonials of
> seats of learning. . . . The university often
> has its eyes set in the back of its
> head. . . .;7

Whitman, it seems to me, had good reason to shrink from
the "professional fellows" who would one day "take hold"
of him. Their lucubrations have spread more darkness
than light about him and his work. If they have
contributed anything to his fame, it is only because, to
quote Rainer Maria Rilke, "fame is the sum of the
misunderstandings that gather about a name." If it had
been up to those who spoke of "Whitmaniacs," of "hot
little prophets," of the necessity of "forgetting
Whitman's disciples," it is certain that neither he nor
his Leaves would have long survived. The counterparts
of the snobs and pedants of aftertimes were present in
Whitman's time as well. They were no doubt the
"plentiful little mannikins" who were, according to the
speaker of "Song of Myself," "positively not worms or
fleas!"

Those who welcomed Whitman sincerely and sustained
his faith, without being instructed by their "betters"

to do so, were of his spiritual kindred. Or, to borrow
Plato's image, they had been "magnetized" by the poet,
who had himself been magnetized by the Muse. It was a
chain in which every link derived its power of magnetism
from its predecessor. If bad taste leads to crime, as
Stendhal said, good taste may lead to a share in
immortality. And it is precisely this share which is
the portion of Whitman's "Beginners." For that is how I
myself think of those "little prophets," "disciples,"
and "maniacs." They are my brothers, but not those who
have labelled them so.

   "Beginners" is the title of one of Whitman's most
indicative Inscriptions to Leaves of Grass, and the
beautiful line in it which best concentrates Whitman's
meaning is this: "How all times mischoose the objects
of their adulation and reward!" Whitman never tires of
reminding us of the unknown soldiers of humanity, of its
unknown saints, almost in the spirit of that
Lamed-Vovnik legend among the Jews which tells us that
this cruel world would not be permitted to survive were
it not for the existence of 36 (the meaning of
lamed-vov) unsuspected humble, righteous men within it.
Whitman put the thought in his own inimitable way in
conversation with Traubel:

> I take it to be one of the main things if not
> the main thing, implied by my philosophy, if I
> may so dignify it, that there is no one man
> anywhere -- that there are countless men on
> all sides, in all countries, who contribute to
> the great result -- most of them in fact
> without a name, unknown, eclipsed by the
> formidable reputations of mostly lesser
> people. It's queer, sad, disconcerting -- how
> that goes: it can't be helped: but we should
> contribute nothing ourselves to such a
> falsifying human habit.

Those much-scorned "hot little prophets," if not true
Beginners in Whitman's grand sense of the word, were
among those without whom there would be no such
Beginners; they were the first small audience which
foreshadowed the later great audiences for the great
poet. It is easy for me to imagine Whitman without his
critics, biographers, professors, but it is impossible
to do so without his disciples. Even Paul Elmer More is
compelled to admit, grudgingly and condescendingly, that
"by eliminating himself and allowing Whitman to speak
his own words, Mr. Horace Traubel, certainly one of the
least tolerable of enthusiasts, has given us a book of
some importance."

   What I am saying must not be taken to mean that the
denigrators of Whitman and the "cool" skeptics about his

poetry do not deserve a courteous hearing. Those who
have looked closely at my book Walt Whitman: The
Critical Heritage will have noticed that I have given
disproportionate representation to the early opposition
to Whitman, almost as if I had sought to include every
negative opinion I could dig up about Whitman but had
passed over many positive ones. There is something to
that suspicion, though if it were wholly true I should
have included (as I did not) academicians like Barrett
Wendell, Bliss Perry, and Paul Elmer More. I do confess
to thinking that, on the principle of immunization,
one's convictions as to the true worth of Whitman are
likely to be strengthened rather than weakened by
reading the worst that has been or can be said about
him. Harold Blodgett thought that Peter Bayne's
devastating attack on Whitman in 1875 deserves
preservation, and I have preserved every word of it
(while abbreviating or excluding altogether many
positive responses to Whitman). The same is true of
Knut Hamsun's satirical, witty, brilliant assault on
Whitman in 1888, which I have said might have amused
Whitman himself had it come to his attention. Until
quite recently, few readers have paid any attention to
Whitman's saying to Traubel, "The idea that anybody
imagines I can't appreciate a joke or even make jokes
seems preposterous." (I dare hazard a wild guess that
he may even have been amused -- as his scholars have not
been -- by the irreverent hoax about his funeral
perpetrated by the poet Guillaume Apollinaire on April
Fool's Day in 1913 in the Mercure de France, a hoax
which, being unrecognized, begot a heated international
literary controversy lasting for more than a year,
leaving behind not only an amusing surrealist fantasy
but a net gain for Whitman on the principle enunciated
by Oscar Wilde that the only thing worse than being
talked about is not being talked about.)*
     The criterion of selections for the "Critical
Heritage" volume perhaps owes something to Tolstoy's
essay What Is Art?, which tells us that the common
denominator of all art is feeling. If that is so, the
common denominator of criticism must be feeling as
well. Not the intellectual rationalizations of feeling
(intriguing as they often are), but sensitivity,
sincerity, and strength of primary feeling. It is out
of such sensitivity and sincerity that the closest thing
possible to a true insight into art originates.
I am speaking of lasting feeling, inspired feeling, the

* For details of the hoax see Walt Whitman Abroad, ed.
Gay Wilson Allen (Syracuse, New York: Syracuse
University Press, 1955), pp. 58-59.

sort of magnetic feeling described by Plato. The critic
speaks "as with authority" only if there is something of
an inner drive or compulsion motivating his utterance.
     My criterion of selections owed even more to the
example and thoughts of Whitman himself. He had, from
the beginning, carefully preserved the negative as well
as the positive reactions to his book, and in the 1856
edition of Leaves of Grass (the one which carried a
sentence from Emerson's endorsement embossed on its
cover) he had bound into the concluding pages of the
volume some of these insulting reviews. From the
beginning, Whitman sensed the value to him of what
Patrick Quinn in The French Face of Edgar Poe calls
"resolute minority opinion." (We must note, however,
that what was minority -- negative -- opinion later on
was the majority opinion to begin with.) To Traubel, he
was always saying things like:

> It was not favorable? What does that matter?
> I like to see, to hear, all that is said
> provided it is serious -- presents a point of
> view: I don't care what side it looks at me
> from so it looks honestly. . . . No one could
> have more doubts of me than I have of myself:
> I'm not sure of anything except my
> intentions. . . . The great function of the
> critic is to say bright things -- sparkle,
> effervesee, probably three quarters, perhaps
> even more, of them do not take the trouble to
> examine what they start out to criticize -- to
> judge a man from his own standpoint, even find
> out what that standpoint is. . . . We must
> face all the objections -- they require to be
> said. . . . What I object to are the sneakers
> -- the men who hit from the rear. Criticism
> is a matter of course, often the best food:
> the right negative word spoken at the right
> time saves many a soul. Criticism is a
> necessary test -- the passage of fire: we
> have got to meet it -- there is no escape.
> . . . I am not thin-skinned about opposition.
> . . .

He was obviously not one of those New York poets
later on who regard the critic as "the assassin of their
orchards." I agree with Mr. Quinn when he observes that

> unless some kind of dialectic were at work, we
> would hear from France nothing but encomiums
> and witness nothing but lavish pouring of
> libations [to Poe], a kind of thing which
> while impressive in its way seldom proves
> especially illuminating. . . . No matter how

sincere, a laudatory note sustained too long
is bound to become taxing, and we are relieved
to hear occasionally contributions in a
dissonant register.

Though the so-called people's democracies have
tried to assimilate Whitman and tend to regard him as
one of their own, they must do so selectively, for if we
look at him steadily and whole it is pretty clear that
he should reject their forceful cultivation of unanimity
of opinion on any subject, including himself. Even in
his time there was beginning to be talk about political
democracy being meaningless if not accompanied by
industrial democracy, but Whitman would have none of
it. Political liberty, he tells us, is the animus of
all liberty. He knows fully what he is saying and all
its consequences. It is one of the deepest thoughts
that has occurred to anyone in our history. For just as
his disciples insisted and later academicians have
frequently not recognized, Whitman was a sage as well as
a poet, and the two are in him inseparable. Could
anyone but a sage have said as he did to his young
friend Traubel: "We must be resigned, but not too much
so: we must be calm but not too calm: we must not give
in -- yet we must give in some: that is, we must grade
our rebellion and our conformity -- both"? Or when he
said on another occasion, in words which seem directly
addressed to anyone who has ever undertaken to speak of
him: "I for my own account find any unqualified
dogmatic generalization offensive: just as much so --
maybe even more -- in my friends than in my enemies."
Let any of us who may ever be tempted to assume
airs, to lay claim to Whitman's "chair" if not to speak
with infallibility on his poetry or person, reflect on
these words and be chastened by them. He would be
speaking in the spirit of Whitman if he were to admit,
as Jules Lemaitre once did, that "whether dogmatic or
scientific, literary criticism is never, in the last
analysis, anything but the personal and perishable work
of one wretched man."

NOTES

1. Gay Wilson Allen, _The Solitary Singer_ (New
York: New York University Press, 1967), pp. 527-8.
2. Ibid., p. 537.
3. Robert Ingersoll, "Liberty in Literature:
Testimonial to Walt Whitman," _In Re Walt Whitman_, eds.
Horace Traubel, R. M. Bucke, and Thomas B. Harned
(Philadelphia: David McKay, 1893), pp. 253-283.
4. Robert Ingersoll, "At the Graveside of Walt
Whitman," _In Re Walt Whitman_, pp. 437-52.

5.   Paul Elmer More, "Walt Whitman," in <u>Shelburne Essays on American Literature</u>, ed. Daniel Aaron (New York: Harcourt, Brace, 1963), p. 253.
6.   Allen, p. 531.
7.   Sources in Traubel remain unidentified.

Part II

Here and Now:
Contemporary Views

5.

Walt Whitman and the New Morality: Contemporary Reconsiderations

JAMES T. F. TANNER

It is especially important that this conference, dealing with the general topic "Walt Whitman: Here and Now," reassess the poet's treatment of moral issues; that is to say, how does Whitman's literary treatment of human morality stand up today, 125 years after the first publication of Leaves of Grass? Let us put the question quite simply: If Walt Whitman could somehow return to America today, what would be his reaction to our moral stance? To avoid the merely speculative nature of such an inquiry, we may observe that numerous passages in Leaves of Grass, Specimen Days, and Democratic Vistas are indeed concerned with the moral future of America; by examining such sentiments and comparing them with current reality, we may approach some understanding of how the good gray poet might regard our behavior in this strange twentieth-century America.

The topic is a large one. To deal with it within the compass of a brief presentation, I have asked myself just what Walt Whitman would have to say about the following four topics: 1) Watergate (or political corruption); 2) women's liberation (or sexual equality); 3) the gay rights movement (or minority rights); and 4) the Vietnam War (or struggle and reconciliation). (You will note that I have attempted to avoid controversial issues!) A consideration of these four general topics will serve to elucidate Walt Whitman's persistent moral concerns.

1. What would Walt Whitman have thought about the great controversy surrounding the Watergate scandal and the implications of political corruption involved therein? There is, of course, little likelihood that he

would have been shocked at the revelations of wrongdoing in high places, or even at the rather callous attitude taken by the bureaucracy toward them. Readers of <u>Democratic Vistas</u> (1871) know that Whitman was not politically naive:

> I say we had best look our times and lands
> searchingly in the face, like a physician
> diagnosing some deep disease. Never was
> there, perhaps, more hollowness at heart than
> at present, and here in the United States.
> Genuine belief seems to have left us. The
> underlying principles of the States are not
> honestly believ'd in. What penetrating eye
> does not everywhere see through the mask? The
> spectacle is appalling. We live in an
> atmosphere of hypocrisy throughout. The men
> believe not in the women, nor the women in the
> men. . . . The official services of America,
> national, state, and municipal, in all their
> branches and departments, except the
> judiciary, are saturated in corruption,
> bribery, falsehood, mal-administration; and
> the judiciary is tainted.;1

Such a description of nineteenth-century America is shocking to us! References to hollowness of heart, disbelief, lack of faith in the principles of the American union, hypocrisy, distrust, bribery, falsehood, and mal-administration seem rather to describe our own state of affairs; we are rather accustomed to regard nineteenth-century America as a pastoral Eden.

But the Watergate scandal is only reminiscent of the numerous and pervasive scandals of the Reconstruction period, particularly those of the Grant administration. And Walt Whitman might even have been delighted to learn of the role of the judiciary (the one arm of government for which he had some small respect) in resolving the Watergate problems. Most important, would he not applaud the great moral outcry against apparently unconstitutional acts committed by the highest officials in the government?

The poet's message rings true even today. The ideal social environment postulated by Whitman remains our own ideal today. The following passage, from "Song of the Broad-Axe," should be required reading for all Chamber of Commerce administrators. The poet here attempts to tell us how to recognize the truly great city:

> The place where a great city stands is not the
>   place of stretched wharves, docks,
>   manufactures, deposits of produce merely,

> Nor the place of ceaseless salutes of
>   new-comers or the anchor-lifters of the
>   departing,
> Nor the place of the tallest and costliest
>   buildings or shops selling goods from the
>   rest of the earth,
> Nor the place of the best libraries and
>   schools, nor the place where money is
>   plentiest,
> Nor the place of the most numerous
>   population. . . .
>
> Where the slave ceases, and the master of
>   slaves ceases,
> Where the populace rise at once against the
>   never-ending audacity of elected persons.
>   . . .
>
> Where outside authority enters always after
>   the precedence of inside authority,
> Where the citizen is always the head and
>   ideal, and President, Mayor, Governor and
>   what not, are agents for pay. . . .
> Where the city of the faithfulest friends
>   stands,
> Where the city of the cleanliness of sexes
>   stands,
> Where the city of the healthiest fathers
>   stands,
> Where the city of the best-bodied mothers
>   stands,
> There the great city stands.
>
> (el. 109-134)

Whitman's regarding the President and other officials as
merely "agents for pay" accords with the current view
that though the President fall, the nation can
endure; and the description of the great city as a place
"where the populace rise at once against the
never-ending audacity of elected persons" lets us know
that he would not be altogether displeased with our
recent behavior. It may be that we continue to
construct the holy city described so forcefully by our
poet.

   2. The linguistic uproar over personal pronouns in
recent years -- the attempt to find some means of
equalizing male and female in references to generic
humanity -- would no doubt evoke a smile on the face of
Walt Whitman. The numerous awkward constructions
throughout his poetry: "he-his, she-hers," "men and
women," "male and female," _et cetera_, testify to his
awareness of this problem in the English language.
Although he did not solve the linguistic difficulties,

he did make it abundantly clear that he was a true
prophet in the area of womens' rights:

> I am the poet of the woman the same as the
>   man,
> And I say it is as great to be a woman as to
>   be a man,
> And I say there is nothing greater than the
>   mother of men.
>   ("Song of Myself," 11. 425-27)

Indeed the poet celebrates all women:

> The wife, and she is not one jot less than the
>   husband,
> The daughter, and she is just as good as the
>   son,
> The mother, and she is every bit as much as
>   the father.
>   ("A Song for Occupations," 11. 33-35)

The sentiments sound simplistic. But the poet felt it
necessary to state them. Simplistic or not, women even
today find it difficult to take their rightful places in
a modern democratic society.

Walt Whitman was not a poet of romantic love.
Robert K. Martin, in his recent book, <u>The Homosexual
Tradition in American Poetry</u>, has suggested that perhaps
because Walt Whitman was homosexual he was therefore
able to view women as something more than mere sexual
objects. In any event his interest in women was social,
moral, political, and humanistic. According to Walt
Whitman, woman would eventually take her place beside
man in all areas of human endeavor:

> Now I will dismiss myself from impassive
>   women,
> I will go stay with her who waits for me, and
>   with those women that are warm-blooded
>   and sufficient for me,
> I see that they understand me and do not deny
>   me,
> I see that they are worthy of me, I will be
>   the robust husband of those women.
> They are not one jot less than I am,
> They are tann'd in the face by shining suns
>   and blowing winds,
> Their flesh has the old divine suppleness and
>   strength,
> They know how to swim, row, ride, wrestle,
>   shoot, run, strike, retreat, advance,
>   resist, defend themselves,

> They are ultimate in their own right -- they
> are calm, clear, well-possessed of
> themselves.
>   ("A Woman Waits for Me," 11. 11-19)

In the face of such forceful sentiments, Whitman might
well be curious to know how we could bear to spend our
time on such questions as whether to admit women to West
Point, whether girls can play baseball in Little League,
whether women can be suitable astronauts, and whether a
constitutional amendment should be approved, giving
women equal rights with men. But there is little doubt
that our poet would applaud our continuing efforts to
admit women to their rightful places in the spiritual
democracy.

   3. If our generation is concerned with inadequate
administration of the laws guaranteeing civil rights and
with insufficient attention to the plight of minorities,
let us remember that Walt Whitman's generation had the
institution of slavery to contend with. And though
Whitman lived to see the end of slavery, the massive
problems confronting the former slaves had scarcely
begun to be dealt with at the time of his death in 1892.

   In the 1960s, the issue of civil rights for
American blacks came to the forefront of our national
consciousness. Surely Walt Whitman's spirit looks on
approvingly as we continue to seek means of redressing
many generations of wrong.

   The decade of the 1970s has seen the emergence of
the gay rights movement, the struggle for equal and just
treatment of a formerly despised minority. How would
Whitman react to this social upheaval?

   He would probably say, "What took you so long?"
This is not the proper forum for debate concerning Walt
Whitman's sexual orientation. Suffice it to say that
modern readers, more sophisticated since the advent of
Freudian psychoanalysis, understand the homoerotic
implications of numerous passages in <u>Leaves of Grass</u> far
better than did Whitman's contemporaries. In the
struggle for the rights of homosexuals, perhaps no
other poet has been so frequently invoked -- and rightly
so.

   Strident in so many other areas, Whitman is never
so in his treatment of homoerotic themes. In the
<u>Calamus</u> section of <u>Leaves of Grass</u> especially, the poet
brings a quiet dignity, a casual acceptance, a moral
tastefulness, and a genuine spirituality to the
subject. The brief poem "When I Heard at the Close of
the Day" is all that anyone could ask for in
spiritualization of physicality:

> When I heard at the close of the day how my
> name had been received with plaudits in

             the capitol, still it was not a happy
                night for me that follow'd,
And else when I carous'd, or when my plans
                were accomplish'd, still I was not happy,
But the day when I rose at dawn from the bed
                of perfect health, refresh'd, singing,
                inhaling the ripe breath of autumn,
When I saw the full moon in the west grow pale
                and disappear in the morning light,
When I wander'd alone over the beach, and
                undressing bathed, laughing with the cool
                waters, and saw the sun rise,
And when I thought how my dear friend my lover
                was on his way coming, O then I was
                happy,
O then each breath tasted sweeter, and all
                that day my food nourish'd me more, and
                the beautiful day pass'd well,
And the next came with equal joy, and with the
                next at evening came my friend,
And that night while all was still I heard the
                waters roll slowly continually up the
                shores,
I heard the hissing rustle of the liquid sands
                as directed to me whispering to
                congratulate me,
For the one I love most lay sleeping by me
                under the same cover in the cool night,
In the stillness in the autumn moonbeams his
                face was inclined toward me,
And his arm lay lightly around my breast --
                and that night I was happy.

Notable in this poem are the many beautiful images of
natural good health, vitality, cleanliness, and purity;
the dissatisfaction with fame juxtaposed against the
acceptance of love cannot fail to elicit a favorable
response from any reader. The love here described is
devoid of selfish and materialistic motives. Love of
any kind has seldom been so chastely celebrated.
     But Whitman did, of course, understand the tendency
of the world to distrust his motives in writing such
poems:

I hear it was charged against me that I sought
                to destroy institutions,
But really I am neither for nor against
                institutions,
(What indeed have I in common with them? or
                what with the destruction of them?)
Only I will establish in the Mannahatta and in
                every city of these States inland and
                seaboard,

>   And in the fields and woods, and above every
>   keel little or large that dents the
>   water,
>   Without edifices or rules or trustees or any
>   argument, The institution of the dear
>   love of comrades.
>   ("I Hear It Was Charged Against Me")

Exactly what were the institutions which the poet had
been accused of seeking to destroy? The family? The
government? The social fabric in general? The poet's
reply is cogent. In establishing the institution of the
love of comrades, no harm is intended for other
institutions. Far from destroying social institutions,
of course, Whitman usually sought to strengthen them.
Indeed, Whitman more than once defended the Calamus
emotion for its social and political benefits.

While it is probable that Walt Whitman would decry
certain excesses in the movement for homosexual rights
-- as he doubtless would excesses of any kind -- it is
clear that he was in favor of a natural love (with
undeniable homoerotic tendencies) which might strengthen
the social order. This desire for a national unity
based on the Calamus emotion is superbly expressed in
the very brief poem "A Leaf for Hand in Hand":

>   A leaf for hand in hand;
>   You natural persons old and young!
>   You on the Mississippi and on all the branches
>   and bayous of the Mississippi!
>   You friendly boatmen and mechanics! You
>   roughs!
>   You twain! and all processions moving along
>   the streets!
>   I wish to infuse myself among you til I see it
>   common for you to walk hand in hand.

Walt Whitman might see today, could he return, some
hopeful signs in this regard.

4. Our century has been steeped in war. War,
indeed, has been one of the causes of massive social and
political disruption in our time. Whitman's knowledge
of war, gained so painfully in the Civil War
hospitals, and presented so compassionately in his
poetry and prose works, is akin to our own. He knew the
horrors of war and its aftermath as well as any poet who
ever lived. And it was the suffering, not the glory,
that he emphasized in his poetry and in Specimen Days.

As disruptive and painful as the Vietnam War and
its aftermath have been for America, Walt Whitman would
no doubt have words of comfort for us. He himself lived
through a far more horrible conflict, one which
threatened the existence of the nation itself. He knew

that atrocities had been committed on both sides (see "A Glimpse of War's Hell-Scenes" in <u>Specimen Days</u>), that war brought out both the best and the worst in human nature, and that somehow human culture would survive. The poet would no doubt understand our frustration and sense of futility. But he would point to the future, as always, and urge us on to greater accomplishments.

Whitman's poems on the Civil War are too well known to require quotation, yet I should like to quote a brief passage from "Song of Myself" to illustrate the poet's common sense as well as his compassionate attitude toward losers of conflicts:

> With music strong I come, with my cornets and
>   my drums,
> I play not marches for accepted victors only,
> I play marches for conquer'd and slain
>   persons.
> Have you heard that it was good to gain the
>   day?
> I also say it is good to fall, battles are
>   lost in the same spirit in which they are
>   won.
> I beat and pound for the dead,
> I blow through my embouchures my loudest and
>   gayest for them.
>
> ("Song of Myself," ll. 361-66)

The proper attitude toward war and its aftermath is one of forgiveness. In our present situation, we need the help of our poet. Indeed, our problems pale when compared to those that Walt Whitman's generation had to suffer.

In summary, Walt Whitman would -- I believe -- be rather more pleased than appalled by what he could witness in America today. His poetic vision of the moral future of America, though certainly not realized in every detail, is at least the ideal toward which we continue to strive.

Could Whitman return today, he would witness our attempts to deal with political corruption, our struggles to open the doors of opportunity to women, our endeavors to strengthen the political and social rights of all minorities, and our earnest aim to overcome the effects of a divisive military struggle. I believe that he would not be altogether displeased.

NOTES

1. <u>Democratic Vistas</u>, in <u>The Viking Portable Library Walt Whitman</u> (New York: Viking Press, 1945), pp. 325-26.

6.
Reading Whitman Psychoanalytically

STEPHEN A. BLACK

Looking backward two or three thousand years, one sees that people have usually regarded literature as something which expresses an author's intentions. To answer the question <u>What does the poet mean?</u>, modern scholars devise increasingly sophisticated methods of editing and annotating texts, of constructing biographies, and of interpreting works. The view of the world implied by such an attitude toward scholarship is that it is both possible and desirable to know another person and to know another's experience. I am aware that a different view of the world is currently favored by many of my academic colleagues, a view which asserts that it is not possible to really know another person, and that the aim of studying literature is to learn about one's self, or to find one's self reflected in an author's words. Although I respect many of my colleagues who hold such views, I do not share their outlook toward scholarship or the world.

Instead, I more nearly accept the admonitions of E. D. Hirsch, Jr., who advises scholars of their ethical obligation to discover "authorial meaning" or "authorial intention." Nearly 20 years ago Mr. Hirsch argued against a then accepted notion that it is a fallacy to concern one's self with an author's intention. Hirsch insists that that is exactly what scholars must do: we must make a "psychological reconstruction" of "the author's subjective stance to the extent that this stance is relevant to the text at hand.";1

When the orthodox scholar tries to follow Hirsch's admonition, to make a "psychological reconstruction" of the artist at work which illuminates intention and meaning, the scholar may have to adopt a psychology

which claims to understand matters beyond the awareness
of the author himself. For sometimes literary scholars
find themselves in the position of elucidating the
intention of a poet who may not want his intention
known, or who does not know it himself. I refer of
course to Whitman.

I will remind you of a famous conversation Whitman
had with Horace Traubel, the subject being the poet's
intention concerning Calamus. Whitman's English admirer
John Addington Symonds had written several letters which
asked Hirsch's question about intention: specifically,
had Whitman meant to write about the physical "love of
man for man." Whitman found the questions irritating,
yet could not seem to dismiss them. He told Traubel:

> Symonds is right, no doubt, to ask the
> questions: I am just as much right if I do
> not answer them: just as much right if I do
> answer them. I often say to myself about
> Calamus -- perhaps it means more or less than
> what I thought myself -- means different:
> perhaps I don't know what it all means --
> perhaps never did know. My first instinct
> about all that Symonds writes is violently
> reactionary -- is strong and brutal for no,
> no, no. Then the thought intervenes that I
> maybe do not know all my own meanings: I say
> to myself: "You, too, go away, study your own
> book -- an alien or stranger, study your own
> book, see what it amounts to." Sometime or
> other I will have to write him definitively
> about Calamus -- give him my word for what I
> meant or mean it to mean.;2

Anyone reading this conversation must decide if
Whitman deliberately lies to Traubel, or if the poet has
somehow forgotten something he once knew. But if one
takes seriously Whitman's own description of his
feelings -- that he doesn't know his own intentions and
never did -- then one may be at a loss to know how to
develop such statements into a notion of authorial
meaning. In my opinion we need a systematic psychology
by which to reconstruct Whitman's intention for Calamus,
and furthermore, it must be a psychology which tolerates
the idea that people may act without full awareness of
their intentions and meanings. If we also try to
fulfill Hirsch's ethical precept, that a scholar should
aim to understand someone else, rather than himself,
then we must also find a psychology which enables a
person to tell the difference between a thought or
feeling of one's own and one that originates in someone
else. The psychology which in my opinion best fits

these criteria, psychoanalysis, has rarely been regarded
as a friend to scholarly orthodoxy, but such may not be
the case.

I must mention at this point that I have been
fortunate during the last five years in having the
opportunity to study psychoanalysis formally in a
training institute, and in acquiring some clinical
training and experience in conducting psychoanalytic
psychotherapy. When I speak of psychoanalysis being
useful to orthodox scholarly aims, I do not necessarily
refer to theories about human "instincts" or human
psychopathology. Rather, I have in mind a certain
attitude which is at the core of the clinical process of
analysis. In my opinion, the most useful thing
psychoanalysis has to contribute to literary studies is
the clinical attitude of "empathic neutrality" or, as
Freud sometimes called it, "evenly suspended attention."

By the even suspension of his attention, the
analyst may avoid fixing his gaze on whatever he might
expect to find and so distorting the patient's
utterances to fit interpretive expectations. The
analyst may, as Freud said, attune his unconscious to
the patient's unconscious. By avoiding thinking about
anything in particular, the analyst may pay attention
not only to the patient's utterances, but also to the
associations (feelings, thoughts, images, desires) that
flit through the analyst's own mind. The analyst's
associations may permit him to understand the patient's
associations at a deeper level than those conscious to
both of them. The analyst, in short, should be
carrying on a kind of double analysis, of himself and
the patient. By means of the double analysis one may
also learn to tell which feelings or thoughts occur in
which person. The confusion may arise through an
unconscious identification with the other person. By
attending to one's own associations while maintaining a
neutral attitude, it is possible to keep in sight the
boundary between Me and Not Me without disrupting the
relationship. One may empathically feel someone else's
experience without becoming confused about who is having
the experience. For shorthand I will call one attitude
"identification," meaning the boundary is lost, and the
other attitude "empathy," meaning the boundary is
maintained.

The attitude I call identification may present
problems to the literary interpreter who wants to know
what the author intends. Identification makes it
difficult to know the difference between the author's
meaning and one's own. Symonds' several inquiries to
Whitman aimed to establish just such a distinction. In
the first letter (1872) Symonds wrote, "What the love of
man for man has been in the Past I think I know. What
it is here now, I know also -- alas! What you say it

can and shall be I dimly discern in your Poems." At
this stage Symonds seems to feel he may not completely
understand Calamus but assumes that it refers to the
form of homosexual love he has experienced. But
eventually something happens which partly convinces
Symonds that his original assumption is incorrect.
Whitman finally wrote Symonds "definitively about
Calamus" -- the celebrated letter condemning as
"terrible," "undream'd," "unreck'd," "gratuitous," and
"damnable" such constructions as Symonds wanted to make
of Calamus, and incidentally claiming, "I have had six
children."

We do not know exactly how Symonds reacted to the
letter, but we do know that in the book he published
after Whitman's death, Symonds presented a different
view of Calamus than he had expressed in the letters.
He seems to take seriously Whitman's denial of conscious
homosexual intent for Calamus and is thus led to
discover something different from his own experience.
Symonds distinguishes not only between fantasy and
physical action, but also between conscious and
unconscious fantasy; he emerges with something very
similar to the idea that Freud would later call
"sublimation" -- the notion that "instinctual energy"
might serve "de-instinctualized" aims.

Now I doubt that Symonds had any interest in
mechanistic theories about "psychic energy," but the
change in his perception of Calamus betokens another
important capacity on his part: that he could behave in
the way a good analyst should behave. He apparently
"listened" to the other person in a relatively open way
and seriously entertained the idea that Whitman might
intend something quite different from what the
identification had led Symonds to expect. As he studied
the poems Symonds evidently tried to think about intense
masculine comradeship which excluded physical love among
men. That is, he tried to think and feel the way
Whitman said he thought and felt. When Symonds became
conscious of, and abandoned his identification with
Whitman, he discovered a new understanding of Calamus,
something different from homosexuality with the sex
taken out. What came out in Symonds' book is a
conviction about Whitman's dream of democratic chivalry,
a democracy of men whose comradely love gave strength,
direction, energy, and an ethical quality to social
organization. Some modern psychologically minded
critics, like Kenneth Burke and Leslie Fiedler, have
accepted most of Symonds' view of Calamus, adding the
psychoanalytic idea that it is because the sexual-action
part of the comradely feeling was kept unconscious that
Whitman could maintain so strong a conviction about his
democratic vista.

My understanding of the interpretive process exemplified by Symonds leads me to reformulate the aim of traditional literary scholarship. The scholar should aim to establish an empathic relationship with the author or work he studies; in this way, the relationship may eventually lead the scholar to achieve an understanding of the topic which is unique to that particular relationship.

But what if we do not have the author present to answer our letters? I believe that we can still adopt an attitude of empathic neutrality toward whatever we read. Consider the Calamus poem, "Whoever You Are Holding Me Now in Hand." As I read this poem over the years, and listen while my students talk about it, I notice that one of the most inescapable aspects of the poem is the demand the poet makes upon the reader. We readers are supposed to be completely accepting, completely tolerant, willing to abandon our own lives and goals. At times the poet wants us to become just like him; at other times we must be his disciples; at one point he seems to ask that the reader be his mother. Many readers react very strongly against demands they find intrusive, arrogant, or infantile. What if one does not want to be what Whitman wants, especially after all those warnings which seem to many people just another kind of indirect seduction. Well, nothing much will happen if we refuse him. He won't love the uncooperative reader, he says, but who cares to be loved by someone so selfish? There is no real problem here, except that by refusing to go along with Whitman we can be pretty certain we will not get an answer to the riddle, What is the one thing without which "all will be useless"?

Let me stop to point out that the reactions I mention are aspects of a relationship a reader feels between himself and Whitman's poem. The reader may be only too glad to abandon a relationship with Whitman, or feel that curiosity about the riddle is the only thing that makes one want to tolerate so demanding a poet. Or the reader may identify with the odd way Whitman makes his demand: "that's the way I feel sometimes."

Or one may be able to direct evenly suspended attention to everything perceived in the poem, and everything perceived in one's own reaction; one might notice the poet's demandingness without either defending oneself against Whitman or identifying with him. One thing the empathically neutral reader may discover, amidst all the unreasonable demands and intense needs for maternal disciples, is a considerable confusion about the poet's own intentions. The organization of this poem, like many others, around a riddle which is never explicitly answered, suggests that the poet may set out to make a poem without knowing exactly where he

will wind up or what his poem will finally say. Perhaps
it would be reasonable to say that Whitman's poetic
intention is often to use his poetic process to discover
what he thinks and feels. Perhaps it is also true that
Whitman intends his poems to establish a relationship
with the reader, to seduce the reader into
discipleship, or to create in the reader a feeling of
vagueness and confusion like that experienced by the
poet. These are some of many statements about Whitman's
intentions that emerge from an empathically neutral
interpretive stance.

To summarize, the possibility of making statements
about literary intention arises when a reader tries to
read literature with the same attitude that a good
analyst should bring to his analysand's sessions: to
evenly suspend attention so that one hears everything
that is said, but avoids the distortion of what one
hears that results from listening only for that which
supports one's predetermined theory. Identifying with a
writer may be an important first step in "knowing" the
writer's meaning, but if the identification is
unconscious, the interpreter will not be able to tell
the difference between his own thoughts or feelings and
the author's. One need not be an analyst to cultivate
an analytic attitude. Symonds never heard of
psychoanalysis, but he did adopt the ethical principle
that when you write a scholarly book, you should try to
write about someone other than yourself. But knowing
something about psychoanalysis may turn out to be useful
to people who wish to follow traditional scholarly
pursuits.

NOTES

1. E. D. Hirsch, Jr., "Objective Interpretation,"
PMLA (Sept. 1960); reprinted in Validity in
Interpretation (New Haven: Yale University Press, 1967),
pp. 238-39.
2. Horace Traubel, With Walt Whitman in Camden
(New York: Mitchell and Kennerley, 1914), vol. 1, pp.
76-77.

7.
Drum-Taps and Nineteenth-Century Male Homosexual Literature

JOSEPH CADY

Surely one of the most pertinent topics that could be discussed at a conference devoted to a contemporary reconsideration of Whitman is the aspect of Whitman that has become more mentionable now because of contemporary social changes -- Whitman's homosexuality and its place in his work. This integral dimension of Whitman was of course once unthinkable and unspeakable, like the subject of homosexuality in society itself. And when the critical silence or equivocation began to be broken, first by Europeans like Roger Asselineau and then by American commentators, Whitman's homosexuality was, predictably, viewed negatively. It was seen primarily as a source of pain for Whitman and chiefly as a point of tension in his work.;1 The only exceptions to this pattern were Malcolm Cowley's daring New Republic essays in 1946, whose positive suggestions Whitman scholars did not then take up.;2 Since the birth of the contemporary gay liberation movement, and under the impetus of open gay scholars, this situation has happily started to change. Robert K. Martin's 1975 article on "homosexual dream and vision" in Whitman's poems was the first extended literary analysis to approach the topic both frankly and as a source of positive feeling for Whitman, and it contains a pointed survey of the earlier unwillingness of most Whitman critics to do that.;3 And in his recent groundbreaking documentary Gay American History, Jonathan Katz has traced Whitman's central place in the early quest for identity and freedom among nineteenth-century Western male homosexuals.;4

My purpose here is to discuss some of Whitman's Drum-Taps poems as documents of nineteenth-century male

homosexual literature. For the most part, the critics
who have given any consideration to the subject have
recognized or implied the strong presence of homosexual
feelings in Whitman's life during the Civil War period,
expressed in his dedicated visiting of the wounded and
strongly suggested in some unpublished manuscripts and
notebook entries of the period and in his correspondence
with soldiers he met during the conflict. At the same
time most of these commentators have seen the Drum-Taps
poems, Whitman's major work of these years, as
desexualized.;5 In this, they may have been encouraged
by Whitman himself, who in a letter to William O'Connor
before the printing of Drum-Taps made the misleading
remark that the collection had "none of the
perturbations of Leaves of Grass.";6 We know that the
word "perturbation" was sometimes associated in
Whitman's mind with homosexual desire -- in an 1870
notebook entry, from the same list of entries in which
he struggled "TO GIVE UP ABSOLUTELY & for good, from
this present hour, this FEVERISH, FLUCTUATING, useless
undignified pursuit of 164" (his code for the initials
of his lover, Peter Doyle), Whitman declared that "it is
IMPERATIVE, that I . . . remove myself . . . at all
hazards from this incessant . . . PERTURBATION.";7
Even though always referring to intense relationships
between men, the moments in the Drum-Taps poems that
imply the greatest personal feeling are usually
interpreted as "completely Platonic emotion" and as
voicing "a universal philosophy of love.";8
      I believe this argument is a misreading largely
based on ignorance of the special conditions and
pressures within homosexual experience during Whitman's
era. The Drum-Taps collection contains several
intensely felt lyrics that, when viewed "from the
inside" of gay experience at that time, emerge as
purposeful homosexual visions. Though of course there
are indications of homosexual feeling throughout
Whitman's work, these most personal of Drum-Taps poems
were the second of two concerted attempts Whitman made
during his career to fashion a homosexual affirmation;
the first had been five years earlier in the Calamus
poems, which, as I have discussed elsewhere, I think are
his major achievement as a homosexual poet.;9 There are
important echoes of Calamus throughout these Drum-Taps
pieces, and I believe they must be understood in the
same way as the earlier collection. But Whitman's main
vehicles in these Drum-Taps poems differ. Emerging
directly out of the war setting itself, the chief means
through which he makes a homosexual statement here are
the motif of "soldier-comradeship" and the elegy
convention.

These two frameworks are often joined in the *Drum-Taps* poems that have a homosexual application, as the actual situation would of course have often determined. *Drum-Taps* is studded with poems in which the speaker or another figure laments the death of a soldier-comrade or the deaths of others who were soldier-comrades; it is primarily through these pieces that Whitman fashions homosexual affirmations in the collection. The best illustration of this approach is one of *Drum-Taps'* most famous poems, "Vigil Strange I Kept on the Field One Night"; other examples are "A March in the Ranks Hard-Prest, and the Road Unknown," "A Sight in Camp in the Daybreak Gray and Dim," "As Toilsome I Wander'd Virginia's Woods," and "Dirge for Two Veterans." A sub-category of this group is the smaller number of poems that represent nursing of the wounded and dying, which echo Whitman's actual experience as a hospital and battlefield visitor; the most obvious example is of course "The Wound-Dresser." Because of limitations of space and since this motif appears less frequently in the collection, I shall not discuss it here, except to say that it works in much the same way as the two vehicles I shall analyze below. Whitman's second major means of making homosexual affirmations in *Drum-Taps* is through soldier-comrade relationships that do not involve a death; the most stirring example of this approach is "As I Lay with My Head in Your Lap Camerado."

When seen within the context of gay experience at Whitman's time, the homosexual meaning and content of these motifs become clear. There was also a homosexual aspect to Whitman's interest in writing about the Civil War in the first place, and this too becomes clear from a gay perspective. Each of these aspects of *Drum-Taps* was a reflection of and a response to the two chief problems of "invention" that gay writers of Whitman's day faced. The first was the task of "inventing" a positive identity, an effort that characterizes much of nineteenth- and twentieth-century homosexual writing. Self-respecting homosexuals of Whitman's day were spurred by a welling positive intuition about their homosexual feelings that was in part the consequence of liberating assumptions about personality and nature inaugurated by the Enlightenment and the romantic movement. At the same time they were faced with an utter lack of accepting and appropriate terms for homosexuality in their general culture, which conceived of it thoroughly negatively and represented it primarily through damning images derived from religion (e.g., "sodomite," "the unspeakable crime against nature").;10 The age's homosexuals thus faced a profound problem of self-understanding, for, when grounded in their autonomous positive feelings, they had no clear sense of "who they really were," at least at the beginning of their development. And, consequently, they were left with an enormous burden of "self-invention," a task that, by the very definition of their art, became a chief concern of the age's homosexual authors -- they had to devise completely on their own a positive symbolism and terminology for gay experience.

The other "invention" the era's gay writers often had to make was self-protective. Their culture placed rigid strictures on any public admission or expression of homosexuality and imposed an absolute ban on any positive and dimensional representation of it. Gay writers of Whitman's day were therefore in what was, to put it mildly, a conflicting situation. On the one hand, they were moved to find a new "speech" for their identity; on the other, they still had to face a culture that considered homosexuality not only morally but literally "unspeakable" and that dealt dangerous personal and social consequences for "speaking" openly about it (as the case of Oscar Wilde at the end of the century would make chillingly clear). Thus, the period's gay authors faced two potentially clashing kinds of "invention" that complicated their enterprise profoundly and often gave their texts a marked intricacy. In addition to attempting the self-invention that the homosexual situation at that time inevitably called for, they had to invent protective strategies that would allow them to pursue that effort while sufficiently guarding themselves from certain social exposure and punishment.

The Civil War obviously had several significances for Whitman, and I believe that among them was the opportunity he sensed its materials would give him to accomplish both of these inventions. The military situation had already proved popular in earlier nineteenth-century gay male writing as a ground for making homosexual affirmations (Byron's Ossianic prose poem, "The Death of Calmar and Orla" [1807], is a good example), and it would continue to be so in later gay male literature (e.g., Wilfred Owen's World War I poems). I believe that in Drum-Taps Whitman, too, recognized the practical advantages that a war setting had for a homosexual writer. Most obviously, it provided a ready made same-sex situation; it was also one of the few available contexts where there already was a sanction for expressing male-male feelings openly. Furthermore, the military situation provided gay writers with a unique balance that was at once permissive and protective. They could depict feelings and actions that could be true of a war situation and that at the same time, through the use of special vocabularies that had a homosexual meaning for them (such as the soldier-comrade motif I shall discuss below), also expressed what seemed to them to be truths about homosexuality. In addition, the often tragic materials of war provided gay writers with an elegiac framework through which they could state homosexual feelings openly and yet "safely."

As noted below, the soldier-comrade motif carried a built-in protectiveness, but I believe that Whitman's use of it in these most personal of the Drum-Taps poems is primarily an example of homosexual self-invention. The homosexual meaning that "soldier-comradeship" came to have for nineteenth- and early twentieth-century gay male writers was a consequence of the complicated task of self-creation that they faced. Strictly speaking, that task is of course impossible for anyone to achieve, and what the authors characteristically did instead was to approximate it as closely as they could. One of the chief courses they took was to make imaginative expropriations from existing popular frameworks, adapting terms from them that they felt were also applicable to or potentially true about homosexuality. One of the most popular results of this process in nineteenth-century gay male literature was the motif from which "soldier-comradeship" derived -- this was the authors' use of the language of "friendship" and the related framework of "comradeship" as representations of male homosexual identity and relationships. Though of course not totally applicable to their situation, for gay male writers these terms had a particular pertinence to it. One obvious connection was that "friend" and "comrade" were the most familiar available terms for close male-male relationships. A more profound and subtle relevance is that these terms also fit nicely with the egalitarian possibilities that gay writers sensed in the homosexual bond (as opposed to the polarity inherent in traditional heterosexual relationships). Though he was not by any means the first nineteenth-century gay author to use it, Whitman had already thoroughly developed and applied the model of "comradeship" to male homosexuality in Calamus, as his empathic "love of comrades" there illustrates. In gay male literature "soldier-comradeship" is a subdivision of this fundamental motif. In Drum-Taps it is simply Whitman's adaptation of the model of basic "comradeship" to the war situation, and it held the same homosexual meaning for him there.

To contemporary readers terms like "friend" and "comrade" might seem like camouflage for franker but "unspeakable" statements, but when we view them within the context of homosexual experience in Whitman's day we can easily see that this is not the case (unless we are thinking of graphic genital or erotic representation, and then we would have to say that most of nineteenth-century heterosexual literature is

"camouflaged" as well). It must be remembered that
there were no accepting or even value-free terms for
homosexuality in Whitman's era (the word "homosexual"
had not even been invented yet), so there was no way
that these terms could be a "cover" for more candid
statements that gay authors wanted to make about their
identity -- they had no positive and fitting terms for
their identity in the first place. Instead, terms like
"friend" and "comrade" were one result of the repeated
attempts nineteenth-century gay male writers made to
solve the problem of homosexual self-understanding.
Exploratory inventions in a cultural vacuum, they were
an example of gay authors' search for models that seemed
to approximate their identity in a way that their
dominant culture's language about them did not and that
gave them an opportunity to visualize the positive
meaning of their feelings more clearly.

At the same time, however, these terms did supply
gay authors with a form of protection, one that
ironically derived from the conditions of oppression
that sought to silence them in the first place. As
already mentioned, only negative conceptions of
homosexuality existed in Whitman's general culture.
This situation ironically allowed gay male writers to
continue to experiment in relative degrees of safety
with images of "friendship" and "comradeship" as valid
possibilities for homosexual identity. For in the
public world of the nineteenth century these terms would
always have an elusiveness. Equipped only with their
culture's negative notions as their means of identifying
homosexuality within their world, outsider-readers would
not be able to recognize, either immediately or
conclusively, the homosexual use that gay authors were
making of these familiar positive terms.
"Soldier-comradeship" could be even less discernible as
a designation for homosexuality than ordinary
"comradeship," even though its notes of intense
attachment and devotion clearly carried a homosexual
meaning for gay writers. For "soldier-comradeship"
carried two levels of familiar meaning that an
outsider-reader would have to penetrate before sensing
its homosexual implication -- the basic "comradeship" I
have just discussed and the literal military situation
to which it also validly applied.

Another common convention in nineteenth- and early
twentieth-century male homosexual literature is the
elegy that doubles as a gay male love poem; the greatest
example in Whitman's time -- and I believe it remains so
today -- was Tennyson's In Memoriam. In dealing with a
war situation Whitman would naturally have occasion to
use this framework. The elegy served gay writers not as
a means of self-invention but as an opportunity for more
open self-expression. It satisfied the other chief

problem of invention that they faced -- the need for
self-protecting strategies. Like the military
situation, the elegy was one of the few available
frameworks that by definition allowed for open
expression of intense same-sex feelings. In gay male
literature the elegy works in a different way from the
"friendship"/"comradeship" motif. Its statements of
homosexual feeling are usually unambiguous, but it
contains a most useful "cover" in the fact that the
praised loved one is dead. This does not make the
sentiments the speaker voices any less homosexual, but
it can throw a gloss of uncertainty over them, offering
a convenient defense against attacks from hostile
readers who may have glimpsed the gay content or
providing anxious readers with a basis for "not seeing"
it in the first place. (This surely must be the chief
reason that In Memoriam was able to become a monument of
Victorianism while at the same time containing so many
daring homosexual statements.)

"Vigil Strange I Kept on the Field One Night" is
the most elaborate example of the way Whitman combines
his two chief vehicles in Drum-Taps to make a homosexual
affirmation. The poem is clearly in the
"soldier-comrade" tradition, and, with the aid of the
background already delineated, we can see that it
carries a male homosexual connotation. An extended
recollection by a soldier speaker about a vigil he kept
by the side of his dead comrade, "Vigil Strange" is also
an excellent illustration of the benefits the elegy gave
to gay male writers of the period. On the one hand, it
provided an opportunity to make outright romantic and
erotic statements, statements that would surely be
recognized by and would inspirit homosexual readers.
"Vigil Strange" contains such intense declarations as
"your dear eyes returned a look I shall never forget,"
"One touch of your hand to mine," "dear comrade, [I]
found your body . . . of responding kisses," "Passing
sweet hours, immortal and mystic hours with you dearest
comrade" and "I faithfully loved you.";11 On the other
hand, the elegy placed that content in a larger
framework that could cloak or defuse it for an audience
of outsiders.

An added complication in "Vigil Strange" is
Whitman's occasional use of the word "son" to
characterize his dead "comrade." On the one hand, this
device could be part of the poem's self-protectiveness,
an attempt by Whitman to distract the reader by creating
the impression of a chaste parental relationship. But
in order to hold to this reading one would firmly have
to ignore the poem's passionately romantic content. A
knowledge of the unique circumstances of gay experience
gives us a way to read this aspect of the poem
differently and as part of a coherence. Even when

recognizing that the word "son" could have a simple
basis in reality in serving to describe a fallen
comrade who was young, Whitman's use of the word here
can also be seen as an expression of homosexual
self-invention, specifically of the way that gay writers
expropriate nearby symbols to their experience. A major
theme of gay experience, and one that gay literature has
yet to develop consciously, is the way that homosexual
lovers can figuratively "parent" each other in the face
of society's lack of models and support, shifting roles
of parent and child in a process of mutual "rearing."
Though it is unlikely that Whitman was aware of his
experience in exactly this way in "Vigil Strange" -- and
without denying the simultaneous protective value of the
term -- it seems to me that his use of the word "son" in
the poem could be an intuitive recognition of this
aspect of the homosexual relation, and by this logic he
could have called himself his comrade's "son" here as
well.

"As I Lay with My Head in Your Lap Camerado" is the
most stirring example in Drum Taps of
soldier-comradeship that does not involve a death, and
it seems to me the most transparent instance in the
collection of Whitman's use of that motif to make a
homosexual affirmation. When viewed against the
biographical and social background I have just
discussed, "As I Lay" emerges as an especially moving
statement of male homosexual love and struggle in an
uncomprehending and hostile world. "As I Lay" first
appeared in the "Sequel" to Drum-Taps, was transferred
elsewhere in Leaves of Grass in 1871 and 1876, and
finally returned to Drum-Taps in 1881. Whitman's
shifting around of the poem clearly indicates its
adaptability to situations other than a military one, a
fact that starts to become clear from its opening
lines. "As I Lay" is dotted with terms that evoke a
literal battle ("weapons," "danger," "death,"
"victorious," "defeated"), but the poem begins instead
with a moment of male-male intimacy and clearly implied
eroticism and with the suggestion of release from an
imposed restraint -- the speaker, about to "resume" a
"confession," lies with his head in his "camerado's
lap. Though not necessarily clear from the text alone,
Whitman's central term "camerado" reinforces this note.
The word certainly echoes the "comrade" tradition, but,
as recent scholarship has pointed out, "camerado" is the
term Whitman typically preferred in situations that had
the greatest intensity and implication of intimacy for
him.;12

As "As I Lay" progresses, it becomes clear that its
theme is not military ardor but "resolute" nonconformity
and that the enemy is not an opposing army but Whitman's
established culture ("I confront peace, security, and

all the settled laws, to unsettle them"). There are two ways in which these lines have a homosexual application. One is that they are linked by the very structure of the poem to a homosexual situation, since they are occasioned by and arise out of a moment of male-male intimacy and eroticism. The other is that their theme directly applies to homosexual experience under oppression and that it had already been so used by Whitman five years earlier in Calamus.;13 "As I Lay" is full of echoes of the earlier collection. Its note of "confession" and its call for militant opposition to established "laws" are also prominent features of Calamus (see, for example, "Scented Herbage of My Breast" and "Whoever You Are Holding Me Now in Hand"). And the situation of the "camerados" here is analogous to the one in which Whitman places homosexual lovers in Calamus' most radical strain -- they are at a maximum distance from their dominant society's "settled" views. In this respect, the Calamus poem that "As I Lay" most resembles is "When I Heard at the Close of the Day," where Whitman has the speaker and his lover withdraw from the "capitol" -- which as homosexuals they must inevitably do -- to a private harmony in nature. In fact, it could be argued that "As I Lay" is the continuation of "When I Heard at the Close of the Day." If we can imagine that Calamus poem as having a "next morning," we can say that "As I Lay" represents the "rude awakening" its gay male lovers would face then. Though by the definition of their orientation they are outside their culture's established conceptions of identity and nature, they are still of course hedged by that society on all sides, and their only honorable recourse is to struggle. It is in this spirit that Whitman ends "As I Lay." He evokes the theme of equality that characterizes much of homosexual writing and, as a pioneer on this "untrodden path," he refuses to guarantee his "camerado" a clear and happy outcome, instead crying, "Dear camerado! I confess I have urged you onward with me, and still urge you, without the least idea of what is our destination, or whether we shall be victorious, or utterly quell'd and defeated."

Homosexual writing up to the present cannot be fully understood outside of the special conditions of the gay situation, especially without reference to the context of gay oppression. Either out of ignorance of its circumstances or simple reluctance to consider its implications, mainstream critics have rarely evaluated the work of a gay writer from this perspective. But, as my discussion has indicated, when we look at the most personal Drum-Taps poems in this way they clearly emerge as examples of gay male literature. They do not represent the "sublimation" of a homosexual identity. Instead, they exemplify the pioneering attempts of that

identity to comprehend and portray itself in the face of
both its culture's thoroughly negative views and its
society's absolute prohibitions. Aided by the materials
that the Civil War gave him, Whitman was able to produce
a number of gay lyrics that, even at their most
militant, possess a distinctive equilibrium. It is not
clear whether Whitman was consciously seeking the kind
of safeguard that the war setting gave him, but it is
clear that he was ironically protected from exposure by
making use of the war's conditions. Through them he
could write a number of pieces that were faithful to the
actual circumstances of the conflict and at the same
time frankly stated homosexual sentiments and truthfully
expressed his developing positive sense of homosexual
identity. It may have been this balance that he sensed
and was trying to express when he cryptically remarked
that Drum-Taps had no "perturbations."

NOTES

1. This view even underlies Asselineau's otherwise
dissenting and pioneering discussion. See Roger
Asselineau, The Evolution of Walt Whitman: The Creation
of a Book (Cambridge, Mass.: Harvard University Press,
1962), pp. 108-28.
2. Malcolm Cowley, "Walt Whitman: The Miracle,"
New Republic, 114 (March 18, 1946): 385-88; "Walt
Whitman: The Secret," New Republic, 114 (April 8,
1946): 481-84.
3. Robert K. Martin, "Whitman's Song of Myself":
Homosexual Dream and Vision," Partisan Review, 42, No. 1
(1975): 80-96. See Martin's The Homosexual Tradition in
American Poetry (Austin: University of Texas Press,
1979) for a continuation and elaboration of his work on
Whitman as a gay poet. I had not yet read this
important book at the time I completed this article; it
is essential reading for anyone interested in this
subject.
4. See Jonathan Katz, Gay American History:
Lesbians and Gay Men in the U.S.A. (New York: Crowell,
1976), pp. 337-65, 499-508.
5. This has been a long-held view in Whitman
scholarship, accepted as early as Frederik Schyberg's
1933 study. For characteristic discussions of Whitman's
sexuality and poetry of the Civil War period, see Gay
Wilson Allen, Walt Whitman Handbook (1946; repr. New
York: Hendricks House, 1962), pp. 70, 162-72, and The
Solitary Singer (1955; repr., with revisions, New York:
New York University Press, 1967), pp. 337-43. Even
Asselineau's franker discussion follows the same view.
See his The Evolution of Walt Whitman: The Creation of a
Personality (Cambridge, Mass.: Harvard University Press,
1960), pp. 149-74. Among more recent scholarship,

perhaps the most astonishing illustration of this traditional outlook is Stephen A. Black's Whitman's Journeys into Chaos: A Psychoanalytic Study of the Poetic Process (Princeton: Princeton University Press, 1975), pp. 223-34. Samuel Cole's "Whitman's War: The March of a Poet," Walt Whitman Review, 21 (September 1975): 85-100, is a rare dissenting discussion, but Cole does not elaborate on his outright statements about the homosexuality of Drum-Taps.

6. Quoted in Allen, Solitary Singer, p. 320.

7. Quoted in Ibid., pp. 421-422.

8. Asselineau, Creation of a Personality, p. 173; Allen; Solitary Singer, p. 339.

9. See my "Not Happy in the Capitol: Homosexuality and the Calamus Poems," American Studies, 19, no. 2 (Fall 1978): 5-22.

10. The study of homosexuality in history is only at its beginnings. At present, the best comprehensive survey of the subject, though flawed by insufficient analysis of the issue, is Vern Bullough's Sexual Variance in Society and History (New York: John Wiley and Sons, 1976). Most of the historical information I mention here can be found in Bullough.

11. All quotations from Whitman are from Leaves of Grass, ed. Scully Bradley and Harold W. Blodgett (New York: Norton, 1973).

12. See Marian Stein, "'Comrade' or 'Camerado' in Leaves of Grass," Walt Whitman Review, 13, no. 4 (December 1967): 123-25.

13. For a detailed discussion of this point and of my other comments about Calamus below, see "Not Happy in the Capitol."

8.

"Hints . . . Faint Clews and Indirections": Whitman's Homosexual Disguises

ALAN HELMS

> "The degree and kind of a person's sexuality
>   penetrates every corner of his being."
> -- Nietzsche, _Beyond Good and Evil_, Paragraph 75.

In 1882, a young Oscar Wilde in a brown velvet suit paid a call on Walt Whitman in Camden. Afterward, Wilde told the friend who had taken him that if the elderberry wine he'd been offered "had been vinegar, I would have drunk it all the same, for I have an admiration for that man which I can hardly express.";1 Oscar Wilde at a loss for words? What did the quickwitted dandy find so admirable about the lumbering, homespun, Good Gray Poet? For one thing, an illustration of his favorite theory: life imitates art. Wilde found a consciously crafted man who had become his own ideal version of himself. For another, Wilde discovered what he had expected to find ever since he had read an early edition of _Leaves of Grass_: a fellow queer, or a fellow Uranian, or however else it was homosexual men saw themselves in the public eye in those days (and how very conscious Wilde and Whitman were of the public eye). Next day, Whitman told a Philadelphia reporter: "We had a very happy time together. I think him genuine, honest, and manly," and later: "He is so frank, and out-spoken, and manly. I don't see why such mocking things are written of him.";2 Whitman's insistence upon Wilde's "manliness" suggests a cautionary tactic designed to dispel suspicion by appropriating the standards by which most nineteenth century American men judged other men. Whitman was, in fact, an extremely cautious man, for he

was a homosexual writing in a homophobic society. In
the Preface to the first <u>Leaves of Grass</u> he starts a
list of "parts of the greatest poet" with the item
"Extreme caution or prudence," an odd requirement for a
poet, especially when stipulated by someone who kept
wanting to "undrape" himself, to become "undisguised and
naked," although it is true he only does so cautiously
-- only "in paths untrodden," or only "apart from other
men,"

> Or else, only by stealth, in some wood, for
>   trial, or back of a rock, in the open
>   air . . .

or

> . . . just possibly with you on a high hill --
>   first watching lest any person, for miles
>   around, approach unawares. . . .
> Here to put your lips upon mine I permit you,
> With the comrade's long-dwelling kiss, or the
>   new husband's kiss,
> For I am the new husband, and I am the
>   comrade.;3

What is strikingly homosexual here is not so much the
phrase "I am the new husband" or even the image of that
lingering kiss, but rather the sense of extreme caution
expressed in "first watching lest any person, for miles
around, approach unawares" -- a caution born of a fear
of exposure, since exposure as a homosexual in a
homophobic society generally guarantees some form of
abuse, judgment, condemnation, even violence. In 1860
Whitman published an epigram which, superficially odd,
goes far toward explaining a basic feature of his nature
and his style:

> He is wisest who has the most caution,
> He only wins who goes far enough.;4

How can one be extremely cautious and at the same time
go far enough? Whitman tells how in <u>Calamus</u> 44, the
penultimate poem of that sequence and the one in which
Whitman is explicit about his need for caution and his
fear of exposure:

> Here my last words, and the most baffling,
> Here the frailest leaves of me, and yet my
>   strongest-lasting,
> Here I shade down and hide my thoughts -- I do
>   not expose them,
> And yet they expose me more than all my other
>   poems.

Whitman will go far enough, cautiously. He will expose
his homosexuality through the agency of his poems; but
since he is afraid of exposure, he will do so cautiously
-- by shading down and hiding his thoughts, by speaking
in what he refers to, in "When I Read the Book," as,
"hints . . . faint clews and indirections."

Granted that the word "indirection" has played an
important role in American poetics (Emily Dickinson,
Robert Frost, and T. S. Eliot all speak of its
importance in their work), and granted that writers of a
mystical tendency sometimes speak in indirection,
through metaphor or allegory. Granted even the
contemporary argument that all literature is to some
degree a form of indirection, it is nevertheless true
that Whitman's homosexuality gave him an additional
reason for employing a mode which for a century and a
quarter has thrown most readers off the track of his
most intimate meanings. Unable to speak directly of his
homosexuality, this extremely sexual poet must employ an
elaborate system of disguises -- hints, clues, and
indirections -- to convey his meaning; in order to
become "undisguised and naked," he must first disguise
himself.

One of Whitman's most successful disguises takes a
form of that linguistic invention which is such a
prominent feature of his style and such an important
part of his excitement. In passages of sexual content,
Whitman often creates a verbal surface of such density
that it interposes itself between us and our
comprehension of what we are reading. Language is
normally used to aid comprehension; in the following
lines, it is used to prevent it:

> Is this then a touch? quivering me to a new
>   identity. . . .
> On all sides prurient provokers stiffening my
>   limbs,
> Straining the udder of my heart for its
>   withheld drip,
> Behaving licentious toward me, taking no
>   denial,
> Depriving me of my best as for a purpose,
> Unbuttoning my clothes and holding me by the
>   bare waist,
> Deluding my confusion with the calm of the
>   sunlight and pasture fields,
> Immodestly sliding the fellow senses away,
> They bribed to swap off with touch, and go and
>   graze at the edges of me,
> No consideration, no regard for my draining
>   strength or my anger,
> Fetching the rest of the herd around to enjoy
>   them awhile,

> Then all uniting to stand on a headland and
>   worry me.

Although this passage is clearly sexual in content, it
is not altogether clear who is doing what to whom.
Distractions abound: the startling image of "the udder
of my heart," that freight train of principles loaded
with ambiguous meanings, the fuzz of syntax toward the
end, the incredibly confusing notion of "deluding my
confusion." Whitman is capable of being plain-spokenly
clear when it suits his purpose -- even as here, where a
line like "unbuttoning my clothes and holding me by the
bare waist" is startlingly clear, and thus performs as a
ruse to keep us reading. But our urgent questions about
this passage -- Who are the provokers? Why is the
speaker angry? How is the sex illicit? -- these never
get answered. The variety of interpretations that have
been "stucco'd all over" this passage attests to
Whitman's success here in shading down and hiding his
thoughts.
     Another obvious disguise occurs in "Song of
Myself," section 11, wherein the shy lonely woman who
desires the twenty-eight bathers joins them in
imagination:

> An unseen hand . . .passed over their bodies,
> It descended tremblingly from their temples
>   and ribs.
> The young men float on their backs, their
>   white bellies swell to the sun. . . .
>   they do not ask who seizes fast to them,
> They do not know who puffs and declines with
>   pendant and bending arch,
> They do not think whom they souse with spray.

Critics point out that an amazing feat of this passage
is Whitman's identification with both subject and
object, the woman and the bathers, but by that same
means it is the speaker who vicariously performs the
masturbation so beautifully described at the end. To my
mind, a more interesting example of Whitman's
identification with subject and object occurs in _Calamus_
29. The poem begins:

> One flitting glimpse, caught through an
>   interstice,
> Of a crowd of workmen and drivers, in a
>   barroom, around the stove, late of a
>   winter night

and we assume that the speaker is the observer who looks
with us into the barroom; but no, for the poem
continues: " -- And / I unremarked, seated in a

corner." Whitman is watching himself, as if to see how
he might appear to a passing stranger glimpsing a
middle-aged man holding hands with "a youth who loves
me, and whom I love." He defuses judgment of this scene
by appropriating to himself the role of outside
observer.

The experience of being simultaneously an observer
and the observed is a common one for homosexuals, and in
this, the passage just quoted is characteristic of the
gay sensibility. In Whitman's poetry, this experience
takes on emblematic significance in the activity of
cruising which appears so prominently in the early work
-- an activity that would seem to be anything but a
disguise, since in cruising we find ways to make our
sexual desires undisguised. Those ways are disguised,
however, in that we only show our desires to a selected
few, usually by communicating them through the eyes:

> Among the men and women, the multitude, I
>   perceive one picking me out by secret and
>   divine signs. . . .
> Some are baffled -- But that one is not --
>   that one knows me.
>
> Lover and perfect equal!
> I meant that you should discover me so, by my
>   faint indirections,
> And I, when I meet you, mean to discover you
>   by the like in you.;5

Cruising is a complicated activity which signifies many
things. It is a disguised exposing; it is also a
blatant hinting, and in that sense it is related to the
many hints at a secret which occur throughout Whitman's
early poetry:

> This hour I tell things in confidence
> I might not tell everybody, but I will tell
>   you,

Whitman says, luring us on through a rhetoric of
seduction which guarantees that we will wonder about
this confidence he hints at but never fully shares.
Some things he promises to tell us in private,
cautiously: " . . . I swear I never will translate
myself at all, only to him or her who privately stays
with me in the open air." Some things he simply will
not tell us: "My final merit I refuse you. . . . I
refuse putting from me the best I am." And some things
he cannot tell us, as in Calamus 36:

> . . . there is something fierce and terrible
>   in me, eligible to burst forth,

> I dare not tell it in words -- not even in
>   these songs.;11

Since "these songs" are the Calamus poems, the remark
"not even in these songs" becomes a clue that <u>Calamus</u>
would normally be an appropriate place for speaking of
"something fierce and terrible in me." By means of such
hints, Whitman makes sure we will try to penetrate to
the meaning of his secret: "My words itch at your ears
till you understand them" ("Song of Myself," 1246).
        Once we come into possession of the entire system
of hints, clues, and indirections which permeates so
much of Whitman's writing through the first three
editions of <u>Leaves of Grass</u>, we are obliged to reassess
our understanding of that writing in the light of
Whitman's homosexual disguises. One result of such a
reassessment is to force upon our attention what is
probably the most obvious of all the disguises:
Whitman's frequent avoidance of gender words, a tactic
allowing him to treat sexual matters in poetry that
lends itself to contrary interpretations, as if the
content were androgynous. The most interesting example
of such a disguise occurs in the famous description of
transcendence at the beginning of "Song of Myself":

> I mind how we lay in June, such a transparent
>   summer morning;
> You settled your head athwart my hips and
>   gently turned over upon me,
> And parted the shirt from my bosom-bone, and
>   plunged your tongue to my barestript
>   heart,
> And reached till you felt my beard, and
>   reached till you held my feet.

This passage gives us a descripton of homosexual love,
but the sexuality is so thoroughly disguised that it is
impossible to prove its homosexual nature without
reference to the whole system of disguises which
provides the context for such an interpretation. The
passage therefore serves as an example of what until
recently was the ultimate triumph for a homosexual
writer -- a disguising of homosexuality so complete that
it becomes invisible, thereby saving straight readers
from the discomforts of fag meanings.
        Whitman's style is thus what Wolfgang Iser calls
"overdetermined," which is to say that the very style of
the writing lends itself to widely varying
interpretations. As soon as you think you have sighted
a clear meaning, it turns into something else in the
view of a different reader. For some readers, Whitman's
homosexuality turns into "adhesiveness"; for others, a
figure of transcendence; for still others, a program of

political action. But for those who read Whitman most
fully and most clearly, it is all these things, while
remaining at the same time fundamentally homosexual, and
all these things -- adhesiveness, transcendence,
political action -- can only be fully understood in the
light of Whitman's homosexuality.

Whitman himself would surely have us read him so at
long last, for anyone who hints repeatedly at a secret
wants to be found out. This exciting tension in
Whitman's poetry between the impulse toward disguise and
the impulse toward exposure explains why it is that
Leaves of Grass creates the impression of cruising the
reader, a book in search of lovers. The remarkable
thing is probably not so much the elaborate disguises
Whitman employs to hide his homosexuality than the
enormous risk he takes in speaking as openly about it as
he does, with an ingenuousness only possible to someone
who lived before Freud. Yet the risk became too great
when it threatened Whitman's cherished dream of
widespread public acceptance, so after the 1860 Leaves
of Grass this extremely sexual poet simply removed the
sex from his poetry, with disastrous consequences for
the poetry. It seems an odd choice, yet what else could
Whitman do? He could either write openly about his
sexuality and thereby surrender any hope of public
acceptance, like Cavafy, or he could remain a public
poet only by sublimating his sexuality out of his art,
like Auden. Given Whitman's enormous desire for fame,
and his time and place, he really had no other choice
than to remove the sex. This haunting lyric poet whose
genius was moved by "cries of unsatisfied love" sings no
such cries after 1860. The rest is one of the most
disappointing and self-destructive chapters in our
literary history.

NOTES

1. Gay Wilson Allen, The Solitary Singer: A
Critical Biography of Walt Whitman, rev. ed. (1967;
repr. New York: New York University Press, 1969), p.
502.
2. Ibid.
3. Calamus 3, Walt Whitman's Blue Book: Facsimile
of the Unique Copy in the Oscar Lion Collection of the
New York Public Library (New York: The New York Public
Library, 1968), p. 371. All quotations from Calamus are
taken from this book.
4. "Debris," Walt Whitman's Blue Book, p. 421.
5. Calamus 41.

9.
Walt Whitman's Pose and the Ethics of Sexual Liberation

M. J. KILLINGSWORTH

Whitman is often considered to have been ahead of his times in the sexual attitudes he reveals in his poetry; he has been portrayed heroically struggling with that grim demon, the "Victorian repressive norm." This image, which in the light of recent histories of sexual attitudes seems oversimplified, derives partly from fact and partly from Whitman's own self-concept -- the pose which gullible admirers have accepted as fact. One aspect of this self-image that has gone unnoticed is its ethical and political origin. Whitman's many defenses of his poetry treating sexual themes were nearly always based on his liberal democratic politics in a curious combination with romantic aesthetic theory.

Whitman was attempting to find a middle way between the libertinism associated with the aristocratic class of the Old World and the prudery associated with the middle class of the New World and the Old. What Whitman settled on has been defined by one intellectual historian as sexual romanticism, a movement toward sexual liberation -- toward an affirmation of the "essential worth of erotic experience" -- but away from the libertinism or sexual materialism represented by the "arch anti-Romantic," the Marquis de Sade. The romantic holds that love purifies sex and thus frees it from the control of religion, the family, and the law; whereas the libertine longs to free sexual enjoyment from love itself.;1 The difficulty of following the romantic way was evident even at its inception. The democrats of the French Revolution discovered that their distrust of the aristocracy came into conflict with their ideals of liberty and tolerance. They were repelled, on the one

hand, by the attitudes and behavior which they
associated with the libertine aristocracy; on the other
hand, their ideal of personal liberty found its way into
their sexual mores; they secularized marriage, legalized
divorce, and reformed old laws restricting sexual
behavior.;2

Having inherited these democratic sexual dilemmas,
Whitman tried to guard against charges of libertinism by
balancing his cries for sexual freedom with solemn
pronouncements about the spirituality of the body. His
ministrations to the soul in sexual poems like "Song of
Myself" and "I Sing the Body Electric" were designed to
balance and justify his materialistic concerns, but more
often than not this tactic produced only contradiction
and confusion. His mystification of birth and
motherhood, for example, interfered with his radical
feminist ideals in the Children of Adam poems. And in
Calamus his dependence on the theme of death as an
emotional intensifier hampered the success of his
political scheme by coloring his joyous poems of
brotherhood with a dark tone suggesting fear or guilt.
In his own lifetime Whitman's defenders would focus on
the spiritual side of his poems, his love ethic or his
mysticism, while his detractors would snatch
materialistic lines out of their context and charge the
poet with libertinism.

Even a sex radical like David Goodman Croly
criticized Whitman for the eroticism of Leaves of Grass,
which he took as evidence of the poet's degeneracy.
Croly thought that sexuality should be discussed in a
disinterested, unimpassioned, "scientific" way, though
Croly's attitude is itself complex. His faith in
science seems materialistic, but it also represents a
concern with middle-class respectability. Scientists,
doctors, professionals -- Croly himself was a journalist
-- were qualified to deal sanely with sex, but a poet?

Croly's critique of Leaves of Grass is found in the
frank but confusing book The Truth about Love, published
in two editions in 1872. His analysis runs as follows:

> If you will carefully note the pleasure which
> greets Walt Whitman among the highly
> cultivated classes, you will see that it is
> with them a case of "reversion" to brute
> life. What a singular phenomenon it is to
> behold these white-cravatted gentlemen . . .
> going into ecstasies over a man "who loves
> the smell of armpits" -- who pictures the wife
> sleeping with her hand upon her husband's
> thigh -- who has raised so many "barbaric
> yawps" over the sublimities of fornication.;3

This criticism would have stung Whitman deeply for two
reasons. First, it implies that Whitman's treatment of
sexuality holds no value in a progressive democratic
society and that it has been rightly rejected by all but
the educated elite. Second, Croly argues that the
acceptance of Leaves of Grass by this class proves the
decadence of the book by association. This is the
argument of a radical egalitarian, a son of the French
Revolution. That Whitman regarded himself as the
paradigm of a true democrat is a fact that needs no
further commentary. That he thought of himself as the
opponent of libertinism and aristocratic degeneracy is
also easily established. His use of health as a moral
category in his poems was based largely on his desire to
make his sexual themes legitimate and to show how sexual
energy could contribute to the positive development of
civilization. In the words of William Douglas O'Connor
-- words approved by Whitman himself before they were
published in The Good Gray Poet -- one of the chief
purposes of Leaves of Grass was to rescue "from the
keeping of blackguards and debauchees, to which it has
been abandoned . . . the general element of . . .
sexuality.";4 Whitman's twentieth-century readers,
moreover, have affirmed that the poet's purpose was
essentially anti-libertine and even non-erotic. Harold
Blodgett, for example, distinguishes Whitman's sexual
poetry from Swinburne's along these lines; he refers to
"the 'fever' of the Poems and Ballads and the 'sanity'
of Leaves of Grass, the eroticism of the one and the
salubrity of the other," Swinburne's "sadistic passion"
and Whitman's "procreative love.";5 There is an erotic
strain in Leaves of Grass, but most often Whitman's
eroticism is only apparent; that is, it is not intended
so much to arouse the reader sexually as to shock him
into an awareness of a sexual life and thus to draw
attention to the poet's serious moral themes. It is a
rhetorical, not actual, eroticism.

     Whitman found it difficult to play the role of the
democrat and sexual liberationist and at the same time
avoid being tagged as a libertine catering to the tastes
of a degenerate upper class. The fact that Leaves of
Grass was as well received as it was among the educated
classes of England was for Whitman a source of comfort
and pride, but it also created difficulties for a poet
who longed to be the voice of the democratic New World.
From such a voice the American public demanded to hear
of their moral superiority over the degenerate Old
World. In addition to David Croly, a number of
prominent literary figures, such as James Russell Lowell
and Thomas Wentworth Higginson, used Whitman's English
popularity against him.;6 There were perhaps some
grounds for the strident and nationalistic moralism of
these critics, for in England, rather ironically,

Victorianism was not so pervasive a force as it was in
America. It is true that the economic domination of the
middle class in England caused bourgeois values to seep
upwards into the aristocracy, just as Methodism produced
much the same effect in the lower classes -- hence
Victorian morality.;7 But among certain segments of the
English upper classes, who were culturally if not
economically dominant, the spirit of libertinism was
still nourished. This spirit was all but utterly
quelled in America because of the complete domination of
the middle class.

When Symonds began to question him about the
Whitman's statements about his English admirers
were nearly always calculated to show his warmth for
them as disciples and "comrades" but also his distrust
of high cultivation. Of John Addington Symonds, Whitman
said: "Symonds is cultivated enough to break -- bred to
the last atom -- overbred: yet he has remained human, a
man, in spite of all." And again: "Symonds has got
into our crowd in spite of his culture." And again:
"That Symonds blood seems to be good stuff: it comes
from the top down rather than from the bottom up, to be
sure (it should come the other way) but nevertheless it
tingles, stirs, thrills with genuine humanism." Of
Edward Carpenter he said: "The best of Carpenter is in
his humanity: he manages to stay with people: he was a
university man, yet managed to save himself in time.";8
This interest in class differences may have been partly
responsible for Whitman's delicacy in dealing with these
Englishmen when they questioned him on the precise
meaning of the apparently homosexual passages of Leaves
of Grass. His secrecy is famous. He told Carpenter,
"There is something in my nature furtive like an old
hen.";9

When Symonds began to question him about the
meaning of the brotherhood theme in Calamus, Whitman was
moved in conversations with Horace Traubel to adopt the
pretense of ingenuousness. He coyly told Traubel: "I
often say to myself about Calamus -- perhaps it means
more or less than what I thought myself -- means
different: perhaps I don't know what it all means --
perhaps never did know.";10

This false ingenuousness also played a part in the
complex psychology behind Whitman's famous reply to the
final pointed question as Symonds phrased it in 1890
after nearly 20 years of indirect questions:

> In your conception of Comradeship, [Symonds
> asked him] do you contemplate the possible
> intrusion of those semi-sexual emotions and
> actions which no doubt occur between men? I
> do not ask, whether you approve of them, or
> regard them as a necessary part of the
> relation? But I should much like to know

whether you are prepared to leave them to the
inclination and the conscience of the
individuals concerned?;11

To this Whitman answered in very direct language:

Ab't the question on Calamus pieces &c: they
quite daze me. L of G. is only to be rightly
construed by and within its own atmosphere and
essential character -- all of its pages &
pieces so coming strictly under that -- that
the Calamus part has even allow'd the
possibility of such construction as mentioned
is terrible -- I am fain to hope the pages
themselves are not to be even mention'd for
such gratuitous and quite at the same time
undream'd & unreck'd possibility of morbid
inferences -- wh' are disavow'd by me & seem
damnable.;12

This passage from the letter makes it quite clear that
in 1890 Whitman did not want his poems used publicly by
homosexuals as a justification for acts which he, the
poet/prophet of democracy, could not -- or could no
longer -- condone. That the young university men of
England were using the poems in this way is evident from
biographical sources.;13 Whitman did not want to be
involved, at least not directly, in the early homosexual
rights movement as it was developing among the educated
classes in England. Furthermore, he might have feared
that Symonds was planning a legal battle, since in the
1890 letter Symonds mentions his preference for the
liberal laws of France and Italy which "protect minors,
punish violence, and guard against outrages of public
decency," but which "are in open contradiction with the
principles of English (and I believe American)
legislation.";14 Whitman was sure, at any rate, that
his answer would be made public in one form or another,
for Symonds left no doubt that he would use any
information provided by Whitman in a study of the poet's
life and works.
     Whitman's response, which has become the great crux
in the interpretation of Calamus, must have been
designed to mislead Symonds in some way. Why else would
Whitman have developed in his letter the elaborate
fiction about his past sexual life? He claimed that "my
life, young manhood, mid-age, times South, &c: have all
been jolly, bodily, and probably open to criticism -- "
and lest there was any doubt that he meant that his
experience was heterosexual, he wrote:

Tho' always unmarried I have had six children
-- two are dead -- One living southern

> grandchild, fine boy, who writes to me
> occasionally. Circumstances connected with
> their benefit and fortune have separated me
> from intimate relations.;15

Of course there is no evidence suggesting the existence of these offspring, and most readers of this letter have concluded that the children were conceived within the poet's imagination. Whitman was as dishonest in the last sentence of his letter as he was in concocting this story of his fatherhood. Even though he had carefully drafted the letter and recopied it before sending it off, he wrote, "I see I have written with haste & too great effusion -- but let it stand." He had also waited to answer Symonds' questions about Calamus until the Englishman phrased his query in a direct way in the letter of 1890; he had been asking the same question in a circumspect way since his first letter to Whitman in 1871. The poet's conversations with Traubel indicate that he had pondered his reply several years prior to writing the 1890 letter.

Whitman did not want to be publicly portrayed as a friend and defender of the upper-class English libertine -- the poet of public school buggery. When he wrote to Symonds that he wanted Calamus to be "construed by and within" the "atmosphere and essential character" of Leaves of Grass, he meant that the poems should be read in their entire context and that any inferences drawn from them should take some account of the moral quality and the democratic principles of the book as a whole. He may also have meant that to deduce a simple sexual meaning from the poems would be to destroy the effect of the whole, an effect he considered complex -- moral and religious as well as political and physical. Symonds' insistence about the meaning of Calamus in particular must have seemed monomaniacal to Whitman. Finally, Whitman might have meant that he wanted Calamus to be read in its relation to the heterosexual Children of Adam poems and in relation to ("construed by and within") the general sexual character of Leaves of Grass.

The most interesting part of this famous letter is the self-concept Whitman projects. His role model might have been any one of the number of heterosexual adventurers among his romantic predecessors. He might have had George Sand in mind, for instance. Once when asked if she disappointed him because of "the latitude she took in the relation of marriage," he replied without hesitating that she did not; "the finest teachers in life," he said, "the most artistic, are the darkest; it is necessary for an artist to see everything -- to go to the depths of life. I don't regret anything about George Sand; her very frailties were the result of

her good qualities. She was impatient of the
goody-good; she wanted something freer.";16 The
implication here is that the artist with a great
imagination necessarily reaches beyond convention,
whether it is artistic, intellectual, or social
convention. In his letter to Symonds, Whitman implied
that though his experience might have been more limited
than Symonds', his imagination was by nature and
inclination less restrained than the Englishman's.
Whitman wrote that "one great difference between you and
me, temperament and theory, is restraint -- I know that
while I have a horror of ranting and bawling I at
certain moments let the spirit impulse, (?demon) rage
its utmost, its wildest, damnedest -- (I feel to do so
in my L of G. & I do so).";17 Symonds took this as a
discreet qualification of Whitman's refusal to authorize
a homosexual interpretation of Calamus, since it
followed the disclaimer in the letter. He makes this
conviction clear in a letter to Edward Carpenter of
February 13, 1893, in which there also appears an
interesting variant for the 1890 letter from Whitman
(which Symonds quotes for Carpenter's benefit). The
variant is important not only because it involves the
key phrase, "the spirit impulse, (?demon)," but also
because it indicates that the letter which Whitman sent
to Symonds and which is no longer extant was in some
significant ways different from the draft which is
printed in The Correspondence of Walt Whitman. Symonds
wrote to Carpenter:

> He rambles on about his being less
> "restrained" by temperament & theory than I
> (J. A. S.) am -- "I at certain moments let the
> spirit impulse (female) rage its utmost
> wildest damnedest (I feel I do sometimes in
> L. of G. & I do so)"
>   That last passage seems meant to qualify
> the first. But if it does so, it implies that
> But if it does so, it implies that those
> inferences [of homosexuality] are not so
> gratuitous morbid & damnable as supposed.;18

Most likely Symonds was right about the
qualification. In fact, Whitman seems to have been
compelled to qualify his denial of the "morbid
inferences." By "spirit impulse (female)" Whitman must
have meant either his unrestrained homosexual emotions
or his sexual imagination, his concept of what it is
like to be female. And, if Symonds has quoted him
correctly, he confessed that he let it rage, both in his
poems and, he implies, in his life -- "I feel, I do so
sometimes in L. of G. & I do so." At any rate Whitman
seems to have been thinking mainly of vicarious

experience of some sort. He wanted Symonds to know the capacity of his imagination and its relation to his emotional experience. "Whatever Whitman's own personal makeup and experience," James E. Miller has remarked, "his imagination and vision were omnisexual. He had the artist's capacity to imagine and recreate many sexual roles, and he showed understanding of them and sympathy for them.";19 This is precisely the image that Whitman himself carefully cultivated.

By posing as the great romantic artist with the boundless imagination Whitman was therefore able to approach themes such as sexual freedom with sympathy and energy, and at the same time he could avoid stating his precise ethical position. He could be a dynamic poet without the responsibilities of a reformer or a moralist. Significantly, Symonds was the only one of his admirers or critics who demanded to be satisfied about the exact meaning of Calamus, and Whitman responded with one of his strongest rejections of the libertine ethic. Yet side by side with this apparent condemnation we find the poet confessing to heterosexual acts he did not commit and admitting that his sexual imagination was violently active. Presumably he not only wanted to avoid being thought of as a libertine, but he was also unwilling to be classified as a middle-class Victorian prude. He was furthermore quite consistent throughout his entire life in choosing the fuzzy ethics of sexual romanticism. He was a liberationist, not a libertine, though without a doubt these two points of view were confused or were condemned together by that dominant group to which they were both opposed -- the middle class, whose ethics have come to be known as the "Victorian repressive norm." Whitman himself differentiated between these three points of view, though he did not call them the bourgeois, the libertine, and the romantic, in his "Memorandum at a Venture," an essay he wrote in 1882 to defend his treatment of sexuality in Leaves of Grass. Whitman rejected both the repressive tendency of the prudes and the erotic tendency of the libertines and outlined his own position in this way:

> The time seems to me to have arrived, and
> America to be the place, for a new departure
> -- a third point of view. The same freedom
> and faith and earnestness which, after
> centuries of denial, struggle, repression, and
> martyrdom, the present day brings to the
> treatment of politics and religion, must work
> out a plan and a standard on this subject
> [sexuality], not so much for what is call'd
> society as for thoughtfulest men and women,
> and thoughtfulest literature.;20

Although Whitman as a public author and as a private
person was not always able to fulfill his goal of
treating sexuality with "freedom and faith and
earnestness," he was largely successful as the poet of
sexual romanticism, as one who took as his subject "the
complete human identity, physical, moral, emotional, and
intellectual, (giving precedence and compass in a
certain sense to the first).";21.

NOTES

1.   Paul Robinson, The Modernization of Sex (New
York: Harper and Row, 1976), p. 194.
2.   Arno Karlen, Sexuality and Homosexuality (New
York: Norton, 1971), p. 161.
3.   David Goodman Croly, The Truth about Love (New
York: Wesley, 1872), pp. 83-84.
4.   William Douglas O'Connor, The Good Gray Poet,
in Richard Maurice Bucke, Walt Whitman (Philadelphia:
McKay, 1883), pp. 118-19.
5.   Harold W. Blodgett, Walt Whitman in England
(Ithaca, N.Y.: Cornell University Press, 1934), pp.
103-4.
6.   Ibid., pp. 3-5.
7.   Karlen, p. 167.
8.   Horace Traubel, With Walt Whitman in Camden
(New York: Mitchell and Kennerley, 1914), vol. 1, pp.
189, 202, 388, and vol. 3, p. 196. Whitman's dealings
with Carpenter and Symonds are also admirably documented
by Jonathan Katz in Gay American History (New York:
Crowell, 1976), pp. 337-65.
9.   Edward Carpenter, Days with Walt Whitman, 2nd
ed. (London: Allen, 1906), pp. 42-43.
10.   Traubel, vol. 1, p. 76.
11.   John Addington Symonds, The Letters of John
Addington Symonds, ed. Herbert M. Scheuller and Robert
L. Peters (Detroit: Wayne State University Press,
1969), vol. 3, p. 482.
12.   Walt Whitman, The Correspondence, ed. E. H.
Miller (New York: New York University Press, 1969),
vol. 5, pp. 72-73.
13.   See, for example, the introduction to Brian
Reade's Sexual Heretics (London: Coward McCann, 1970).
14.   Symonds, vol. 3, p. 482.
15.   Whitman, Correspondence, vol. 5, p. 73.
16.   Grace Gilchrist, "Chats with Walt Whitman,"
Temple Bar, 118 (1898): 204.
17.   Whitman, Correspondence, vol. 5, p. 73;
Whitman's italics.
18.   Symonds, vol. 3, pp. 818-19.
19.   James E. Miller, "Whitman's Omnisexual Vision,"
in The Chief Glory of Every People: Essays on Classic
American Writers, ed. Matthew J. Bruccoli (Carbondale:
Southern Illinois University Press, 1973), p. 241.

20.   Walt Whitman, "A Memorandum at a Venture," in *Prose Writings of Walt Whitman*, ed. Floyd Stovall (New York: New York University Press, 1964), vol. 2, pp. 491-93.

21.   Ibid.

10.
Walt Whitman, Feminist

HAROLD ASPIZ

Every reader of Whitman's poetry knows that the Whitman
persona is an "accepter" of women, in the same sense
that he "accepts" men, animals, "the commonest weeds by
the roadside," and all phenomena in nature. But a
historic approach -- comparing his views about women
with those of the feminists and marriage reformers who
were his contemporaries -- reveals him as a feminist
whose utterances about women are meaningful and perhaps
still inspiring today.

In fairness to the poet, we have no right to expect
his feminist values to jibe with feminist thought in the
1980s; the most advanced thinkers of a century ago will
be found sadly disappointing when judged by such
criteria. However, Whitman's ideal of athletic,
self-reliant women, eligible to participate on equal
terms with men in all phases of public life and to
become happy wives and the mothers of well-conceived,
painlessly birthed children and to grow into magnificent
old age, harmonizes with the avant-garde feminist
opinion of his era. Although the poetic portraits of
women in Leaves of Grass rarely reach the pinnacle of
artistic expression, we must not be misled by D. H.
Lawrence's devastating comment that Whitman's athletic
matrons are only so many faceless muscles and wombs or
by Richard Chase's taunt that the poet's women figures
are only males surrounded by a female nimbus. For
Lawrence and Chase misread Whitman's intention: to
introduce into literature an image and concept of
womanhood that was entirely opposed to the svelte,
enfeebled, and fashionable "lady" who was the reigning
heroine of Victorian literature. (How Whitman
abominated that word "lady," always insisting on

"woman"!) The enervated heroine of fashionable
literature, the stylish "monthly-magazine-made" girls,
said Henry Adams, "had not a feature that would be
recognized by Adam.";1 But in depicting the beauty of
fully developed, healthy women, Whitman sought to
promote woman's dignity and independence which, he felt,
were essential to the development of a democratic
order. Despite certain limitations in his outlook which
now seem obvious, he was guided by a positive feminism
in Democratic Vistas and predicated the success of
social evolution in America on the existence of "perfect
Women, indispensable to endow the birth-stock of the New
World.";2
     Whitman consistently maintained that women are
equal to men and, by virtue of their capacity for great
motherhood, may indeed be endowed with finer physical
faculties and superior sensitivities -- a sentiment not
unfamiliar to readers of such feminist manifestos as
Margaret Fuller's Woman in the Nineteenth Century. In
the first edition of Leaves of Grass, "Song for
Occupations" salutes

     The wife, and she is not one jot less than the
          husband,
     The daughter, and she is just as good as the
          son,
     The mother, and she is every bit as much as
          the father.

                                        (el. 33-35)

A selection in the second (1856) edition -- afterward
reworked as "A Poem of Remembrance for a Girl or a Boy
of These States" -- counsels the youth of America to

     Anticipate the best women;
     I say an unnumbered new race of hardy and
          well-defined women are to spread through
          all These States,
     I say a girl fit for These States must be
          free, capable, dauntless, just the same
          as a boy. . . .
     The creation is womanhood;
     Have I not said that womanhood involves all?
     Have I not told how the universe has nothing
          better than the best womanhood?

"Song of the Open Road," which first appeared in that
same edition, envisions a procession of splendid women
marching beside the men toward a hopeful future:
"Journeyers with their womanhood, ample, unsurpass'd,
content." And An American Primer, also written in 1856,
perceives that a feminist consciousness must have an
impact on the English language:

> In America an immense number of new words are
> needed to embody the new political facts
> . . . words to answer the modern, rapidly
> spreading, faith of the vital equality of
> women with men and that they are to be placed
> on an equal plane, socially and in business,
> with men.";3

Amidst the dark days in the Washington military
hospitals, when he was so deeply moved by the heroism of
the soldiers, Whitman declared: "I think sometimes to
be a woman is greater than to be a man -- is more
eligible to greatness, not the ostensible article, but
the real one." The prose preface to the 1872 edition of
the poems defines America as "not the Man's Nation only,
but the Woman's Nation -- a land of splendid mothers,
daughters, sisters, wives." Nevertheless, Whitman often
expressed the fear that unless America produces masses
of healthy and well-sexed women who have learned to
treat their bodies with dignity, America's great future
will be jeopardized. Without this "gift of gifts" --
without "the beauty, health, completion" of splendid
motherhood, "the ultimate human problem" could go
unsolved.

While it is impossible in a few minutes to suggest
the scope of Whitman's feminism, it is clear that
Whitman wanted women to be proud of their sexuality,
physically strong, self-reliant, and capable of splendid
motherhood. Indeed, this capacity for motherhood is the
key to his thinking and to that of many feminist
reformers of his day. In poems and in various prose
comments he implied that the woman must bring sexual
passion to the marriage bed and must approach motherhood
in the healthiest way. He stressed the wholesomeness
and nobility of the woman's sexual yearnings long before
he wrote Leaves of Grass; insisted in his famous letter
to Emerson that the prevailing prohibitions on the
expression of sexuality hinder the advancement of women,
warp our literature, and thwart democracy; and asserted
three decades later that these prohibitions were
blocking "the movement for the eligibility of women amid
new spheres of business, politics, and the suffrage."
He maintained that sexual passion (the woman's equally
with the man's) makes life worthwhile and that it must
find free expression in all phases of human endeavor.

A sizable literature of marriage reform asserted
that woman did indeed possess sexual passions as strong
as man's and that their free expression was the first
step in her liberation and development. For instance,
the historian Richard Hildreth observed in 1844 that the
sexual urge "probably is more powerful in women than in
men" and that all the physical and moral punishments in
Victorian society are designed to make woman deny her

sexuality. Writers like Orson S. Fowler, Dr. H. T.
Trall, Dr. Edward H. Dixon, Elizabeth Cady Stanton, and
others with whose writings and persons the poet was
familiar, made female sexuality the cornerstone of
female liberation. Not surprisingly, women are often
shown in <u>Leaves of Grass</u> in the full expression of their
sexuality. "Without shame the man I like knows and
avows the deliciousness of his sex," proclaims the poet
in "A Woman Waits for Me": "Without shame the woman I
like knows and avows hers." Section 5 of "I Sing the
Body Electric" (which the poet had once entitled
"Bridalnight") describes a woman in the midst of the
passionate and sensuous "bridegroom night of love,"
which culminates, as do all the wholesome matings in
<u>Leaves of Grass</u>, in the birth of a perfect child; the
woman's magnetic sexuality is proof and emblem of her
womanly excellence. Physical ripeness characterizes
Adam's eugenic bedmate in "From Pent-Up Aching Rivers"
as well as the sensuous "full-grown" lily-woman in
"Faces," who invites the "limber-hipped" hero-father to
fill her "with albescent honey" and who later reappears
in the poem as the contented grandmother of many
stalwart farmers and farmers' wives.
     A pair of statements by the marriage reformer H. C.
Wright, who published a daring volume the very year
<u>Leaves of Grass</u> first appeared, may put Whitman's
sentiments into a clearer perspective. Wright argued
that

> Maternity is a divinely appointed mission, --
> to be a mother is a sacred trust. To
> reverence this trust and come into close
> communion with the heart of all life replaces
> fear and dread with joy and satisfaction.
> This is in agreement with nature's plan, a law
> of the spirit. Acknowledgment of and
> obedience to this law lessen or entirely
> overcome the usual sufferings of pregnancy and
> of parturition.

And Wright also insisted that only the most sexually
dynamic matings, in which both married partners form
"but one existence, one life, one eternity" of sexual
harmony, can bring about the parentings of perfect
children. "Passional intercourse is meant to be an
ecstatic expression of the soul," he said.;4
     Small wonder that the words "mother" and "mothers"
together occur over 100 times in <u>Leaves of Grass</u>, where
they are fraught with Whitman's reverence for motherhood
as the sacred key to the evolutionary mystery. The
mother -- in youth, in childbirth, in old age -- is
exalted in "Song of Myself," whose 21st section asserts
that "there is nothing greater than the mother of men."

In other poems, Whitman undertakes to portray "the
Mothers of These States" as the proper emblem of the new
America, declaring that "none of the emblems of the
classic goddess -- nor any feudal emblems -- are fit
symbols for the republic." Typically, the poet pictures
Mother America surrounded by her sons and daughters:

>A grand, sane, towering, seated Mother,
>Chair'd in the adamant of Time. . . .

And he concludes "Faces," a poetic vision of
ameliorative evolution, with the portrait of an old
Quaker grandmother, the contented "mother of many
children," so unlike the "Venus women" -- the
fashionable ladies whom the poem deplores:

>Behold a woman!
>She looks out from her quaker cap, her face is
>   clearer and more beautiful than the sky.
>   . . .
>The melodious character of the earth,
>The finish beyond which philosophy cannot go
>   and does not wish to go,
>The justified mother of men.

Whitman's sentiments belong to a rich philosophic
tradition. Echoing Whitman's very line, "The daughter
and she is as good as the son," his great contemporary
Elizabeth Cady Stanton declared:

>We must educate our daughters to think that
>motherhood is grand. . . . If you suffer, it
>is not because you are cursed by God, but
>because you violate his laws. What an incubus
>it would take from woman could she be educated
>to know that the pains of maternity are no
>curse upon her kind. . . . But one word of
>fact is worth a volume of philosophy; let me
>give you some of my own experience. I am the
>mother of seven children. My girlhood was
>spent mostly in the open air. I early imbibed
>the idea that <u>a girl is just as good as a boy</u>
>and I carried it out.";5

And 40 years after Whitman penned his lovely tribute to
fulfilled maternity, the Scottish altruist and geologist
Henry Drummond wrote:

>Mothers are the chief end of creation. In
>plants the mother species head the list.
>Beyond the mother with her milky breast the
>Creator does not go: that is his goal. In as
>real a sense as a factory is meant to turn out

locomotives or locks, the machinery of nature
in its last resource is meant to turn out
mothers.;6

The fact that Whitman named robustness and
athleticism as feminine virtues and assigned these
traits to the idealized women in Leaves of Grass need
not reflect some psychic quirk. Such notions were
common among reformers. Orson S. Fowler, the
phrenologist whose works the poet knew very well (these
included such titles as Love and Parentage, Amativeness,
and possibly Creative and Sexual Science), advocated
vigorous physical exercise for women and opposed
corsetry, sedentary habits, and stimulants of all kinds,
including romantic fiction and dancing parties -- in
much the same way that Whitman did in newspaper pieces
and in poems -- on the grounds that they thwarted the
development of the healthy and wholesome mother. Dr.
Edward H. Dixon, a surgeon whose Woman and Her Diseases
the poet had reviewed in 1847 and whose New York-based
magazine The Scalpel he read regularly in the 1850s,
also held that the fashionably soft and listless
feminine lifestyle caused debility and reproductive
ailments. D. H. Jacques, author of a simplistic tract
which the poet warmly endorsed, insisted that women must
work hard, run, walk, swim, row, dance, and engage in
gymnastics. Jacques defined feminine beauty (as did
Whitman) in terms of female sturdiness, broad limbs,
ample bust, and large pelvis -- those physiological
characteristics which, he thought, best promoted healthy
motherhood. He illustrated his tract with line drawings
of the life-sized matronly nudes by the American
sculptor Hiram Powers which, he said, best illustrated
this ideal.
    Powers' statues exhibit the physical amplitude and
apparent ripeness for motherhood which caused the poet
to praise them -- traits which also characterize the
portrayals of women in Whitman's writings. For example,
the heroine of Franklin Evans is said to be "about
twenty-five, and very handsome, not with the unformed
and unripened loveliness, but in the rich swell, the
very maturity of physical perfection." What Whitman
called "a poem illustrative of the women under 'the new
dispensation' . . . the best mothers -- the healthiest
women -- the most lovely women," is sketched in "A Woman
Waits for Me":

They are not one jot less than I am,
They are tanned in the face by shining suns
        and blowing winds,
Their flush has the old divine suppleness and
        strength,

> They know how to swim, row, ride, wrestle,
>   shoot, run, strike, retreat, advance,
>   resist, defend themselves,
> They are ultimate in their own right -- they
>   are calm, clear, well-possess'd of
>   themselves.

It is possible to parallel that appeal for athletic women in the statements of many reformers, including Whitman's beloved Frances Wright, Elizabeth Cady Stanton, and Dr. H. T. Trall, friend alike of Amos Bronson Alcott, Thoreau, and Whitman. Dr. Trall's book _The Illustrated Family Gymnasium_ (1857), which Whitman reviewed, prescribed vigorous gymnastic exercises for men and women alike. Trall's _Sexual Physiology_ (1871), a fascinating pro-feminist volume, not only stresses athletics but declares that any young man looking for a fit marriage partner should study Hiram Powers' nude statues to discover how the mother of his children ought to look.

Whitman rejected the ideal of romantic love in favor of marital chastity: "the chastity of maternity," "the chastity of paternity," "the chaste blessings of the well-married couple." For chastity was a code word in reformist literature, generally implying a marriage of regulated sexuality in which the woman is not compelled to pregnancy until she is passionately ready for it. The word is used in that sense by such reformers as Robert Owen, John Humphrey Noyes, Dio Lewis, and Ezra H. Heywood, author of such pamphlets as "Uncivil Liberty, An Essay to Show the Injustice and Impolity of Ruling Woman without Her Consent." (Anthony Comstock, who condemned _Leaves of Grass_ as an obscene book, sent Heywood to prison on obscenity charges; but Whitman insisted that Heywood was "a brave man -- a man more sinned against than sinning.") And Whitman enshrined the beauty of chaste, well-poised motherhood in the striking 11-line portrait in "Song of the Broad-Axe" of the woman who moves unsullied among the "gross and soil'd men" of the city:

> She is the best belov'd, it is without
>   exception, she has no reason to fear, and
>   she does not fear. . . .
> She is silent, she is possess'd of herself,
>   they do not offend her,
> She receives them as the laws of Nature
>   receive them, she is strong,
> She too is a law of Nature -- there is no
>   stronger law than she is.

A draft version of the poem specifies the law which the woman embodies: "She too was a law of nature. . . . [S]he was maternity."

This same verse reappears as the epigraph of Eliza W. Farnham's Woman and Her Era (1864), a neglected classic of militant feminism, which asserts that "honor to womankind and reverence for maternity are conditions of permanency to any people, nation, or race," and argues that woman is biologically the most advanced and virtuous form thus far evolved by nature and that she is destined to become intellectually and spiritually superior to man as soon as she has divested herself of the prohibitions forced upon her by a male-dominated society. (This same work, incidentally, proclaims Whitman to be the only genuine poet of woman -- the sole poet in the history of the world who has envisioned an era in which woman shall have triumphed.) Whitman's feminism is most cogently expressed in Democratic Vistas, which may be perceived, in part, as a feminist manifesto. Its theoretical premise (like that of Mrs. Farnham's Woman and Her Era) is that woman's potential for personal excellence is symbolized by her capacity for motherhood. Deploring the materialistic post-Civil War society, with its conspicuous distrust between the sexes, Whitman insists that social progress (the new "sociology") is predicated largely on the evolution of a new womanhood. "I have sometimes thought," he writes,

> that the sole avenue and means of a
> reconstructed sociology depended, primarily,
> on a new birth, elevation, expansion,
> invigoration of woman, affording for ages to
> come (as the conditions that antedate birth
> are indispensable), a perfect motherhood.
> Great, great, indeed, far greater than they
> know, is the sphere of women. (Democratic
> Vistas, p. 372, 55n)

Basic to a "reconstructed sociology," Democratic Vistas asserts, is "achieving the entire redemption of woman out of these incredible holds and webs of silliness, millinery, and every kind of dyspeptic depletion -- and thus insuring to the States a strong and sweet Female Race, a race of perfect Mothers." (Democratic Vistas, p. 372) Here Whitman joined ranks with the mainstream feminist reformers who argued that fashionable dress, modish behavior, and husband hunting render women frivolous, rob them of self-respect, and make them view their situation through the conventional lenses of a male-oriented society. To gain the "perfect social equality" to which they are entitled by nature, Whitman said, American women must reject the romantic allurements which block their way and

        become the robost equals, workers, and it may
        be, even practical and political deciders with
        the men -- greater than men, we may admit,
        through their divine maternity, always their
        towering emblematic attribute -- but great, at
        any rate, as man, in all departments; or,
        rather, capable of being so, soon as they
        realize it, and can bring themselves to give
        up toys and fictions and launch forth, as men
        do, amid real, independent, stormy life.
        (Democratic Vistas, p. 389)

Like Mrs. Farnham, Whitman denounces conventional literature for its failure to show "woman protray'd or outlin'd at her best, or as perfect human mother," and deplores "the stock feminine characters" of the romantic novelists and poets "which fill the envying dreams of so many poor girls, and are accepted by our men, too, as supreme ideals of feminine excellence to be sought after." By way of suggesting the sort of women whom modern writers should delineate, Democratic Vistas presents four thumbnail portraits which are said to be "frightfully out of line" with traditional literature: a poor but self-supporting, intellectually alert domestic worker; a married woman who conducts "a mechanical business" but retains "the charm of her womanly nature"; a cheerful, "physiologically sweet and sound" housewife and mother; and a fulfilled and lovely octogenarian like those whom Whitman had previously enshrined in such poems as "Faces" and "A Song of Joys." These sketches of well-adjusted women, Whitman asserts, are his artistic response to the revolutionary "mutterings" which he can hear in the air. "The day is coming," he prophesies, "when the deep question of woman's entrance amid the arenas of practical life, politics, the suffrage, etc., will not only be argued all around us, but may be put to decision and real experiment." (Democratic Vistas, p. 401)

Now, more than a century later, that day of decision and "real experiment" that Whitman envisioned has become part of our reality.

        NOTES

        1.   D. H. Lawrence, Studies in American Literature (1923; repr., New York: The Viking Press, 1964), p. 167; Richard Chase, Walt Whitman Reconsidered (New York: William Sloane Associates, 1955), p. 115; The Education of Henry Adams: An Autobiography (Boston and New York: Houghton Mifflin, 1918), p. 384.
        2.   Walt Whitman, Democratic Vistas, Prose Works, 1892, vol. 2, ed. Floyd Stovall (New York: New York University Press, 1964), p. 364. Subsequent references to Democratic Vistas will be noted in the text.

3.   Walt Whitman, _An American Primer_, ed. Horace Traubel (Boston: Small, Maynard and Co., 1904), p. 12.

4.   Henry C. Wright, quoted in Alice B. Stockham, _Karezza: Ethics of Marriage_ (Chicago: A.B. Stockham and Co., 1896), pp. 60-61; Wright, _Marriage and Parentage: or, The Reproductive Element in Man_ (1855; repr., New York, 1974), p. 271.

5.   Quoted from "a speech to ladies" by Elizabeth Cady Stanton, in Alice B. Stockham, _Tokology: A Book for Every Woman_ (Chicago: Stockham Publishing Co., 1905), p. 172.   Stanton's italics.   The book dates possibly from around 1883.

6.   Henry C. Drummond, _The Ascent of Man_, quoted in Stockham, _Karezza_, p. 70.

11.
Whitman's World View:
A Contemporaneous Message

HOWARD L. PARSONS

Whitman voiced ideas about man, society, and the
universe that in many ways characterize the general
perspective of the modern mind as affected by the ideas
of science. He anticipated the big picture of the
cosmos -- energetic, pulsating, multitudinous,
evolutionary, creative, many-layered, knowable,
mysterious, individuated, and organized. For those who
share and appreciate this perspective today, his message
is therefore contemporaneous.

Unlike many scientists, Whitman was strongly
affected by German idealism, mediated to him by his
reading of Thomas Carlyle and Emerson. Yet he
transmuted it in a uniquely American way. He was, first
of all, a boy and youth in rural Long Island and
Brooklyn, absorbing images of grass and trees, birds and
sky, ships and sea, and "the blab of the pavement" --
going to Quaker meetings, hearing the Bible read,
reading novels and poetry. Systematic science and
philosophy -- and the pseudosciences of phrenology,
animal magnetism, and hydropathy -- later supervened on
these formative feelings and images, providing a general
framework.;1 In time came the influence of the
secession war, while the whole was borne along in the
tide of the sentiments of national expansion.

The idealistic principle of the unfolding of the
grand Idea in history through specific individuals and
historical movements seemed relevant and right. The
"law over all, and law of laws," Whitman declared,
writing of his hope for the unification of Americans, is
"the law of successions.";2 It is spiritual progress
toward higher unity.

He conceived the cosmos to be a creative process
whose unfolding individual parts are unified in their
origins, interconnections, and destiny -- a great
originator, receptacle, transformer, and preserver of
the individual creatures.

Through his wide reading in journals and books
Whitman was acquainted with some of the leading ideas of
nineteenth-century science -- the electromagnetic field
theory; the theory that atoms combine in unitary
proportional weights; the cell theory; the refined
formulation of the law of conservation of energy; and
the theory of biological evolution.

But most scientists then still proceeded from the
premises of the traditional cosmology, namely,
mechanical materialism -- the view that reality consists
of isolated bits of matter, occupying definite spaces
and having definite boundaries, which act and
react at a distance toward other material bodies
according to fixed external laws.;3

The poet was expressing his sense of connectedness
with all things, of the unification of processes in a
field, of the material and energetic continuity of all
things, of the fact that nothing is lost in its
energetic character but only transformed into a new
form, of the evolution of physical and biological
energy. Whitman bypassed the abstractions of nineteenth
century mechanical materialism and, like Wordsworth and
Shelley and Keats, went directly to his experience with
people and nature. For this, of course, Whitman did not
need all the theories. But for him they did illustrate,
extend, and confirm his direct intuition.

What are the general ideas that define Whitman's
outlook?

1. <u>The ultimacy of change and incessant
transformation</u>.

> All is procession,
> The universe is a procession with measured
>   and perfect motion.;4

Whitman sings of the open road, the Brooklyn ferry,
pioneers on the march, explorations and railroads,
flood-tide and ebb-tide, sailings and voyages, passage
to India, journeys to the stars. There is always a
starting from Paumanok or somewhere else, a setting
forth into the unknown, toward "the horizon far and
dim," a search and a longing -- a motion of migrants,
cities, continents, oceans, and nebulae, a motion mixed
with hopeful certainty and expectant, curious
uncertainty -- a deeply American theme.

Whitman is striving to come to terms with the fact
of change, with the presence of Permanence in Change and
the inherence of the One in the Many. In a world of

nature, into which we are inextricably tucked, the
supernatural is "of no account." Space, time, and the
flow of events in and out of us define our being as
becoming. Time must be taken seriously. We always
existed in some sense, and we always will exist, since
the Spirit of which we are made cannot be created or
destroyed and we are indissolubly bonded to the whole
environment, to the flow of history and the evolution of
nature.

Like the astrophysicist, Whitman can find no
absolute center in such a universe of processes. "There
is no object so soft but it makes a hub for the wheel's
universe." Each self is "divine," the center of its
cosmic environment, the place where the energies of the
cosmic field have converged into just this
particularity.

2. <u>The realization of value in space-time.</u>
Whitman saw that we are space-time energies in the
midst of energies, in the field of the cosmos. There is
no other reality -- either before, under, above, or
after the cosmos. (Did Einstein read Whitman? Did he
cry, "Salut, O Camaredo!"?)

For us, as for all creatures in this cosmos, to
realize any value we must do so here and now with just
this body and environment of bodies.

> There was never any more inception than there
>   is now,
> Nor any more youth or age than there is now,
> And will never be any more perfection than
>   there is now,
> Nor any more heaven or hell than there is now.
> ("Song of Myself," 40-44)

All this is holy -- "I make holy whatever I touch
or am touched from."

Experience has two alternating modes, receptivity
and activity, "influx and efflux." To exist in the
receptive mode is to be open and sensitive, not
asserting or contending, not inviting or refusing,
witnessing and alertly waiting:

> what I am
> Stands amused, complacent, compassionate,
>   idle, unitary.

The other mode is active affirmation of the self's
powers reaching out to the world to form links of love,
links of social and political reform, links with
nature. Even if we fail in the active mode, we can
always rely on the receptive, "watching and wondering"
at the procession within us and around us, marvelling at
the miraculous drama in which we are immersed.

Whitman himself required some time to balance the efflux and the influx, to develop the rhythm of ecological alternation in living. In youth he related himself to society and cosmos by starting from the unique person with his own indomitable instincts. Later, transformed by his war experiences, he reversed the emphasis.

This attitude of poetic, social, and ecological outreach stands over against the selfish commercialism and acquisitive materialism that Whitman excoriated.

3. <u>The unity of individualities in creative interchange and in the whole.</u> The universe for Whitman is a fecund, inexhaustible spawning of individualities. But the diversity is held together through a process of interactive integration of parts.

The "me imperturbe . . . aplomb in the midst of irrational things" cannot just stand still; it must be "self-balanced for contingencies." But this speculative vision is not only cosmological; it is a serious social and political proposal, an ideal of what the States and their unformed swarms of people might become, bound together by the "adhesiveness of love."

In Whitman's universe, the countless things are as autonomous as wild game, spontaneous and free, but they are set within a context of omnipresent law. Freedom is the Hegelian appreciation of such law. The individual differentiated things stand over against, contradict, interpenetrate, and change one another. Yet everything is in its place -- the ugly, perverse, and evil things, defects and failures, the maculated, morbid, demonic things.

In the mood of poetic passivity, the One prevails; in the mood of anger against injustice, it is individuality and struggle. We are apt to forget Whitman's social radicalism, his long anti-slavery stand, his poems to revolutions and revolutionaries, his work as bodhisattva care-taker and wound-dresser in the Civil War.

Whitman takes evolution seriously; the stuff and form of which he is composed were always present; he was sown like a seed in the primeval atomic soil of the universe. "Afar down I see the huge first Nothing, I know I was even there." He traces his embryo through all stages: nebula, orb, strata, "vast vegetables," sauroids. "I am the acme of things accomplished, and I am the encloser of things to be."

The space of geographical North America -- such space is room enough and more, for all the sons and daughters of the race, each a "simple separate person," all together "En-Masse."

4. <u>The creation of our identity with the world.</u> As a poet assuming various roles, Whitman himself discovered his identity in three modes. The first mode

is receptivity. He is "passive, receptive, silent." He
wants with his negative capability to wiggle his way
down into the barks of trees and the skins of wild
animals, to feel existence as they do,

> To confront night, storms, hunger, ridicule,
>   accidents, rebuffs, as the trees and
>   animals do.
>
> ("Me Imperturbe," 8)

He waits, he listens, he is the child who becomes the
world that he looks upon. He loafs and invites his
soul, he sings and celebrates what has come unbidden to
him in the very bud of his unopened being. "I am the
man, I suffered, I was there." Second, Whitman's poetry
is in the attitude of action and a prophetic cry to
action. He urges and charges the reader to affirm his
or her self -- to "claim your own at any hazard," to put
forward your own unique identity, to reveal yourself --
to "come forth!" The poet's speech unfolds covered buds,
forcing them out with the voice of the beast, the
"barbaric yawp" -- "the dirt receding before my
prophetical screams."
     Third, Whitman is a nurturer. The matrix and
atmosphere of maternity lie under and around all that he
writes. From childhood he had developed a deep identity
with his own mother. He expresses a tender,
appreciative solicitude for the children of Adam and all
things. He is "the caresser of life wherever moving."
He gathers in and mothers all creators in the great
household of Space. "I moisten the roots of all that
has grown."
     In what sense are we identical with each thing and
with the whole? First, we are compounded out of the
same materials. "Every atom belonging to me as good
belongs to you."
     Second, we interdepend with all things in one way
or another. Air, liquids, solids pass in and out of us
in the rhythm of ecological sustenance. Experience is
an alternation of sensing and responding. "How is it,"
Whitman asks in the spirit of Shakespeare, "I extract
strength from the beef I eat?"
     Third, we are the products of inorganic and organic
evolution. The individual person carries within his
body the record of past evolutionary stages.

> I find I incorporate gneiss, coal,
>   long-threaded moss, fruits, grains,
>   esculent roots,
> And am stucco'd with quadrupeds and birds all
>   over. . . .
>
> ("Song of Myself," 670-71)

Fourth, we respond to one another with both
recognition and attraction. We intuit our being in
others, and we are drawn to them to deepen and affirm
the bond of identity. We recognize ourselves in
others. The animals

> bring me tokens of myself, they evince them
>   plainly in their possession.
>
> ("Song of Myself," 693)

Whitman would be enthusiastic about parapsychology,
telepathy, Kirlian photography, communication with
animals, and the prospects of interplanetary
communication. A man with the imaginative audacity to
take up hydropathy and Spurzheimian phrenology would
surely be sympathetic to the far more "far-out"
hypotheses of our own scientific age.

The universal force that makes all things cleave
together Whitman calls "love." This is "a kelson of the
creation," a ubiquitous "adhesiveness." He grasps for
scientific images and ideas to illustrate his point. "I
sing the body electric." "I have instant conductors all
over me," and "I Am He That Aches with Amorous Love":

> I am he that aches with amorous love;
> Does the earth gravitate? Does not all
>   matter, aching, attract all matter?
> So the body of me to all I meet or know.

"I make appointments with all," cries the poet --
because I make appointments with myself -- heroes,
kept-woman, sponger, thief, heavy-lipp'd slave,
veneralee. We can say of the infant what Whitman says
of himself:

> I merely stir, press, feel with my fingers,
>   and am happy,
> To touch my person to some one else's is about
>   as much as I can stand.
>
> ("Song of Myself," 617-18)

The motif of sensory and extrasensory communion
with others is unceasing. To touch and be touched, to
see and be seen, to kiss and be kissed, to smell and be
smelled ("The scent of these arm-pits aroma finer than
prayer") -- this is the divine consummation, this is
what we came for.

He is here stating something profound about the
human need for creative interaction in the many
modalities of feeling --

> What is it I interchange so suddenly with
>   strangers? . . .

    What gives me to be free to a woman's and
        man's good-will? what give them to be
        free to mine?

    5. <u>The natural equality of people, and the</u>
<u>validity of democracy</u>. Cosmic democracy and the
material and psychic identity of people with one another
are the base and proof for social democracy. The common
life, the rhythm of "the common day and night -- the
common earth and waters," the common work of people --
it all has "the democratic wisdom underneath like solid
ground for all." Whitman repudiated imperialism,
chauvinism, racism, slavery, and sexism. He was a
socialist, internationalist, and equalitarian.
    6. <u>The right and necessity of revolution</u>.
Whitman's revolutionary views came out of his conviction
that persons are and ought to be fulfilled as
independent beings in community. He had a radical
belief in the rights of others to be free of economic,
political, and other oppression. He condemned the
exacting of surplus value from the laborers:

    Here and there with dimes on eyes walking,
    To feed the greed of the belly the brains
        liberally spooning. . . .
    Many sweating, ploughing, thrashing, and then
        the chaff for payment receiving,
    A few idly owning and they the wheat
        continually claiming.
                ("Song of Myself," 1070-71, 1073-74)

He has within him the cry of the people for liberty:

    Through me many long dumb voices,
    Voices of the interminable generations of
        prisoners and slaves,
    Voices of the diseas'd and despairing and of
        thieves and dwarfs,
    Voices of cycles of preparation and
        accretion. . . .
    Of the deform'd, trivial, flat, foolish,
        despised,
    Fog in the air, beetles rolling balls of dung.
                ("Song of Myself," 508-11, 514-15)

The revolutionary poet is ready to

    beat the gong of revolt, and stop with
    fugitives and them that plot and conspire.

CONCLUSION

Whitman's ideas were organically connected to his images, which in turn sprang naturally out of his lifelong sensitivity to persons and nature. The power of his poetry derives from his skill in communicating in vivid images his experience of relatedness to the people, things, and events of his world -- as well as from the immense social, ecological, and cosmic vision inherent in that experience. Faithful to his direct intuitions and earnest to communicate his intuited world as honestly and as forcefully as possible, Whitman expressed a world, his intimately felt world, that we today feel is our own. We feel that both because Whitman's words carry us immediately to the depths of our own experience and because the vision that held his experience and its imagery together in general and rough form is the same as ours. That is the perspective of the modern sciences when broadly generalized.

One may speculate that Whitman would have been a great poet without the sciences and philosophy that he learned and used. That is quite possible. Yet the experience itself, as he underwent and expressed it, has within it, sometimes implicit, sometimes explicit, the rudimentary structures that situate and inform us about our being and the world's -- about change, transformation, value, creativity, interchange, identity, and equality. That modern science at the fullest reach of its generality points to these as categories of the world tells us not so much about the continuity of science as about the penetrative power of a poet to find the base of things and celebrate it in immortal language.

We have not explored the psychological processes through and by which Whitman did this semi-metaphysical thing. Whitman's way of perceiving and conceiving formed early and went on slowly and steadily. At the time of his Preface to the first edition of _Leaves of Grass_ the main vision was together:

        Love the earth and sun and the animals,
        despise riches, give alms to everyone that
        asks, stand up for the stupid and crazy,
        devote your income to others, hate tyrants
        . . . go freely with powerful uneducated
        persons, and with the young, and with the
        mothers of families.

But this simple, pure, whole vision would, with deprivation, disappointment, loneliness, and ostracism, be deepened and matured. Whitman's natural empathy toward people and things was rendered still more tender and poignant by his decision to break with his past, to

be the new "Walt," to go it alone, to defy
respectability, to be obedient to the unblossomed and
requited soul within. Whitman was early quickened and
awakened to his need for others and nature. Like all
great persons and poets, he generalized his state. He
felt a kinship with the yearning for unity in all beings
in our common voyage toward universal community. His
poetry, beautiful for its expressive qualities, was
turned toward message and mission. Through it he
reached out to give love and encouragement to others, to
tell them that someone understands and cares:

> The untold want, by life and land ne'er
>   granted,
> Now voyager sail thou forth to seek and find.
>   ("The Untold Want")

NOTES

1. Frederik Schyberg, _Walt Whitman_, trans. Evie
Allison Allen (New York: Columbia University Press,
1951), pp. 67-68. Vernon Louis Parrington, _Main
Currents in American Thought_, vol. 3 (New York:
Harcourt, Brace, 1927), p. 74.
2. Walt Whitman, _Democratic Vistas_, _Prose Works,
1892_, vol. 2, ed. Floyd Stovall (New York: New York
University Press, 1964), p. 381.
3. Alfred North Whitehead, _Science and the Modern
World_ (New York: Macmillan, 1926).
4. All quotations of the poetry, unless otherwise
indicated, are from _Leaves of Grass_, 1891-92 edition.

Part III

Whitman's Poetics

12.
Whitman's Body, Whitman's Language

JON ROSENBLATT

In a remarkable passage from An American Primer, Whitman
speaks of his favorite words, "kosmo words," as if they
were actually bodies. They show themselves, he says,
with "foreheads, muscular necks and breasts. -- These
gladden me! -- I put my arms around them -- touch my
lips to them." In another passage, which continues the
comparison between language and body, he claims that "a
perfect writer would make words sing, dance, kiss, do
the male and female act, bear children, weep, bleed,
rage, stab, steal, fire cannon.";1 These passages are
not isolated instances of Whitman's sexual and physical
feeling for words; language becomes nothing less than
the double of the human body in his work. Throughout
the notebooks of 1850-55 and the first edition of Leaves
of Grass Whitman establishes an equivalence between
language and body that takes romantic organicism one
step beyond its previous limits. Whitman no longer
speaks of an analogy between organic life and poetry but
of an identity between the human body and poetry. This
identity then becomes the basis for Whitman's poetic
strategy in which the poet, the poem, and the reader are
linked together as one being through the
spiritual-physical presence of language.

The physicality of language in Whitman's poetry and
poetics is not, then, a simple extension of romantic and
Emersonian doctrine about the organic nature of poetry.
The corporeal qualities of speech and poetry contribute
not only to the aural effects of Whitman's work but also
to its essential structure and metaphysic. Nothing
confuses our understanding of Whitman's radical
innovativeness in the history of poetry more than the
treatment of his aesthetic as a repetition of what

Emerson said about the relationship between language and
things and what the English romantics did with organic
analogies. I want to show briefly that Whitman
initiates one of the key doctrines of modern poetry --
the view of language as a kind of self-contained body of
changing meanings -- and anticipates the collapse of his
own realistic aesthetic that grounds language on the
body.

We have been repeatedly told that Emerson's view of
language and poetry is essentially the same as Whitman's
and that Emerson's failure to write great poetry derives
from his temperamental inability to follow his own
aesthetic. Yet Whitman does not hold the same position
toward language that Emerson does. In his essay
"Nature" Emerson argues that three fundamental
relationships govern words in relation to things: words
derive their meanings and forms from physical phenomena;
physical phenomena symbolize spiritual facts; and nature
as a whole symbolizes spirit. According to Emerson, the
physical world has been converted through language into
a system of spiritual realities. Thus, the word _right_
originally meant _straight_; _wrong_ meant _crooked_; and
spirit meant _wind_. When we go all the way back to the
origin of language, in Emerson's Swedenborgian view, we
come upon a universal vocabulary of natural symbols that
is common to all languages. The poet taps this
reservoir of primordial unconscious knowledge, which is
the property of both the race and the individual.
Following Swedenborg, Emerson argues that the universe
must be ultimately read as the book of the spirit, and
that nature in its entirety is nothing other than the
articulated form of mind and of those ideas which are
the permanent truths of the universe.

Emerson's reliance upon Swedenborg and the
idealistic neo-Platonic tradition produces this account
of language and reality; but it is an account that
Whitman only partially follows in his aesthetic. To
begin with, Whitman perceives of language as a
perpetually changing organism that constantly generates
new meanings in the world. Whereas Emerson emphasizes
the permanent, fixed relationship between meaning and
word and between symbol and meaning, Whitman sees that
the allegorical fixing of interpretation threatens his
own celebration of an evolving, expanding cosmos. _An_
American Primer is a remarkable testimony to Whitman's
organic conception of language. The greatest enemy to
language, according to the _Primer_, is the grammarian,
who would straitjacket words, preventing the constant
mutation of old words and the coinage of new ones.
Evidently, Whitman would never have used neologisms and
foreign words in his poetry without believing that
language cannot be fixed in a single form; it is a
self-regulating, or, as he might have said, a

"self-supplying" system of organically based relations.
Rather than embracing the Swedenborgian doctrine of
allegorical correspondences between body and truth, or
the less dogmatic Emersonian version, Whitman
understands language as nothing other than process and
growth. He agrees with Emerson's conception of a
universal sign system upon which the poet draws, but he
does not perceive this system as fixed by
correspondential laws governing idea and nature.
Whitman's symbols are in flux, as in the sixth section
of "Song of Myself," when the leaf of grass becomes
everything from a personal sign of Whitman's disposition
to a "uniform hieroglyph" to the "hair of graves" to a
symbol of the eternal regeneration of nature. Just as
the movement of the personal self down the open road
cannot be fixed by a social or natural law, so the
movement of language into the future cannot be
predetermined by linguistic, social or religious
interpretation.

     It is not my intention to cast Emerson in the role
of doctrinal allegorist to Whitman's symbolist, since
Emerson himself moved toward an organicist aesthetics in
his later writing, abandoning his allegiance to
Swedenborgian theory.;2 But the differences between
Emerson and Whitman as poets and as theorists of poetic
language still remain fundamental differences. When
Emerson thinks of the relationship between words and the
materials that they label, he thinks of objects and
things that have imprinted their form on language. In
contrast, Whitman conceives of language as a
specifically bodily phenomenon. For Whitman, poetry is
not only organically derived, as the "leaves of grass"
metaphor suggests, but also corporeally shaped by the
body. What distinguishes the claims of the first
sections of "Song of Myself" from Emersonian aesthetics
or English Romantic doctrines is Whitman's assertion
that his openness to bodily reality alone produces his
poems and that only the reader's similar "nakedness" can
open him to the nature of poetry. When Whitman says
that his poetic voice is a product of evolutionary
inheritance from his ancestors and that "my tongue,
every atom of my blood [is] form'd from this soil, this
air" (1. 6), he is insisting upon the corporeal origin
of poetry. If the tongue, which produces speech, is
physical, why should poetry itself not be physical? The
poetic voice is not a mental phenomenon that enters the
physical world from above or below; it is a bodily
production. Whitman's evolutionary conception of
spiritual development blends here with his aesthetic
notion of the poet. Language is as much a body as the
poet who produces language is a body.

     What is missing from Emerson's poetry is Whitman's
explicit use of poetry as a mediating agency that

converts poetic language into a body and that
understands the human body as a language. This
equivalence between body and language is central to
Whitman's poetry and provides it with a tremendous
energy, which is precisely what is lacking in Emerson's
poetry. Whitman understands each of his encounters with
the reader as a relationship between different parts of
the same body. As a result, his language responds to a
pressure that is absent in Emerson's: the need to make
poetry convey the poet's bodily presence directly to the
reader so that reader and poet recognize each other as
sharing the same body. Whitman's poems accomplish this
quasi-physical contact with the reader through several
well-known techniques: direct address to the reader,
use of colloquial expressions that, paradoxically,
defamiliarize the poetry; constant reiteration and
parallelism that "weight" the language so that it seems
"physical." The effect of these techniques and of the
repeated assertions of metaphysical oneness is to
persuade the reader to recognize Whitman's language and
body as his own. Bodies and words meet in the field of
the Whitman poem and seem to share a common selfhood.
Whereas Emerson believed in the same doctrine of the
unified self as Whitman, he never pushed the identity of
opposites -- body and soul, language and body, present
and future -- as Whitman did into the bodily realm.
Whitman substantializes words, poems and readers so that
they all become, in the fiction of his work, real
bodies. Whitman himself passes into the poem as if it
had become his second body.
     Whitman's poetry develops what I have come to call
the tropes of embodiment. It presents the poet as if he
had a second body, the poem itself, which can then be
touched by his reader. The poem-as-body offers Whitman
the possibility of purifying his own mortal body, which
has failed to provide him with the guiltless sexual
contact with others that he desires. The body-poem thus
converts the divided self, split between a
transcendental universality and a fragmentary
personality, into a unified linguistic body. This
doubling occurs throughout "Song of Myself" and such
poems as "Whoever You Are Holding Me Now In Hand" and
"Not Heaving from My Ribb'd Breast Only." These poems
incorporate the body within them as if song and body
could be literally one. The trope of embodiment also
dominates "So Long," Whitman's death-bed poem, which
foresees the moment of death when the poem will jump
from behind his "screen" of flesh into our arms.
"Camerado," says Whitman to his reader

          this is no book.
     Who touches this touches a man. . . ."

                                             (1. 55)

The corporeality of the book or poem allows Whitman to turn the isolated poetic self, which is threatened by sexuality and mortality, into a bridge that unites the poet to his present and future readers.

This desire to convert the poem into a text that possesses both a linguistic message and a sexual physicality involves Whitman in the reciprocal presentation of the human body as a poem. If the poem is a kind of body, then the body must be a kind of poetry. The two assumptions mutually support each other in the early notebooks and in the first edition of Leaves of Grass. In one of the notebooks, Whitman writes:

> The body of a man, -- that is of my model -- I
>   do not reject what I find in my body -- I
>   am not ashamed -- Why should I be
>   ashamed?
> The body of a woman, that is my perfect
>   model. . . .;3

"I Sing the Body Electric" makes the most extreme case in Leaves of Grass for viewing the organs and physical functions as inherently poetic. In his most optimistic moments, Whitman views the human body as the perfect aesthetic model for poetry and the fundamental source for all that men are or know.

In the fully developed version of the tropes of embodiment -- the poem-as-body and the body-as-poem -- Whitman envisions a universe that has been unified through poetry. Words and bodies become equivalent manifestations of a single, limitless, renewable energy. The universe is absorbed within the individual, as in "A Child Went Forth," and then converted into physical motion and direction. Political and social forms of organization appear as organic structures based upon the human body; and, in Whitman's criticism, literary developments are judged favorably depending upon the physical vitality that they manifest. The poet remains the great legislator of Whitman's universe because he has physicalized the spiritual and spiritualized the physical. Language and body have become one. It is not accidental that Whitman was fascinated by astrology and phrenology. Whatever disciplines showed mind and body to be a single energy field fired his imagination.

Yet it should be evident that the equivalence between language and body was fated to be destroyed by the inevitable differences between symbolic and organic systems. If it is true, as I have been arguing, that a great degree of Whitman's originality lies in the radical claims that he makes for the body, then his growing mistrust of the body in the 1860s and 1870s may well account for the decline in the quality and adventurousness of his poetry. The crisis that overtakes him in 1857 through 1860 is recorded with great intensity in a relatively neglected poem, "As I Ebb'd with the Ocean of Life," which shows that Whitman's entire method of reading the world as a series of shifting signifiers that are unified in the poet's self is on the verge of collapse.

In Whitman's time, the use of "types" or correspondences was the basis for systematic thought like Swedenborg's and Emerson's and for the poetic or novelistic structures of Balzac and Baudelaire. Whitman understood, however, that correspondential thinking is purely mechanical unless it captures the movements of real bodies between the poles of the correspondences, between what we have come to call the signifier and the signified. Whitman could thus adopt a correspondence or "type" only if he could see himself as embodying the object (signifier) without being permanently fixed with the domain of a given meaning (signified). The domain of the signified must always be in flux, as in the sixth section of "Song of Myself," so that the identification of the self with every life-form will not be restricted. The process of finding a "type" or likeness for the self in Whitman is always one of discovery and transformation, since the type will be a temporary manifestation of a mutable body. The beginning of "As I Ebb'd" shows Whitman in the process of "seeing types" for the self as he walks along the shore of Long Island (Paumanok), but the second section reveals the problematic nature of correspondences:

> As I wend to the shores I know not,
> As I list to the dirge, the voices of men and
>   women wreck'd,
> As I inhale the impalpable breezes that set in
>   upon me,
> As the ocean so mysterious rolls toward me
>   closer and closer,
> I too but signify at the utmost a little
>   wash'd-up drift,
> A few sands and dead leaves to gather,
> Gather, and merge myself as part of the sands
>   and drift.

According to the procedures of "Song of Myself," the signifier must come to embody the transcendent facts of existence: our bodily participation in spiritual totality. But sand is a signifier for separation and distance. The sand-drifts that ebb and flow with the ocean tides signify for Whitman a perpetual, ungrounded flow rather than the grounding of the self in a great world body. The correspondence, which is a form of identification for the poet, places Whitman within this

shifting play of sand as he is hurled from the waves,
which are symbolized as a maternal force in the poem, to
the shore, which is paternal, and back again. Between
male and female, ocean and land, mother and father, the
poet shuttles back and forth like a homeless body.
Having taken on the "body" of the shifting sand, Whitman
has defined himself as nothing other than a signifier
that cannot recombine with its lost origins. He has
pictured himself as an adult who is a fragment of his
material, biological past and of a prior, lost unity.
To put this another way: the temporal succession of
changes in the self has ripped apart the unity of
signifier and signified that was previously governed, in
"Song of Myself" and other poems, by the trope of the
poem as a body.
    The vision of fragmentation and "drift" occurs in
"As I Ebb'd" because of Whitman's impossible assertion
of identity between language and body and between body
and language. For the domain of the poem, understood as
a corporal form, is the ideal mediation of self and
other of object-world and self; but the domain of the
body, understood as a poem, necessarily collapses and
decomposes into smaller and smaller material units. The
sand-drifts cannot stabilize themselves in the shape of
a coherent body because they constantly dissolve into
ever-diminishing pieces of sand.
    In "As I Ebb'd" Whitman faces the ultimate threat
to his vision of a coherent, eternal exchange between
his own body and the transcendent principle of the
universe. Since he identifies himself with the sand
drifts, in the form of a correspondence, he can only
follow the "drift" of this signifier into dissolution
and inexpressibility. But as a poet, he has based his
entire aesthetic and metaphysic upon the equation of the
body, the world, and the self. Initially in "As I
Ebb'd," his "electric self" is "seized by the spirit
that trails" through the water, which is to say, Nature;
but when he walks on the shore and thinks "the old
thought of likenesses," he finds only

        a little wash'd up-draft,
    A few sands and dead leaves to gather.

This fragmentary sign of a fragmentary body calls into
question, as it must, the entire series of
identifications which had grounded "Song of Myself."

    O baffled, balk'd, bent to the very earth,
    Oppress'd with myself that I have dared to
        open my mouth,
    Aware now that amid all that blab whose echoes
        recoil upon me I have not once had the
        least idea who or what I am,

> But that before all my arrogant poems the real
>   Me stands yet untouch'd, untold,
>   altogether unreach'd,
> Withdrawn far, mocking me with
>   mock-congratulatory signs and bows,
> With peals of distant ironical laughter at
>   every word I have written,
> Pointing in silence to these songs, and then
>   to the sand beneath.
> ("As I Ebb'd," 25-31)

The real "Me" who mocks the "electric self" which
produces poetry is simply that transcendental Self that,
in other Whitman poems, hides behind curtains, watches
the world as a theater, and distances itself from all
merely material forms. The entire function of Whitman's
"songs" is to bring this transcendental Self into the
world so that it becomes one with all individual selves
and bodies, but here it remains distant, mocking,
laughing, and condescending. By pointing first to
Whitman's poems and then to the sand, the real Me
suggests that Whitman's poems express nothing more
permanent or truthful than the shifting, ungrounded
sands. Just as Whitman's body, identified with the
sand-drift, seems to be purposeless and fragmented, so
Whitman's poems, identified with sand, appear
meaningless and irrelevant to the real Me. Poem and
body are again identified, but in this case they are
both dominated by the character of the signifying
object. Rather than controlling the world through the
unifying identification of language and organism,
Whitman now experiences the domination of the natural
world in its decomposing aspects. Within the triad of
real "Me," "electrical self," and Nature, the poet can
only experience himself as drifting helplessly with
nothing more than a mouth, producing sounds of no
lasting significance. The great poems of the first
edition of <u>Leaves of Grass</u>, which had served to answer
the question of identity for Whitman, are now revealed
as producing only "echoes" which thus send their answers
back to him: "I have not once had the least idea who or
what I am." This is a major reversal for a poet who had
celebrated, with the greatest certainty, the identity of
the self.

The triadic drama of transcendental Self, poetic
self, and Nature is completed at the moment when Nature
attacks the poet for his pride:

> I perceive Nature in sight of the sea, taking
>   advantage of me, to dart upon me, and
>   sting me,
> Because I was assuming so much,

            And because I have dared to open my mouth to
                sing at all.
                               ("As I Ebb'd," 32-34)

Caught between the two great universals, the natural
world and the world of spirit, the poet can hardly dare
to raise his voice to speak and to form a self.
Fragmented into drifting material pieces, broken by
natural and spiritual attacks, Whitman loses the courage
which had allowed him to assert universal analogies and
identities between his own body and the cosmos. Like
Samuel Taylor Coleridge in "Dejection: An Ode," Whitman
faces a major block to writing that he attempts to
overcome through the articulation of the blockage
itself. Only by dramatizing his humiliation and lost
confidence can he transform this triadic structure into
a new, unified vision of identity.
    This transformation occurs according to one of the
characteristic processes of Whitman's poetry: the triad
is converted into a sequence of dyadic relations which
can then be understood as identities. In "Out of the
Cradle Endlessly Rocking," the triad of child, male, and
female bird initially becomes the dyad of singing male
bird and listening child, then of the whispering ocean
and the poet, and finally of the poet ("solitary
singer") and audience, who are joined into a single
body-poem. The triadic corresponds, psychologically, to
the oedipal situation, which is then converted into a
relation of son to mother (the ocean) and, eventually,
resolves into the corporalized language of the poem in
which lost mother, father, and poet-son become one in
the body of the poem. The conflicts between the poet
and the various representatives of the mother and the
father can thus be resolved into the unitary figure of
the speaking "voice" of the oceanic poem, which is both
male and female, old and new, temporal and atemporal.
    The structural resolution of "As I Ebb'd" involves
the same sequence of conversions. Whitman "submits" to
the choice of the sand-drifts as the true correspondence
for the self. Rather than fighting against the
inevitable identification of the body with a "friable"
piece of the landscape, Whitman embraces it as the
proper sign of physical smallness and mortality: "You
tangible land! Nature!" he says in the 1860 edition,
"Be not too rough with me -- I submit! -- I close with
you. . . . " To "close" with the land is, as the next
stanza makes clear, to return to a dyadic relation with
the father. The phallic, fish-shaped island of Paumanok
provides the larger body with which Whitman can merge.
If the sand-drift is small and homeless, the land itself
becomes the new bodily shape which the poet assumes. By
"throwing" himself onto the "breast" of the father and
"clinging" to him, Whitman abolishes the distance and

alienation of the triadic, oedipal structure, which had
left him isolated from both the real Me and the natural
world, and substitutes the one-to-one relation of the
dyad. Mediation between these opposites occurs through
identification with a larger body and the literal
exchange of breath, voice,and body between the father
and the son:

> Kiss me, my father,
> Touch me with your lips, as I touch those I
>   love,
> Breathe to me, while I hold you close, the
>   secret of the wondrous murmuring I envy,
> For I fear I shall become crazed, if I cannot
>   emulate it, and utter myself as well as
>   it.

By 1867 Whitman had decided to excise the final
line of this passage, probably because of the admission
to "craziness" on his part; but this line is crucial to
understanding the emotional intensity of the poem.
Whitman's "fear" is precisely that the reciprocal
relation between world-body and poet is false and that
the limited, fragmented self utters his poems rather
than the world spirit. If he cannot believe that the
land-father speaks through him, then he cannot affirm
the reciprocity of world and self, which is to destroy
the entire structure of identities and analogies
developed in the first edition of <u>Leaves of Grass</u>. For
this reason he imagines himself as so physically close
to his father that their breath and bodies seem
commingled. In this extraordinarily intense expression
of union with the father, Whitman returns to his
biological origins so as to recapture a voice for his
poetry <u>which is not his own but the world's</u>. Just as
"Out of the Cradle Endlessly Rocking" locates the
origins of his poetic voice in the birdsong of a bereft
male bird, so "As I Ebb'd" finds the secret voice of
poetry in the "murmuring" of the father and the
"moaning" of the mother-ocean. The "electric self,"
proud of its creations and its assertions of identity
but guilt-ridden and self-negating, dissolves back into
the originating relation to nature out of which it was
formed and thus overcomes the guilt which prevented it
from speaking. By turning his separateness as a body
into the avenue for merger with the world's body,
Whitman converts the now-diminished self back into the
giant Self of Nature.

This procedure wards off the attacks of Nature on
Whitman by making ocean and land the equivalents of
mother and father; but it does not resolve the relation
to the transcendental Self, which has become infinitely
distant from the self. The criticism of "As I Ebb'd"

has been divided over the question of whether Whitman
resolves the relation to the "real Me," but the notion
of resolution becomes irrelevant once we realize that
the last section is <u>not a resolution but a dissolution</u>.
The poem dissolves the body and self of the poet into
the scene in front of him, thus making him identical
with the processes of the natural cosmos. The
transcendental Self, which is imagined as "You, up
there, walking or sitting," is infinitely distant from
the natural world from which the poet "gathers" his
reality. The great last section of "As I Ebb'd"
converts the negation and fragmentation of the self and
sand-drift into a trope of identification between the
natural world and internal process:

> Me and mine!
> We, loose windrows, little corpses,
> Froth, snowy white, and bubbles,
> (See! from my dead lips the ooze exuding at
>   last!
> See -- the prismatic colors, glistening and
>   rolling!)
> Tufts of straw, sands, fragments,
> Buoyed hither from many moods, one
>   contradicting another,
> From the storm, the long calm, the darkness,
>   the swell,
> Musing, pondering, a breath, a briny tear, a
>   dab of liquid or soil,
> Up just as much out of fathomless workings
>   fermented and thrown,
> A limp blossom or two, torn, just as much over
>   waves floating, drifted at random,
> Just as much for us that sobbing dirge of
>   Nature,
> Just as much, whence we come, that blare of
>   the cloud-trumpets;
> We, capricious, brought hither, we know not
>   whence, spread out before You. . . .

What is typically overlooked in commentary about
this passage is that Whitman now simultaneously
perceives and is the dead, fragmented pieces of bodies,
straw, and sand. The poem, which began with a search
for correspondences between the self and the seashore
scene filled with straw, chaff, and splinters of wood,
now returns to the scene from another perspective.
Since the initial correspondence had objectified and
fixed Whitman within the domain of external isolation
and separation, the only escape is to interiorize the
objects and signifiers as if they were actually his own
body. The poem ends by coming full circle back to the
flotsam and jetsam with which he began, but this time

correspondence gives way to a totally mobile identification with everything around him. Paradoxically, the attempt to ground the self in a stable correspondence with the transcendent through natural objects had ended by creating a diminished, guilty, split-off body. By embracing the entire flux of reality as if he were already dead and broken up into colors, windows, and bubbles, Whitman no longer remains split off from existence. What had been negatively imagined as fragmentation, isolation, and objectification -- the sand, the drifts, the chaff -- becomes the positive substance of the poet's vision. The contradictions of perception and conception, motion and stasis, are converted into a unity which affirms both the inner, emotional chaos and the eternal, fragmentary chaos as part of a single "drift."

It is crucial to Whitman's development that in "As I Ebb'd" he admits that the natural universe, as well as the inner self, cannot find a unified, necessitated ground. The origins of self are random events over which we have no control; but we do know that the processes that govern our inner being are identical to the processes that govern the ebb and flow of life itself. In this identification Whitman can rest assured that the self again possesses the universe as its own. The exultant shout at the beginning of the passage -- "Me and mine!" -- recreates the self at the level of the drifting, pulsing flow of the life force. This is not the exultant Self that had declared its transcendent embodiment of the cosmos. Rather, Whitman has withdrawn to a position in which the fragmentary body can reclaim its identity-in-negativity and participate in the cosmic drama of emergent identity.

The importance of "As I Ebb'd with the Ocean of Life" as a rethinking of Whitman's relation to the world has largely escaped criticism because the poem does not fit into any of the usual categorizations of Whitman's work as transcendentalist, Emersonian, or Vedantic. The concluding section of "As I Ebb'd" introduces a new form of interpenetration between the body and its world because it specifically leaves the divine, super-conscious Self outside the objective sphere. Whereas the 1855-56 poems and most of the Calamus poems had successfully imagined the body-poem as mediating the spatial-temporal distances between transcendentalist Self and objects (natural and human) through the tropes of embodiment, "As I Ebb'd" does not envision a stabilized unity or synthesis. The "real ME," which had rejected words as inadequate expressions of truth, is transferred into the Heavens to become a bodiless, silent eye (or "You") in its own reality. The poet's creative self, which he calls the "electric self," after Emerson, is thus split off from the super-conscious and must find its body-object within nature. But since the natural is dominated by the "drift" of every object into segmented units that are in perpetual flux, the self can only affirm its identity by literally confusing itself with the fragmenting, dissolving body of the world. This synthesis is not a static embodiment in an object, symbol, or poem-body but a completely mobile sequence of identities, in which neither the origin nor the end of the body-self can be known. Because the transcendental Self no longer grounds the world in the form of a coherent body, Whitman can only embrace the disintegrated flux as a groundless ground, a self-evolving unity-in-disunity. Nothing guarantees that these individual fragmented units express the nature of reality. Correspondences between one element of the universe and a psychic or spiritual truth cannot accurately define reality, just as individual words can no longer definitively embody the object-world.

The movement in Whitman away from the self-confident tropes of embodiment of the earlier editions of <u>Leaves of Grass</u> seems to me to presage one of the fundamental developments of modern poetry. Just as Whitman initiates the modern conception of the bodily origin and ground of poetry, which would be elaborated by D. H. Lawrence in England and William Carlos Williams, Charles Olson, and Robert Creeley in this country, so he registers the decomposition of the body of symbolic meanings which has supported the entire Western tradition. What makes Whitman so central a poet for us today is his recognition of the contradictory postures in which the transcendent Self must find itself. Convinced of its universal validity, the self seeks to make its home in every physical or human form that exists. Yet this search for home in a completely embodied universe faces a threat to its desire for stabilization both from the outside and the inside, from death and from sexuality. The impulse toward unification of the world and self can ground itself either on the body or on language, but every assimilation of one to the other will eventually be destroyed by the internal fragmentations of both these terms. Modern writers like Stephane Mallarme, James Joyce and Samuel Beckett have taken language as an autonomous realm, turning it into a gigantic, even monstrous body. Other writers, notably such Latin American poets as Pablo Neruda and Octavio Paz, have sought to follow the Whitmanic example by using the body as a source of gorgeous and vital metaphors. But in both cases, Whitman's example stands as a strange and wonderful contrast: Whitman is both at the beginning and at the end of thetranscendental project of modern poetry. He perfectly embodies the contradictory passions of a transcendentalism that has made its home in the body.

NOTES

This essay was written during an NEH Fellowship in Residence at New York University with Professor Anna Balakian.

1. Walt Whitman, Collected Writings (New York: New York University Press, 1972), vol. 6, pp. 739, 742.
2. Richard P. Adams, "Emerson and the Organic Metaphor," in Interpretations of American Literature, ed. Charles Fiedelson, Jr., and Paul Brodtkorb, Jr. (New York: Oxford University Press, 1959), pp. 137-152.
3. Walt Whitman, Daybooks and Notebooks (New York: New York University Press, 1977), vol. 3, p. 782.

13.
Running Aground in Barnegat Bay: Whitman's Symbols and Their Rhetorical Intentionalities

GREGORY M. HAYNES

Contemporary estimation of Walt Whitman has directed our attention to his poetic achievement as either language experiment or symbol-making. In his language experiment, Whitman creates a transparent text; the immediate relationship between poet and reader allows him to address us directly, openly proposing a renewal of perceptual vitality. The most characteristic technique of such a poem is the extended catalogue, a random naming of phenomena which, though thematically unified, bespeaks not a selective consciousness, but an expansive consciousness. Correctly linking the word to the thing allows a direct call for us to invest imaginatively in this dross of reality. The transparent text erects no masks of persona, no structures of irony, but rather promotes the pragmatic phenomenology of the Protestant fundamentalist sermon -- Whitman seizing his reader and showing him how to perceive the world afresh:

> I know perfectly well my own egotism,
> Know my omnivorous lines and must not write
>   any less,
> And would fetch you whoever you are flush with
>   myself.
>
> ("Song of Myself," Sec. 42)

In his symbol-making, on the other hand, Whitman creates an autonomous text that stands between us and the author. This is a poetics of embodying form, by which the world exists reshaped as mythos within the poem as artifact. Language is molded into its own structure, preceding our imaginative participation in it, and

cohesive symbolic interrelationships require, in spite
of Whitman's own denigration of aestheticism, a
self-conscious aesthetic response. Yet how do we
reconcile these two divergent tendencies in Whitman's
poetic imagination -- language experiment, and
symbol-making; the poem as medium for message, and the
poem as artifact; exhortation, and closure;
transparency, and ambiguity?

In many poems, the chasm separating these two
Whitmans is not without a natural bridge. The
anthologies invariably include "A Noiseless Patient
Spider" along with those obligatory snippets of "Song of
Myself." The authorial fiat of that emblem of the
spider, the predominance of the poet's own voice, the
cognitive determinacy of subject -- these indeed seem
consonant with the rhetorical strategy of "Song of
Myself." And the more complex symbolic structures such
as "Out of the Cradle Endlessly Rocking" allow a
prominent sense of the poet's self communicating
directly to the reader. Can this be said, however,
about "Patroling Barnegat"? Not inserted as the
penultimate piece in the Sea-Drift sequence until 1881,
"Patroling Barnegat" is perhaps Whitman's greatest
achievement as an artificer of symbol. The poem
possesses an ambiguity which pushes to the limit the
availability of message. How can we reconcile this poem
with the poet of rhetorical immediacy? What is Whitman
doing to his unique poet-reader relationship? This will
be our concern as we turn to "Patroling Barnegat."
Since I will examine the poem in detail in the following
pages, I reproduce it here in full.

> Wild, wild the storm, and the sea high
>   running,
> Steady the roar of the gale, with incessant
>   undertone muttering,
> Shouts of demoniac laughter fitfully piercing
>   and pealing,
> Waves, air, midnight, their savagest trinity
>   lashing,
> Out in the shadows there milk-white combs
>   careering,
> On beachy slush and sand sprits of snow fierce
>   slanting,
> Where through the murk the easterly death-wind
>   breasting,
> Through cutting swirl and spray watchful and
>   firm advancing,
> (That in the distance! is that a wreck? is
>   the red signal flaring?)
> Slush and sand of the beach tireless till
>   daylight wending,

> Steadily, slowly, through hoarse roar never
> remitting,
> Along the midnight edge by those milk-white
> combs careering,
> A group of dim, weird forms, struggling, the
> night confronting,
> That savage trinity warily watching.

Reading literally, the poem describes a coast patrol watching for wrecked vessels during a storm. In the years before the Coast Guard was established, the Revenue Marine served only as a Federal maritime law enforcement agency, so the search for and rescue of wrecked vessels and their victims were the responsibility of local townspeople. For commerce emanating from New York harbor, the New Jersey coastline was particularly dangerous; spectacular disasters, some costing hundreds of lives, occurred during midnight storms in these unchartered waters. In the mid-1840s, for example, wrecked vessels washed up on the New Jersey shoreline at the rate of one per week.;1 Whitman may have heard about Barnegat Bay even before the excursions of his Camden days; separating a 30-mile stretch of New Jersey from the Atlantic, the inlet is located mid-way between the two locales of his early and mature life -- Long Island to the north, and Camden to the south. At any rate, Barnegat Bay, in particular, gained a reputation for danger in the late 1830s with the arrest and conviction of a group of thieves who plundered some of the wrecks on its shore. The New York press quickly fed the rumors of false lights luring vessels to disaster, survivors being robbed, and even corpses being held for ransom.;2 The currency of these stories about Barnegat Bay reveals the address this poem is making with its ghoulish diction of "a group of dim, weird forms" and "shouts of demoniac laughter." Whitman had a penchant for resurrecting the lore of the place in his poetry, and the Gothic horror of this piece would have fulfilled the expectations of a mid-nineteenth-century audience coming to a poem entitled "Patroling Barnegat."

The historical context of this poem, however, does not sufficiently explain Whitman's method of courting ambiguities within the poem -- ambiguities of diction and syntax, of grammatical subject and pronoun reference. These ambiguities and the gaps they create for interpretation will guide my review of the reading experience of the poem. The world line one evokes is an orchestrated tempest of juxtaposed natural forces. The violence of the storm from the sky is met by the agitation of the bay. After this visual juxtaposition comes the audial perception in the next two lines. The gale locates the causative force behind the tempestuous scene, and the sounds of this gale are delineated in

detailed particulars. Primary among these sounds is a
roar, for this is the overpowering impression, the one
most readily apprehensible. Next is observed an
undertone, a more subtle auditory perception, one
apprehensible only through a more sustained
contemplation of the wind -- that is, one not likely to
be an initial impression. This signals an
intensification of perception and a progressive analysis
of the sound of the wind. Both the "steady" roar and
the "incessant" undertone provide a continuous level of
sound. Whitman orchestrates these with a staccato of
"shouts of demoniac laughter" in line 3. This is an
important development in the complex of these audio
impressions. Whitman has moved out of the confines of
commonly attested perception by identifying something
that cannot be named, but only described in quasi-human
terms. The shift in the poem is actually not quite so
abrupt; the seeming anthropomorphizing began in the line
preceding, where the undertone was observed as
muttering. This fact suggests a possible scheme for the
process of perception through lines 2 and 3. First, in
the movement from roar to undertone to demoniac
laughter, the lines evince a gradually intensified and
refined focus upon the audio impression of the wind.
What first would seem obvious shifts to a more subtle
nuance. Concomitant with this refinement, though, is a
departure from anything resembling wind. Unspecified
muttering and then laughter specifically demonic are
anthropomorphic qualities imposed by a human mind. So
while there is a greater exploration of the auditory
effect of the wind as a thing in itself, there is as
well a movement away from anything normally recognizable
as wind. Lines 2 and 3 have located the cause of the
storm in the gale, but within this process of
identification there has occurred a skewing away from
empirically demonstrable cause to suggestions of some
force perhaps superhuman and certainly malign.;3
     Just this kind of movement is characteristic of the
entire poem. It seems as if the awesome potential of
that vague suggestion of the demonic results in the
confused perception of line 4. Here the former
progressive analysis of perception breaks down into a
chaotic list of elements present. It is as though the
speaker were so overwhelmed by that momentary intuition
which his auditory perception led him to that he must
struggle just to name the things before him at random.
"Waves, air, midnight" is a perceptually frustrated and
cognitively depleted listing of the elements of this
storm. We do not need to be reminded of the presence of
waves; the mention of air seems vastly inappropriate --
it makes no substantive contribution; and "midnight"
provides a significant though belated temporal
circumstancing of the scene. Yet these confusedly

groping perceptions are erected in the conclusion of
line 4 into an apprehension of a force we never
anticipated: the "savagest trinity."

This is the poem's first climax in emotional
movement and rhythmic cadence, and it deserves some
attention. How did the poem attain this apprehension?
The seemingly random and confused catalogue of waves,
air, and midnight, though perhaps just one of Whitman's
occasional infelicities, seems to provide an emotional
rebound from the intuition of demonic laughter in the
preceding line. And out of this confused reaction
emerges a more refined recognition of that something we
seemed to hear before. That unknowable force discerned
through its cacaphony now has a name. But how Whitman
has earned this new identification in line 4 is
uncertain. I suggest that there may be a perceptual
logic in what the speaker sees; those apparently random
designations of waves, air, and midnight might in fact
comprise a movement of the eye from the bay to the
natural element coming in direct confrontation with it,
upwards to the sky in all its immensity. It may be that
the visual impression of the heavens in their awesome
blackness, their snow-streaked stillness, implacably
lording over the uncontrolled turmoil of this localized
scene, may have provided the necessary catalyst to an
apprehension of both savagery and trinity. Indeed,
recognitions and disclosures in this poem seem possible
only by erratic shifts in sensory perception.

But regardless of what may be a tenuous logic, the
conclusion of line 4 provides the climax of what we have
seen so far. What began as a description of a storm has
opened new dimensions through the suggestion of a savage
trinity. Yet significantly, this climax is not merely
one of revelation, for it heightens the problematic
nature of the poem. It is not a solution -- it is the
beginning of our questions. What is this "savagest
trinity"? Whitman was fond of exploiting the term
"trinity," with its culturally loaded associations. And
he valued the savage and fierce as a source of
knowledge. The operatic trio in "Out of the Cradle
Endlessly Rocking," for example, includes a "savage old
mother." But is the "savagest trinity" here the waves,
air, and midnight? The superlative adjective
necessitates the existence of more than one trinity.
Besides, line 4 is grammatically ambiguous: it is
"their" savagest trinity. The most likely referent is,
I think, the "shouts of demoniac laughter." In that
case, the waves, air, and midnight are but the savagest
of instruments issuing from that unnamed demonic
source. The reappearance of "savage trinity" in the
final line suggests a number of possibilities. "A group
of dim, weird forms" (patrolmen or plunderers) watching
"that savage trinity" (waves, air, and midnight); or

"that savage trinity" (patrolmen or plunderers) "warily"
watching "a group of dim, weird forms" (the "milk-white
combs" of the waves); or "that savagest trinity" (maybe
the source of demonic laughter, maybe not) watching the
"group of dim, weird forms" (traces of wrecked vessels
and/or patrolmen and/or plunderers). The ambiguities
created by diction and participial construction, and the
uncertainty whether any human beings present have come
to rescue or destroy, are both heightened by the
suggestiveness of "watching," with its contingency, its
lack of finality, its illusory purpose. So, what seemed
like a revelatory moment is in fact highly ambiguous.
The climactic fourth line has exaggerated the dichotomy
of revelation and obfuscation.
        The pattern I have observed may be fruitfully
applied to the remaining ten lines. Lines 5 and 6
juxtapose the visual sensations of white against black,
first out in the water, then on the beach. The
suggestion of similitude between the water and the land
is strengthened by the next two lines describing
someone's "breasting" the wind -- a "death-wind,"
significantly. For the first time in the poem, the
actual occasion is seemingly telescoped to a group's
struggling through the storm on the beach. Yet the
adverbial modifier "where" beginning line 7 could
describe not only the beach in the preceding line, but
the waters in the line before that. Thus the forceful
"breasting" and careful "advancing" which we would
ascribe to a human agent on shore could in fact describe
the movement of the waves, or of something amidst those
waves. What Whitman sets up, then, is a dynamic
principle whereby identifications continually slip away
from us and ambiguities predominate. Line 10, the
momentary suspicion of a wreck off shore, ushers in the
only intelligible idea of the poem (aside from the storm
itself, of course). Whitman's parenthetical enclosure
of this line betrays his self-consciousness in violating
the incantatory rhythm and hypnotic optics of the
verse. But the momentary Husky-Haughty Lips, O Sea,"
11. 16-17). The comparison to these lines penned in
1884 highlights the technical control in "Patroling
Barnegat" and indicates its thematic prominence in the
poet's memory, judging from other echoes in the later
piece from <u>Sands at Seventy</u>.
        4. The eventual substitution of "midnight edge"
for "midnight beach," a phrasing Whitman retained even
at an advanced stage of composition, is just part of the
evidence which textual history reveals of Whitman's
engagement with this poem. His other major alteration
was the positioning of the penultimate line, which had
been interpolated between lines 10 and 11:

> Slush and sand of the beach, tireless till
>   daylight wending,
> A group of dim, weird forms, struggling, the
>   night confronting,
> Steadily, slowly, through hoarse roar never
>   remitting,
> Along the midnight beach, by those milk-white
>   combs careering,
> That savage trinity warily watching.

-- thus the private version Whitman gave to R. M. Bucke on June 3, 1880 (Trent Collection, William R. Perkins Library, Duke University). The earlier line order does not clarify the ambiguities noted, but it does serve to illustrate the gradually crystallizing conception of the work. This arrangement dissipates an otherwise evolving perceptual process. Whitman evidently recognized that the potential of the second line above would best be realized only by making it an integral part of those final lines, transforming them beyond mere repetition of earlier images. In his final revision for inclusion in the 1881 Leaves of Grass patroling a beach. The semantically restricted "midnight" of line 4 has here become a "midnight edge";4 which, set next to those reappearing "milk-white combs," makes the visual impact of precariousness and precipitate disaster. Any efforts to confine the poem to rational statement are defeated by the subsequent appearance of "dim, weird forms." And with this, Whitman has moved from symbolist to symbologist, initiating inquiry into the nature of created and received meaning. Has perceptual indistinctness carried the mind itself beyond incongruities which can be rescued? Not for nothing does this image of struggling forms recall the earlier suspicion of a wrecked vessel. The image may call forth the symbolic topos of life as a precarious journey upon a storm-tossed sea. But the perceptual scrambling of "dim, weird forms" explodes any symbolic determinacy, and we are left holding in our laps, not the face of Whitman looking up at us, but a ballooning ontological conundrum.

I have closely analyzed this little verse of Sea-Drift to demonstrate that it can sustain this kind of imagistic dissection. Indeed, the poem calls for it as a necessary aesthetic response. But we must understand this manifestation of Whitman's poetic powers not as occasional experimentation, or as a tendency during his late career, but as a strain present from his first emergence as a mature poet. Lines such as "baskets cover'd with white towels swelling the house with their plenty" in "Song of Myself" (Sec. 3), and the idee fixe of Children of Adam -- "The swimmer swimming naked in the bath, or motionless on his back lying and

floating" -- were present in Whitman from the start.
Such lines are moments in his poetry which erode from
the doctrinally locatable to the suggestive, the
elusive, the problematic. As a conspicuous line in
"Song of the Open Road" (Sec. 10), "The stale cadaver
blocks up the passage -- the burial waits no longer,"
approaches the mythic in its almost purely emotive
relationship to thematic context.

    "Patroling Barnegat" is a critically unrecognized
poem that concentrates and amplifies what is diffuse
throughout Whitman's work. The availability of message,
the relationship of word to thing, of poet to reader,
seem to be less than explicit, or at least less than
certain. How then, to answer our question, can we
reconcile such a performance as "Patroling Barnegat"
with the Whitman of rhetorical immediacy and the
transparent text? Any attempt at such a reconciliation
would likely involve a re-examination of Democratic
Vistas, where he defines poetry as the spiritual
expression of the material. Whitman inherited this
dictum from the transcendentalists but put it to the
test more extensively than any of them. Such a
re-examination will require a discussion larger in
scope. Suffice it to say that the idea of poetry as the
spiritual expression of the material possesses
consequences for Whitman's own role as poet, his
expectations for his audience, and ultimately, his
conception of the nature of vision. It allows him to
envision the poet as both transmitter of transcendent
realities and privileged possessor of immanent
potentialities. Whitman shifts from the role of
transmitter of spiritual essences to the role of source
of symbolic creation. As the bard proclaiming
universal revitalization, he uses mundane experience as
the raw material of the poem, and the poem, in turn,
serves as a transparent rhetorical medium allowing the
poet to speak directly to his reader. Yet that same
prophetic impulse in Whitman produces verses in which
the symbol is ascendant, the poet transforms mundane
experience, and rhetoric is ancillary to the open-ended
logic of a symbological inquiry. In the first case,
prosaic catalogues such as we find in "Song of Myself"
require a poesis in the reader's mind, and in the second
case, finely honed, intellectually elusive images such
as we find in "Patroling Barnegat" emerge the product of
poesis in the author's mind. But whether we must look
to Whitman's theoretical formulation of poetry or
elsewhere, it is evident that the prophetic tradition of
revitalization of self means for our American bardic
poet a revitalization of poetry. The paradoxical quest
for Whitman and some of his successors has been the
search for a poetic form expressive of both rhetorical
immediacy and self-sustaining symbol. This quest has

been the aesthetic frustration and the human triumph of
Whitman's poetics.

     NOTES

     1.   Francis Bazley Lee, New Jersey as a Colony and
as a State (New York: The Publishing Society of New
Jersey, 1902), vol. 4, pp. 329-42.
     2.   For this resurrection of Barnegat Bay's
notorious history, I am indebted to Adeline Pepper's
nutshell expose in Tours of Historic New Jersey (New
Brunswick, N.J.: Rutgers University Press, 1973), p.
124.
     3.   Cf. "And serpent hiss, and savage peals of
laughter,/And undertones of distant lion roar" ("With
Husky-Haughty Lips, O Sea," 11. 16-17). The comparison
to these lines penned in 1884 highlights the technical
control in "Patroling Barnegat" and indicates its
thematic prominence in the poet's memory, judging from
other echoes in the later piece from Sands at Seventy.
     4.   The eventual substitution of "midnight edge"
for "midnight beach," a phrasing Whitman retained even
at an advanced stage of composition, is just part of the
evidence which textual history reveals of Whitman's
engagement with this poem. His other major alteration
was the positioning of the penultimate line, which had
been interpolated between lines 10 and 11:

     Slush and sand of the beach, tireless till
          daylight wending,
     A group of dim, weird forms, struggling, the
          night confronting,
     Steadily, slowly, through hoarse roar never
          remitting,
     Along the midnight beach, by those milk-white
          combs careering,
     That savage trinity warily watching.

-- thus the private version Whitman gave to R. M. Bucke
on June 3, 1880 (Trent Collection, William R. Perkins
Library, Duke University). The earlier line order does
not clarify the ambiguities noted, but it does serve to
illustrate the gradually crystallizing conception of the
work. This arrangement dissipates an otherwise evolving
perceptual process. Whitman evidently recognized that
the potential of the second line above would best be
realized only by making it an integral part of those
final lines, transforming them beyond mere repetition of
earlier images. In his final revision for inclusion in
the 1881 Leaves of Grass (Barrett MS), Whitman deleted
the commas in nearly half the lines, thereby
rhythmically accentuating the description and minimizing
the ordering influence of prose-logic punctuation. The

sheer number of alterations at this late date, even
after the poem's appearance in both The American (June
1880) and Harper's Monthly (April 1881) -- the revised
directions to the printer, the carefully cut lines
pasted in their present order, the evidence of five
different writing instruments -- reveals that this poem
was one of the most deliberated additions, both in
composition and placement, to the Sea-Drift section.

14.

The Lament in
"Song of the Broad-Axe"
DAVID CAVITCH

Within a week after the first publication of Leaves of
Grass, in which Whitman was proclaiming himself the
liberator of all the downtrodden spirits in the world,
the poet's begrudging father died on July 11, 1855, as
if erased by his inspired son's declarations of
independence. He had been seriously ill for a few
years, partly paralyzed, according to one newspaper
obituary notice, and he had suffered so many "bad
spells," as Mrs. Whitman called them, that on the day
the final attack developed the family was not aware of a
critical change in his condition. Walt and two of his
brothers, George and Jeff, spent the day away from the
house, presumably separately working, until they were
bidden home. Walt and Jeff arrived too late, and Mrs.
Whitman reported in a letter to her absent daughter in
New Hampshire that "they felt very much to blame
themselves for not being home but they had no idea of
any change." Mrs. Whitman appears to have remained
characteristically placid and encouraging toward her
children, while with the same demeanor she projected
upon them the burden of any "blame" that she felt. The
anticipation of the father's death had been absorbed
dispassionately into the family routine for a long time
before it happened. The old man's removal was
apparently a relief to all members of the household, who
found it easy to stop caring about the unappreciating
and dour invalid.
     In the immediate aftermath of his father's death,
which was all too calmly accepted by most of the family
under Louisa's emotional influence over the household,
Whitman felt badly unnerved by suggestions of
indifference and possible treachery in nature. The

apparently invulnerable calm of the inhuman world roused
his fascinated horror, which he expressed in a poem
responding to his father's death. Written after the
interment of his father's wasted body, "This Compost"
dwells on Whitman's shock and revulsion over facing the
facts of the corpse and burial while nature serenely
remains unaffected by the grotesqueness of man's
mortality. The earth's complacency frightens him, and
he scarcely knows whether the chemistry of decomposition
that distills the sour dead in the earth produces
healthful nurture or subtle poison. He recoils in
fright from contact with the earth he loves: "Something
startles me where I thought I was safest." The word
"something" begins the poem with a flourish of dramatic
mystery about the cause of his uncharacteristic
behavior. The poem reveals that his father's death is
the unnameable "something" that startles him into
renewed anxiety over the natural world that he usually
regards as maternally protective.

Overcome with revulsion from the thought of mortal
decay, Whitman cannot take off his clothes to touch the
woods, the pastures, the grass or sea where the rotting
corpses seep and drain, or expose himself to the air
that must be made infectious by the gas of decomposing
bodies. Deprived of nature's customary, sensual
caresses, his fearful recoil into himself away from the
places in which he enjoyed his securest pleasures is a
symptom of his grief, an interpretation which is not
evident to him, but which the rhetoric of the first
stanza reveals as his anger over bereavement. He is
abusively gross about the foul carcasses: resentful
over man's weakness and nakedness; and he is angry that
the earth placidly receives yet more putrefaction of the
dead.

> Something startles me where I thought I was
>   safest,
> I withdraw from the still woods I loved,
> I will not go now to the pastures to walk,
> I will not strip the clothes from my body to
>   meet my lover the sea,
> I will not touch my flesh to the earth as to
>   other flesh to renew me.
>
> O how can it be that the ground itself does
>   not sicken?
> How can you be alive you growths of spring?
> How can you furnish health you blood of herbs,
>   roots, orchards, grain?
> Are they not continually putting distemper'd
>   corpses within you?
> Is not every continent work'd over and over
>   with sour dead?

```
Where have you disposed of their carcasses?
Those drunkards and gluttons of so many
     generations?
Where have you drawn off all the foul liquid
     and meat?
I do not see any of it upon you to-day, or
     perhaps I am deceiv'd.
I will run a furrow with my plough, I will
     press my spade through the sod and turn
     it up underneath,
I am sure I shall expose some of the foul
     meat.
```
                                        (ll. 1-16)

Throughout the stanza he feels desolated and hostile over a death and burial that have unmanned him but which the earth accommodates as usual. The second full sentence of the stanza directs his vehemence against the earth's imperturbable capacity to hide the dead, and perhaps indeed its readiness to snatch men away into oblivion. He speaks as if he will shock, interrogate, challenge, bait, threaten, and eviscerate the earth into disclosure of the enormity of death and corruption within it.

In the plot of the poem, he falls back from his turbulent, dangerous impulse to expose the whole earth as a sickening charnel house. A new season of growth in the springtime restores his wonder over the mystery of natural regeneration. He marvels that the full-grown crops of summer are "innocent and disdainful above all those strata of sour dead." Feeling himself innocent of and superior to any blame for mortality, he relaxes into enjoyment of the pleasures of bodily life, resuming his walks and sea-baths, just as Whitman actually did following his father's death, and he renews his sweet tastes of fruit and his hours of repose upon the grass. Solaced by the earth's chemistry of resurrection -- the poem in 1856 was originally titled "Poem of Wonder at the Resurrection of the Wheat" -- Whitman follows almost to the end a simple reciprocating pattern of experiencing first loss and then consolation in witnessing the renewal of the world. But the final six lines of the poem carry their meaning beyond the logical structure of consolatory verse. Whitman remains transfixed by the earth that immunely refines human corruption into fresh air and bounteous goods. He is frightened by its impervious resilience; nature is distressingly unmindful of any values but her own equilibrium:

```
Now I am terrified at the Earth, it is that
     calm and patient,
It grows such sweet things out of such
     corruptions,
```

> It turns harmless and stainless on its axis,
>   with such endless successions of diseas'd
>   corpses,
> It distills such exquisite winds out of such
>   infused fetor,
> It renews with such unwitting looks its
>   prodigal, annual, sumptuous crops,
> It gives such divine materials to men, and
>   accepts such leavings from them at last.
>
> (11. 42-47)

Ostensibly, the poem calls into doubt and then reaffirms procreative life and the on-going vitality of Whitman's father who will prevail over death through resurrection in his son. But in these final lines the poem lingers disquietingly over the curious impassivity of the earth that overcomes, and indeed, perhaps drains away the vigor of men. The earth remains steady "on its axis"; it takes no harm or stain from the poisons and degradations of absorbing the dead. It coolly presides over death, while continuing its hermetic activity of provision as usual; its "unwitting looks" anticipate the inconsequence of individuals who are everlastingly diminished, shamed, and replaced: "It gives such divine materials to men, and accepts such leavings from them at last." This poignant disparagement of mortal men expresses pity for the disappointment of everyone's high hopes of life, but Whitman also conveys a strong sense of danger in the power of the earth to deactivate and reconstitute the very substance of men. To come to think of men as earth's compost, as he does throughout the poem, is to reflect the earth's irrational denial of their humanity.

Whitman does not, however, attain a very high level of recognition of the meaning of his feelings and his symbolic material. He did not come close enough to identifying Louisa in the attitudes of the earth, and consequently he did not incur the directly personal threat of the earth's power over him, nor did he feel horrified by an inevitable sense of complicity in whatever he found blameworthy in his mother. The irony of burying the dead in the fruitful earth is an entirely conventional, elegaic subject that Whitman treats in a fairly conventional way; he suggests but does not develop more revelatory meanings in the usual imagery of springtime and burial and the distress and consolation of the mourner. But when Whitman responded to his father's death with less conventional poetic elements, he more clearly acknowledged his complicated personal feelings and the ambiguous family relationships that underlay his bewilderment and his suspicion that the heart of nature was destructively possessive toward men and manhood. In "Song of the Broad-Axe" he works with

his more characteristically original imagery of
democratic society, and he is able to take hints from
his social observations of the veneer of femininity over
the coarseness of mid-century American life. What he
uncovers unnerves him deeply in the poem. "Song of the
Broad-Axe" at first develops and then disguises a
spectacle of masculine, workaday power that is sapped by
feminine, decorous complacency.
    Whitman begins the poem with a riddle: that is,
the axe is described with abundant use of suggestive
metaphors that make it a distinctly enigmatic, poetic
expression of meanings yet to be unravelled. The
deliberate symbolism is emphasized and set off from the
rest of the poem by the stylized prosody of the opening
six lines of pronouncedly metered verse and insistent
rhyming:

> Weapon shapely, naked, wan,
> Head from the mother's bowels drawn,
> Wooded flesh and metal bone, limb only one and
>   lip only one,
> Gray blue leaf by red-heat grown, helve
>   produced from a little seed sown.
> Resting the grass amid and upon,
> To be lean'd and to lean on.

(11. 1-6)

The exaggerated figurativeness of the language draws
attention to the forthcoming paradox, which Whitman
intends to demonstrate, that the overtly phallic object
that has represented man's law and masculine power
throughout the ages contains an inner core of feminine
power, which expresses nature's law.
    The axe, as Whitman develops its meaning, is the
great instrument with an organ-range of creative and
destructive acts from ancient times to the present. It
is the most common, most flexibly usable tool of the
individual will, an extension of personal strength and
impulse that can be multiplied thousands of times into
armies and hordes; or that singly can be invested with
the power of monarchs to execute traitors and rivals and
to arrogate property in the name of the king; or as used
by countless millions the axe clears forests, builds
houses, bridges, ships, and cities. Whitman makes the
axe altogether symbolic of the immanent but undervalued
human spirit in every use and feature of the implement.
Even the materials from which it is made, unlike the
materials of aristocratic wealth, come from lands that
do not produce obvious riches like crops, gold, timber,
grazing for cattle; the ores that are smelted and forged
into the axe are hidden in the earth under the apparent
barrenness and severity of the "Lands of iron -- lands
of the make of the axe." Its original sources lie

unseen within places that are forbidding, austere, and
not counted precious.
     The uses of the axe that are celebrated in
Whitman's catalogue method in stanza 3 indicate a world
at work without stint or relief. For 69 lines humanity
is shown striving to inherit the earth through skills,
trades, occupations, greed, and ambitions, always
employing the axe as the instrument of material
achievement. The external facts of civilizations are
defined by the work of the axe that exerts "the power of
personality just or unjust."
     At the height of glorifying the productive work of
the axe -- and extolling all the material values of his
family of Brooklyn housebuilders -- the argument of the
poem turns to dwell on the ephemeralness of man's
accomplished works and of the visible world generally.
What seems substantial and fixed in the world is only
transitory; material achievements indicate chiefly the
immaterial powers that form them. "Muscle and pluck
forever!" Whitman calls out as he redirects his praises
away from man's feats of muscle to celebrate the human
pluck that rises and rises again through the falling
monuments of the ages. Echoing Emerson's idealism,
Whitman dismisses the works of the axe because they do
not last -- "Do you think a great city endures?" he
asks. Only the spirit that the axe expresses is real
and immortal. The universal occurrence of the axe
amidst the changes of the mutable world indicates that
"nothing endures but personal qualities." The aphorism
in that line sounds more like a sentence by Emerson than
Whitman's usual verse. The Emersonian accents in his
tone continue as Whitman asserts that the axe symbolizes
not only the individual will but specifically the
natural democracy of the great spirit of mankind,
because only the vigor of individuals survives and
endures through the pomp and decay of empires.

          What do you think endures?
          Do you think a great city endures?
          Or a teeming manufacturing state? or a
               prepared
               constitution? or the best built
               steamships?
          Or hotels of granite and iron? or any
               chef-d'oeuvres of engineering, forts,
               armaments?

          Away! these are not to be cherish'd for
               themselves,
          They fill their hour, the dancers dance, the
               musicians play for them,
          The show passes, all does well enough of
               course,
          All does very well till one flash of defiance.

> A great city is that which has the greatest
>   men and women,
> If it be a few ragged huts it is still the
>   greatest city in the whole world.
>
>   (ll. 100-109)

When he has established the moral and social
significance of the symbol as distinctively democratic,
the continuation of the poem becomes partly repetitive
and concentric as Whitman reiterates the themes
developed in the first half; but as he elaborates on the
clarified meaning of the axe, his perspective changes to
a more visionary outlook that discerns a general truth
about the way all of nature, not just the axe, expresses
the supremacy of the spirit. He once again notes the
unpromising landscape that contains the hidden, common
ore; he again recounts through history the service of
the axe to the living and the dead; he sees again the
emblem of the American future in the scourge of the
world's past, now washed clean of its blood and
disgraces; and the rapid condensation of these
particular symbolic facts about the axe projects upon
the poem's own evidence a pattern of nature's ceaseless
externalizations of inner essences. He finds the
meaning of experience in nature's process of giving
increasingly revealed, objective form to profoundly
subjective spirit. The essences of all created things
come into his view like special penumbra redefining
their now hallowed shapes. These _shapes_ rise in the
vision he has gained to see into the spiritual core and
dimension of the world. "The shapes arise!" he repeats
through the final 54 lines, as these shapes which are
the essences of things express directly and radiantly
the reality of internal life.

> The shapes arise!
> Shapes of factories, arsenals, foundries,
>   markets,
> Shapes of the two-threaded tracks of
>   railroads,
> Shapes of the sleepers of bridges, vast
>   frameworks, girders, arches,
> Shapes of the fleets of barges, tows, lake and
>   canal craft, river craft,
> Ship-yards and dry-docks along the Eastern and
>   Western seas, and in many a bay and
>   by-place,
> The live-oak kelsons, the pine planks, the
>   spars, the hackmatack-roots for knees,
> The ships themselves on their ways, the tiers
>   of scaffolds, the workmen busy outside
>   and inside,

>   The tools lying around, the great auger and
>   little auger, the adze, bolt, line,
>   square, gouge, and bead-plane.
>
> (11. 207-15)

He sees a world transformed into the embodiment of spirit; from huge factories to small tools, the implements themselves have become wholly personal, while remaining concretely external objects. These lines of inspired perception of details resound with echoes of Whitman's beatific vision in "Song of Myself," in which he recognized love immanent in the plenitude of the universe and enjoyed spiritual intimacy with starkly objective nature. But in "Song of the Broad-Axe" the beatific quality of his vision turns melancholy as the celebration of commercial manufacturing concludes with its imagery of man's production, skillfulness, designs, and mastery. Whitman cannot bring the joy of spiritual work back to man's ordinary existence at home without resuming tones of deep depression. The shapes of domestic life that subsequently arise are shadowed with pathos, frustration, and suppressed rage. The routines of ideally contented home life are intermixed with the miseries of dying, family strife, drunkenness, criminality, punishment, and despair. The shapes that arise in stanza 10 are the enclosing or rejecting structures of beds, coffins, houses, courtrooms, taverns, prisons, gallows, and doorways of forced exits and ignoble entrances. The places are all closely associated with parents, spouses, the old and young generations, children and outcasts. It is as though Whitman can find no place at home for his essential shape to arise amidst the bitter chaos of his private life. Facing that diminished and oppressive world, Whitman recognized figures of his brothers trying to find the natural balance, the order and sanity of their life even though they understood nothing of the emotional turbulence that beset them. In the first version of this poem, which passed through several stages of revision as Whitman struggled with the painfully intractable materials of its concluding portion, the shapes arise of "full-sized men" -- that is, adults who are still thought of as being children. They want to know what is being asked of them, imposed on them, what more they can give to forestall the constant indications of their debts and guilt:

>   Their shapes arise, above all the rest -- the
>   shapes of full-sized men,
>   Men taciturn yet loving, used to the open air,
>   and the manners of the open air,
>   Saving their ardor in native forms, saying the
>   old response,

> Take what I have then, (saying fain), take the
>   pay you approached for,
> Take the white tears of my blood, if that is
>   what you are after.;1

Whitman dropped this entire passage and removed
from the poem this expression of his sympathy for his
inarticulate brothers, speaking for himself among them,
who with reason complain about the strangely demanding,
restless family atmosphere in which affection is
gainsaid, or unacknowledged, yet further expression of
it is implicitly required as "pay you approached for
. . . the white tears of my blood."
   The intense ambivalence of being in that situation
is directed toward the mother at home. Her shape
immediately arises in the next ten lines that Whitman
retained without any revision. She is portrayed as the
center of equanimity, poise, and justice; she knows
everybody's concealed thoughts, yet she remains
undistressed. She is impassively generous, secure,
inviolate; and amidst the disorder of relationships
that seem to direct hostility against her, she is the
calm law of nature itself:

> Her shape arises,
> She less guarded than ever, yet more guarded
>   than ever,
> The gross and soil'd she moves among do not
>   make her gross and soil'd,
> She knows the thoughts as she passes, nothing
>   is conceal'd from her,
> She is none the less considerate or friendly
>   therefor,
> She is the best belov'd, it is without
>   exception, she has no reason to fear and
>   she does not fear,
> Oaths, quarrels, hiccupp'd songs, smutty
>   expressions, are idle to her as she
>   passes,
> She is silent, she is possess'd of herself,
>   they do not offend her,
> She receives them as the laws of Nature
>   receive them, she is strong,
> She too is a law of Nature -- there is no law
>   stronger than she is.

> (11. 239-48)

Some of the mother's preternatural powers appear as
mere idealizations of womanhood in the final version of
the poem, which lacks the preceding expression of her
son's anguish. But in the light of the original verses,
the fact that she knows everyone's secret thoughts,
remains insulated against harsh criticism, denies the

grossness of other people's suffering and anger,
exercises her will without any hesitation or particular
response to individuals -- all these qualities of
majestic self-possession are maddening and desolating
traits when they are seen from the eyes of a child,
however old, who feels trapped by his love and hate,
neither of which ever gets through to her. The
apparently benign, sweet temper of the woman suggests,
from the viewpoint of a family in distress, a callously
impervious will to please herself. That view of her
character, or "shape," explains Whitman's quick change
of tone to melancholic thoughts of humiliation,
degeneracy, and oblivion as soon as the plot of the poem
brings him home with his band of working brothers where
the door shuts behind them upon the promise of
achievement and freedom in the vigorous world of other
men. But these negative aspects of her essence are
disguised and idealized as the equanimity and grace of
female sensibility that expresses the impersonal
awfulness and strength of Nature itself in its spiritual
essence. The shape of the new American woman is
presented as the underlying basis of reality; her
revealed shape is the ultimate expression of human
depths made evident, of the invisible world made
visible, of the inchoate personality given perfect
form. Acknowledgment of her supremacy completes the
symbolic work and revelatory meaning of the broad-axe.
     In another tussle with his ambiguous and
disturbingly aggressive feelings in the concluding
section, Whitman initially included a portrait of his
own shape, or self, arising immediately after his
mother's. In the first version of the poem, the brawny
shape of the new American man, resembling Whitman in
every feature and trait that he popularly projected as
his own, balances the female shape with equal strength
and poise -- and outmatches her by offering much more
personal affability and sensual responsiveness. He
celebrates his own image, trying for the second time
within this poem to achieve the harmonious
self-acceptance that he expressed in "Song of Myself,"
in which his acknowledgment of his inner core of
feminine sensibility led to transports of relief and to
doting on himself in liberated pleasure. But the
imaginative structure of "Song of the Broad-Axe" is not
similar to that of "Song of Myself." The analysis and
translation of the symbolic meaning of the axe lead
Whitman to recognize a deceptively untrustworthy
feminine shape that denies him, but which he
nevertheless associates with his matching self. He
faces a malign egotism that is ambiguously both outside
and inside him; and he experiences not relief but the
burdens of his inadequacy, resentment, and guilt. He
refused to face the full intensity of the negative,

hostile feelings he uncovered by exploring that symbol
of manhood; and despite all the revisions, he never went
far enough to connect his exposed anger to feelings of
frailty which were likely after the death of his father,
or to any other anxiety, specifically the threat of
emasculation by the cutting axe. In this threatening
capacity the axe as an expression of a powerful will
could suggest to him both mother and father as a
combined parental force. But as far as his insight
takes him, the feelings in this poem lead him unhappily
away from transcendence, and away from fulfilling
himself through identification with the social units of
family and nation that he tries to embrace. His initial
self-portrait as a triumphantly representative man who
embodies and enriches the culture that formed him is
evidence of his failure to admit what the poem
demonstrates, that the mother-in-the-axe is no warm
breast of nature, such as he wished her to be. When he
eventually dropped the 18-line passage of ostentatious
self-description, and dropped as well the passage
expressing himself as a deeply troubled son and brother,
he left a curiously warped but intense poem, in which
flashes of his creative intuition outleap his intention
to poeticize Emerson's dogma that the external world
symbolizes spirit. But Whitman could not entirely
accept the personal meanings of this symbol which he
translated back to its origins in his private life.

The calm possessiveness of the earth in "This
Compost" and the withering complacency of the woman in
"Song of the Broad-Axe" express Whitman's horrified
suspicion that he was betrayed in his deepest trust. He
saw from a childish perspective the destructive
self-centeredness of his mother who remained a
threatening presence as long as she lived, despite their
mutual dependence. He never again undermined his
idealization of his mother by openly expressing such
severe resentment of woman in his poetry. His sense of
loss in the death of his father did not emerge openly as
mourning until three years later, in his Sea-Drift
poems, in which he seeks a reconciliation with the
spirit of his father; and his entire work thereafter
turns predominantly elegaic over all the sons and
fathers lost in the family conflict of the Civil War.

NOTE

1. Leaves of Grass, Facsimile Edition of the 1860
Text, ed. Roy Harvey Pearce (Ithaca, N.Y.: Cornell
University Press, 1961), p. 140.

Part IV

Whitman and America

15.
Whitman's Democratic Vista
in the First *Leaves of Grass*

JEROME LOVING

Ralph Waldo Emerson's anger over the passage of the
Fugitive Slave Law of 1850 is well known. Not one given
to what was considered profanity in Victorian America,
he declared in his journal, "I'll not obey it, by
God.";1 Daniel Webster, the hope of New England against
slavery, had let the country down. As the Quaker poet
John Greenleaf Whittier would remark in "Ichabod!"
Webster had become a

>   bright soul driven,
>   Fiend-goaded, down the endless dark,
>   From hope and heaven.

As for Emerson, "The word liberty in the mouth of Mr.
Webster [now sounded] like the word <u>love</u> in the mouth of
a courtesan." With Webster's concession to the South,
it appeared that the high principles of the founding
fathers were already forgotten by the middle of the
nineteenth century. Following the election as president
of Nathaniel Hawthorne's Bowdoin classmate Franklin
Pierce, Emerson confided to his journal:

>   The head of Washington hangs in my dining room
>   . . . & I cannot keep my eyes off it. . . . We
>   can imagine him hearing the letter of General
>   Cass, the letter of Gen Scott, the letter of
>   Mr. Pierce, the effronteries of Mr. Webster
>   recited. This man listens like a god to these
>   low conspirators.

The actions of such politicians "soft" on slavery led him to conclude that "the Union is no longer desirable.";2   Indeed, Emerson's concern over the decay in national leadership may have played an important part in his solitary recognition of Whitman's genius in the first edition of Leaves of Grass.   Of course, Emerson recognized Whitman's ability to absorb into his poetry native American materials ("our Negroes and Indians, our boats and our repudiations, the wrath of rogues and the pusillanimity of honest men"), but he also perceived the political theme he had called for -- Whitman's celebration of "our stumps and their politics."

     Malcolm Cowley has branded this theme Whitman's "bumptious American nationalism,";3 but a closer examination will show that Whitman's knowledge of politics through his work as a journalist played an important part in the making of his first book of poetry.   Between 1838 and 1850 he worked for more than a dozen newspapers, in a journalistic era when most newspapers represented a particular political point of view.   Ultimately, the association caused him to become pessimistic about the health of democracy.   Like Emerson he came to lament the lackluster political spirit that contrasted sharply with the examples of statesmen of the previous century.   Shortly before he was fired as editor of the Brooklyn Daily Eagle in 1848, in fact, he compiled a list of representative men whose example he thought the present-day politicians should have been following.   His gallery included Andrew Jackson, Silas Wright, Zachary Taylor, George Bancroft, Jefferson Davis, George Washington, and Thomas Jefferson.;4   These individuals, he believed, had stood up for democracy and represented the "average" American far better than the likes of Pierce and Webster.

     Whitman feared for the cause of liberty in the 1850s, and his frustration found its way into the 1855 Preface.   In a passage from that curious manifesto -- one that might be subtitled "When Liberty Goes" -- he defined the first stage of America's demise as when "the memories of old martyrs are faded utterly away . . . when the large names of patriots are laughed at in the public halls from the lips of orators."   Whitman's Preface was probably written in haste,;5 but its sentiments accurately reflect the democratic vista in the first Leaves -- in poems that celebrate the "common people," the working men and women who were generally unrepresented in the political arena of the 1850s.   In this light the book may be considered Whitman's answer to the politicians of the day.   A letter written in 1852, for example, shows that he viewed the election of Franklin Pierce as a dark chapter in American history. Prior to the fall election, he urged Senator John Parker Hale, the free-soil party choice for the presidency, not

to decline the nomination. "Out of the Pittsburgh
movement, it may be," he told Hale,

> that a real live Democratic party is destined
> to come forth, which, from small beginnings,
> ridicule, and odium (just like Jeffersonian
> democracy fifty years ago), will gradually win
> the hearts of the people, and crowd those who
> stand before it into the sea. Then we should
> see an American Democracy with thews and
> sinews worthy of this sublime age.

In the 1855 Preface the "sublime age" became the
"age transfigured," and the Preface introduced poems
that celebrated what Emerson had sought in the American
epic. It is perhaps not unreasonable, therefore, to
theorize that the animus of the first Leaves was formed
sometime between the passage of the Fugitive Slave Law
and the election of Franklin Pierce in 1852 -- as
Whitman became as disenchanted with American politics as
Emerson during the same period. Whitman believed he
knew the average far better than did the currently
elected officials. He told Hale in the same letter:

> How little you at Washington -- you Senatorial
> and Executive dignitaries -- know of us after
> all. How little you realize that the souls of
> the people ever leap and swell to any thing
> like a great liberal thought or principle,
> uttered by any well-known personage -- how
> deeply they love the man that promulges such
> principles with candor and power.;6

The "great liberal thought" was "pushed into the sea,"
of course, by the victory of Pierce, and Whitman's
idealization of the American average in Leaves of Grass
becomes closely associated with his disapproval of
American politics under the leadership of Pierce.
Although we find no outright condemnation of national
leaders in the first Leaves, the politicians are in the
Preface more or less sacrificed in the poet's praise for
the divine average. In fact, they are almost forgotten
in Whitman's enthusiasm for the average. His political
anger, as it were, was simply absorbed in the process.
And yet his anger was in part the basis for his
democratic vista in Leaves of Grass.
     Evidence of this is found in one of the most
remarkable essays the poet ever wrote, "The Eighteenth
Presidency! Voice of Walt Whitman to Each Young Man in
the Nation, North, South, East, and West." Whitman's
criticism of both presidential candidates seeking to
succeed Pierce in 1856 suggests that the pamphlet, which
was not published in the poet's lifetime, was written

after the first publication of <u>Leaves of Grass</u>. But the
essay probably began to germinate around 1854, shortly
after the passage of the Kansas-Nebraska Act. This
hotly debated bill nullified the Missouri Compromise of
1820, which had forbidden the extension of slavery in
the remaining and unsettled portions of the Louisiana
Purchase. It led to much bloodshed in Kansas, and
Whitman referred to the violence in "The Eighteenth
Presidency!" Further and more convincing evidence of a
pre-1855 draft, however, comes from Clifton J. Furness'
<u>Walt Whitman's Workshop</u>, where a version of the pamphlet
was published in 1928. Furness writes:

> A preliminary germ of this pamphlet: "The
> [blank] th Presidency. Voice of Walt Whitman
> to the mechanics and farmers of These States,
> and to each American young man, north, south,
> east and west." . . . Then follows the
> introductory paragraph, in which he spoke of
> "more than five millions" of workingmen. This
> seems to indicate that the plan was originally
> conceived a good while before the campaign of
> 1856, since in the completed version the
> number had increased to "some six millions."
> The pamphlet was probably the fruit of a long
> slow growth, like many another of Whitman's
> creations.;7

Whitman's thesis in the final draft of "The
Eighteenth Presidency!" calls for the average workingman
to come forth and usurp the political offices of the
"swarms of dough faces, office vermin, kept editors,
attaches of the ten thousand officers and their parties,
aware of nothing further than the drip and spoil of
politics -- ignorant of principles, the true glory of
man." What is important about the pamphlet, however, is
its exaggeration of the qualities of the average
American, the same kind of idealization we find in
<u>Leaves of Grass</u>. I see no reason, therefore, to doubt
that the earlier version carried the same political
tenor and that Whitman drew upon it in the composition
of the 1855 <u>Leaves</u>.
In <u>Democratic Vistas</u> (1871) Whitman would complain
that the "people are ungrammatical, untidy, and their
sins gaunt and ill-bred." Then he was concerned about
the postwar bent for materialism ("a vast and more and
more thoroughly-appointed body and then left with little
or no soul"), but in the 1850s he believed that the
national leaders were materialistic and that the nation
sorely needed leadership from "the real America." In
fact, in "The Eighteenth Presidency!" he looked for and
anticipated a man like Lincoln, not simply one of the
average. He had enough political savvy to qualify his

statement about the American "blacksmith or boatman" who would come out of the West to occupy the White House. Not only should this individual be heroic, Whitman declared, but "shrewd, fully informed," as the future poet himself was about the realities of American democracy. He would vote "for that sort of man, [but only one] possessing the due requirements."

Had Whitman not believed in the reality of such a leader, I believe that he could not have written Leaves of Grass. Hence, a crucial element in the book, as I have said, was his anger or pessimism over the expansion of slavery into Kansas. Yet it was not slavery or its effect on the black man that most concerned him. Whitman sought a leader who would restore the dignity of the white man and woman. "In fifteen of the States," he wrote in "The Eighteenth Presidency!,"

> the three hundred and fifty thousand masters
> keep down the true people, the millions of
> white citizens, mechanics, farmers, boatmen,
> manufacturers, and the like, excluding them
> from politics and from office, and punishing
> by the lash, by tar and feathers, binding fast
> to rafts on the rivers or trees in the woods,
> and sometimes by death, all attempts to
> discuss the evils of slavery in its relation
> to the whites.;8

On the surface, Whitman sounds like an abolitionist (as he would in section 10 of "Song of Myself," where the poet cares for a runaway slave), but like Lincoln he placed the integrity of white America above the need to abolish slavery. Slavery was an evil primarily because "the true people," the white divine average, were degraded by having to perform in the North what was the work of the slave in the South.

Such a bifurcation in his concern over slavery, then, helps to explain Whitman's ambivalence on the question of race. Claims for the poet's "racism" are largely based upon three editorials he wrote between 1842 and 1858. In the first he defended slavery against British criticism. Citing the harsh conditions the average English laborer's family had to endure, he wrote, "Everything bears the impress of cheerfulness and content" in the American slave's shanty.;9 In 1848 he once again put the welfare of the nation ahead of the abolition of slavery by supporting the annexation of Texas as either a free or slave state.;10 His most blatant concession appeared in 1858 when he asked, "Who believes that the Whites and Blacks can ever amalgamate in America? Or who wishes it to happen? Nature has set an impassable seal against it.";11

In "Song of Myself" Whitman describes his celebration of America as a "meal pleasantly set": . later, the line was changed to read "equally set." And in all editions the celebration included "the heavy-lipped slave," but it is significant that this individual is placed among other low life in America: "the kept woman and sponger and thief" and the "veneralee." In other words, these individuals are not really on the same level as the jour printer, the duck-shooter, or the trapper. The "meal," then, is "equally set" only in the sense of potential -- the potential of the "heavy-lipped slave" and other unfortunates to take their places among the "divine average." As Whitman would write of another low-life character in "To a Common Prostitute," this woman is not excluded from his catalogue of Americans, but his assignation with her must wait until she has emerged from the degradation of her profession. "My girl," he announced, "I appoint with you an appointment, and I charge you that <u>you make preparation to be worthy to meet me</u>" (emphasis added).

Ironically, even "A Boston Ballad," composed in 1854 in response to the Anthony Burns incident, paid little attention to the plight of the black man. Rather, the emphasis was on the erosion of the principles established by the country's forefathers and the resulting effete patriotism of their "great grandsons." In harsh satire -- uncommon in Whitman's poetry -- he ridiculed the fact (reported in the New York <u>Tribune</u> of June 3) that it required "10,000 troops under arms" to escort one fugitive slave from the Boston courthouse to the "black-bellied clipper" for his forced return to Virginia. All the while, the citizens who had previously rioted in protest to the implementation of the Fugitive Slave Law in their city stand by, Whitman observed in his poem, and thereby allow the principles of their great-grandfathers to be mocked by the procession. But Whitman's satire was double-edged, for he also ridiculed the founding fathers themselves:

> What troubles you, Yankee phantoms? What is
>   all this chattering of bare gums?
> Does the ague convulse your limbs? Do you
>   mistake your crutches for firelocks?

Actually, Whitman is attacking not the forefathers themselves but the dissipation of their democratic legacy by the politicians of his day. Through their nefarious influence, they had undermined the spirit of "the old martyrs," a spirit Whitman believed made the American average divine and worthy of celebration. Now -- because of the Fugitive Slave Law -- Americans are helpless to uphold the dignity of their patriotic

great-grandfathers. In "A Boston Ballad" Brother
Jonathan, once shrewd but basically honest, becomes a
surrogate for Daniel Webster. "Clear the way there
Jonathan," Whitman declares in his opening line -- to
suggest that by abiding by Webster's compromise
Bostonians were clearing the way for slavery in the
North. And he closed the poem with this stinging
remonstrance:

> Stick your hands in your pockets Jonathan --
>   you are a made man from this day,
> You are mighty cute -- and here is one of your
>   bargains.;12

Slavery, therefore, was wrong to Whitman's thinking
primarily because it degraded white Americans. Its
expansion through the Fugitive Slave Law and the
Kansas-Nebraska Act was also wrong because it violated
the Constitution, which originally permitted slavery
only in South Carolina and Georgia. Finally, it was
wrong because it prevented the black man from achieving
his potential in the New World. But this final concern
carried a low priority in Whitman's first book. In
fact, during the Civil War he lamented the deaths of
white Americans -- both North and South. In an argument
with his abolitionist friend William Douglas O'Connor,
Whitman is alleged to have said: "This war must stop.
. . . I don't care for the niggers . . . in comparison
with this slaughter.";13 In Democratic Vistas he also
opposed the passage of the Fifteenth Amendment, which
gave the black man the right to vote. Like Emerson, he
believed that reform had to begin with the individual
and declared in that essay that America needed not the
enfranchised Negro but the "enfranchised man.";14
Whitman's democratic vista in the 1855 Leaves,
therefore, extolled the average and called upon his
political involvement. Yet it was essentially the white
average, not the white below-average or the degraded
black slave, that he summoned forth in his book. For
these unfortunates their rendezvous was not as yet fitly
"appointed."

NOTES

1.   Journals and Miscellaneous Notebooks of Ralph
Waldo Emerson, ed. A. W. Plumsted et al. (Cambridge,
Mass.: Harvard University Press, 1975), vol. 11, p. 412.
Cited below as JMN.
     2.   JMN, vol. 11, p. 346; vol. 13, p. 63.
     3.   Walt Whitman's "Leaves of Grass"; The First
(1855) Edition, ed. Malcolm Cowley (New York: Viking
Press, 1959), p. xxvii.

4.   Walt Whitman, Gathering of Forces, ed.
Cleveland Rogers and John Black (New York: G. P.
Putnam's Sons, 1928), vol. 2, pp. 180-98.
    5.   Joseph Jay Rubin, The Historic Whitman
(University Park: Pennsylvania State University Press,
1973), p. 306.
    6.   The Correspondence, ed. Edwin Haviland Miller
(New York: New York University Press, 1961), vol. 1,
pp. 39-41.
    7.   Walt Whitman's Workshop: A Collection of
Unpublished Manuscripts (Cambridge, Mass.: Harvard
University Press, 1982), pp. 92-113, 227n. Quotations
from this tract, however, are taken from a later and
more reliable text, Walt Whitman: The Eighteenth
Presidency!, ed. Edward F. Grier (Lawrence, Kans.:
University of Kansas Press, 1956).
    8.   Grier, pp. 22, 21, 24-25 (emphasis added).
    9.   Walt Whitman of the New York "Aurora," ed.
Joseph Jay Rubin and Charles H. Brown (Westport, Conn.:
Greenwood Press, 1972), pp. 126-27.
    10.   Thomas L. Brasher, Whitman as Editor of the
Brooklyn "Daily Eagle" (Detroit: Wayne State University
Press, 1970), pp. 91-92.
    11.   Walt Whitman, I Sit and Look Out: Editorials
from the Brooklyn "Daily Times," ed. Emory Holloway and
Vernolian Schwarz (New York: Columbia University Press,
1932), p. 90.
    12.   Emphasis added. See Stephen D. Malin, "'A
Boston Ballad' and the Boston Riot," Walt Whitman
Review, 9 (Sept. 1963): 51-57.
    13. Jerome Loving, Walt Whitman's Champion: William
Douglas O'Connor (College Station, Tex.: Texas A&M
University Press, 1978), pp. 86-87.

16.

The American Context of
Democratic Vistas

ROBERT J. SCHOLNICK

Walt Whitman's Democratic Vistas (1870) is known today
primarily -- perhaps even exclusively -- for its
uncompromising and biting attack on the failures of
American society in the immediate postwar years.
Cleanth Brooks, R.W.B. Lewis, and Robert Penn Warren,
for instance, in their anthology American Literature:
The Makers and the Making, describe the book as

> a major document -- the first thoroughgoing
> survey of the American Republic in "The Gilded
> Age," that period of chaotic economic
> development, of financial greed and many kinds
> of gross corruption following the Civil War.
> . . . Among others, Mark Twain, Henry James,
> and Henry Adams would also give an account of
> this disreputable but fascinating moment in
> our national history; but none would offer as
> scathing an indictment of postwar America as
> Whitman.;1

His report of his examination of contemporary America --
made "like a physician diagnosing some deep disease" --
is so powerful that this section, which appears early in
the text, may color our reading of the entire work.;2
We may forget, then, that Democratic Vistas, while
magnificent in the force of its denunciation of
immediate problems, remains our most far-reaching and
inspiring "defense" of American democracy. The
greatness of the work is due to its ability to combine a
realistic and unsparing evaluation of both the
contemporary failings and the structural weaknesses of
democracy with a full statement of its spiritual

potential. One key to this unique balance may be found
in the unusual factors influencing its composition over
a period of some three years, from 1866 to 1870.

The initial impetus for Democratic Vistas was
Horace Greeley's publication in the Tribune for August
16, 1867, of the complete text of Carlyle's Shooting
Niagara, an intemperate, even savage, attack on
democratizing tendencies in England and America. The
same day Greeley published an editorial defending
American democracy from Carlyle's attacks, and this was
followed by many others, including an essay by E. L.
Godkin in the Nation.;3 On September 7, Whitman wrote
the editors of the Galaxy, two brothers, William C. and
Francis P. Church, that he had in composition, an
article, (prose,) of some length -- the subject
opportune -- I shall probably name it Democracy. It is
partly provoked by and in some respects a rejoinder to,
Carlyle's Shooting Niagara.";4 The editors encouraged
Whitman to proceed with the project, and the three major
divisions of Democratic Vistas were conceived as
separate essays for the Galaxy. "Democracy" appeared in
December 1867, "Personalism" in May 1868, but the third,
"Literature," was not published, perhaps because of its
length. However, in preparing these essays for
publication as a separate volume, Whitman made a number
of significant additions and deletions. He removed
three paragraphs, written in a splendid imitation of
Carlyle's own style, directly attacking the cantankerous
old Scotsman. And he added, at the beginning of the
volume, the passages condemning the business, political,
and social corruption which he saw engulfing America,
turning it into "a sort of dry and flat Sahara" (p.
372). Clearly, Whitman's diagnosis, his reading of what
he saw under "the moral microscope," had changed (p.
372).

Whitman explained his changing perspective in a
footnote he added to the published volume:

> I was at first roused to much anger and abuse
> by this essay [Shooting Niagara] from Mr.
> Carlyle, so insulting to the theory of America
> -- but happening to think afterwards how I had
> more than once been in the like mood, during
> which this essay was evidently cast, and seen
> persons and things in the same light, (indeed
> some might say there are signs of the same
> feeling in these Vistas) -- I have since read
> it again, not only as a study, expressing as
> it does certain judgments from the highest
> feudal point of view, but have read it with
> respect as coming from an earnest soul, and as
> contributing certain sharp-cutting mettallic
> grains, which, if not gold or silver, may be
> good hard, honest iron. (Pp. 375-76)

In the Galaxy article he had, in a sense, apologized for appearing to preach to the converted, explaining that "a portion of our pages we indite with reference toward Europe, more than our own land, perhaps not absolutely needed for the home reader." But with the addition of the condemnatory passages at the beginning, there can be no doubt of his intention to include the "home reader." He changed the sentence to read "A portion of our pages we might indite with reference toward Europe, especially the British part of it, more than our own land, perhaps not absolutely needed for the home reader" (p. 382). The addition of the conditional "might" changes the force of the sentence and serves to direct attention back to the American audience.

Just as Whitman was not alone in responding angrily to Carlyle, so he was not -- contrary to our general impression -- the first contemporary writer to denounce the corruption of the new period. Probably the most prominent writer to take up this theme was E. L. Godkin. In "Commercial Immorality and Political Corruption," published in the North American Review for July 1868, he observes that "many thoughtful men . . . in England, America, and France" are asking if not "all the great communities in the Western World [are] growing more corrupt as they grow in wealth.";5 Focussing on the American business community, Godkin convincingly demonstrates both the growing commercial immorality and political corruption and the close connection between the two. If we are to believe Godkin, then, a strong moral disapproval of postwar American society was widely felt, and both he and Whitman were in fact speaking for "many thoughtful men." Whitman's intellectual movement, from an optimism so strong as to lead him to strike out against aristocratic critics of American democracy to a position of discouragement as the failure of Reconstruction and scandals of local and national politics became evident, was hardly unique. Godkin, Henry Adams, and Charles Eliot Norton traversed much the same course.

Whitman's jeremiad, unlike, say, Godkin's, received little immediate attention, for when the complete text of Democratic Vistas appeared in an edition published by James Redpath, it was met with what Gay Wilson Allen has called "a conspiracy of silence.";6 There is evidence, however, that this changed with the inclusion of the work in Specimen Days and Collect, published in 1882. The distinguished Unitarian minister O. B. Frothingham, for instance, in an essay entitled "Democracy and Moral Progress," published in the North American Review in July 1883, quotes extensively from Whitman's condemnatory passages at the outset of his essay as a means of setting the tone for his own critical evaluation. Calling Whitman "perhaps the most ardent democrat living," Frothingham correctly remarks that "he is severe because he hopes so much, and sees so much at stake in the experiment of liberty.";7

A writer who anticipated both Godkin and Whitman in this argument is the little-known Eugene Benson (1839-1908). A painter as well as an active magazinist, Benson saw himself as a "literary frondeur," a writer always poised to attack the "honored Mumbo-Jumbos" of society. His essay "To-Day," published in the _Galaxy_ for November 1867, takes issue with virtually every aspect of the emerging "secular creed" of the postwar years, particularly the identification of material with moral progress. Benson insists that while the material progress may have "added to our comforts," it has brought with it a pervasive corruption and "moral inertia." As would Whitman three years later, Benson argues that a nation is to be evaluated not by its material achievements, but by its moral and spiritual health, and from this perspective he lamented the decline:

> We exist, and multiply mechanical forces, and
> increase in wealth, and the only correction of
> the grossness of our prosperity is now and
> then the disturbance of an ethical question
> involved in political action; but what have we
> to show as an illustration of that ultimate
> life for which the noblest of the race have
> agonized and struggled? . . . The more tools,
> the greater our work and wealth; but we have
> become dead to noble sensations.;8

Denouncing the domination of business, he sadly concluded that "manufactures and trade" are the real gods of the people.

"To-Day" is one in a series of six essays Benson published in the _Galaxy_ that treat many of the same themes as _Democratic Vistas_. The first five appeared before Whitman's "Democracy": "About the Literary Spirit," August 15, 1866; "Literary Frondeurs," October 1, 1866; "Literature and the People," April 15, 1867; "Solitude and Democracy," June 1867; and "To-Day." The final essay in the series, "Democratic Deities," appeared in November 1868. Although Benson, who became a permanent expatriate in Italy in 1873, did not identify these essays as a group, they develop a consistent theme and so may profitably be considered together. In view of the importance of the _Galaxy_ to Whitman at this time as a lucrative outlet for both prose and verse and as the publisher of John Burroughs' important "Walt Whitman and His _Drum-Taps_," which appeared on December 1, 1866, it is likely that Whitman read the magazine regularly and was familiar with

Benson's work. Since both Benson's approach and many of
his conclusions anticipate Whitman throughout, it is
likely that a reading of Benson contributed to the
formative thinking which preceded the actual writing of
Democratic Vistas.
     Although personally committed as an artist to
painting, Benson, like Whitman, looked to literature as
the primary vehicle through which the modern spirit
would express itself. The first three essays in this
series consider the broad question of the function of
literature in a democratic society. With the failure of
the established social institutions, Benson looked to
the writer to create an image of a world beyond the
materialism which was so abhorrent to him and to
stimulate critical thinking about social values.
Measuring contemporary writing against his lofty
expectations, he describes it, as would Whitman, with an
abusive scorn. He blames the "thin and lifeless"
qualities of American writing on the failure of the
writers to establish a vital connection with the actual
life of the people. Paradoxically, he argues, the
American "reverence for majorities" has been
inappropriately transferred from politics to literature
and is responsible for a "dreadful monotony and . . .
low level of conformity.";9 Whitman also attacked the
levelling down in contemporary writing: "To-day, in
books, in the rivalry of writers, especially novelists,
success (so-call'd) is for him or her who strikes the
mean flat average, the sensational appetite for
stimulus, incident, persiflage, &c., and depicts to the
common calibre, sensual exterior life" (p. 408). Both
writers insisted that very little of the great streams
of material pouring forth from the nation's printing
presses could actually be called literature.
     As the deprecatory reference to novelists in the
passage quoted above suggests, Whitman did not envision
an important role for prose fiction. He speaks instead
of the need of "powerful native philosophs and orators
and bards, these States, as rallying points to come, in
times of danger, and to fend off ruin and defection"
(p. 422). Novelists are left out of the picture.
Benson, on the other hand, understood the potential of
prose fiction. In "Literature and the People" he
presciently recognizes that the novel would serve as
"the great modern medium of intercourse" between the
writer and the people. Writing shortly before the
appearance of John William DeForest's Miss Ravenel's
Conversion (1867), generally regarded as the first novel
in American realism, Benson lamented the "dearth of
novelists on this side of the Atlantic" and recognized
that the development of the novel in America lagged
behind its growth in Europe.;10

Benson was an appreciative reader of Whitman, and in some respects his broad literary philosophy may have been influenced by Whitman. Clearly, he shared Whitman's dedication to a democratic literature: "man in the free exercise of his faculties, free to choose his happiness, is the grand idea which must be set forth in literature for the people.";11 From this perspective, he praised Whitman himself as potentially the great liberating poet, although he observed that it is still too early to form a final estimate of a body of work "which may be more and it may be less than what contemporary advocates [John Burroughs] claim.";12 Appropriately, in an editorial dated January 3, 1868, the Nation identified Benson and Whitman as the two leading proponents of an independent national literature, a concept in which it did not see much merit.

As a "literary frondeur," Benson saw himself as a critic of the culture as a whole and as such was centrally concerned with the concept of culture. In "Personalism" Whitman observed sadly that "culture" was then the great modern word and that contemporary writers never seemed to tire of insisting that Americans acquire as much of it as possible: "To prune, gather, trim, conform, and ever cram and stuff, and be genteel and proper, is the pressure of our days" (p. 394). Whitman argues for a "radical change of category, in the distribution of precedence." Culture must be understood, he insists, not as something apart from the people, but as the reflection of their actual lives and values. Any "programme or theory" must be of "a scope generous enough to include the widest human area. It must have for its spinal meaning the formation of a typical personality of character, eligible to the uses of the high average of men -- and not restricted by conditions ineligible to the masses" (p. 396). Of all contemporary writers, Benson's position on this subject is closest to Whitman's. The focus of his treatment of the question was an attack on the literary establishment, "the proper gentlemen who sit in editorial chairs.";13 This group finds itself far more drawn to things British than to American life and so is guilty of attempting to impose foreign standards on its own land. They form "a separate and selfish class deriving their intellectual capital from an older society, and from a civilization different from the hybrid and half-developed but virile civilization of our own land.";14 Both Whitman and Benson, then, utterly detested the attempt of the leading editors and writers to force American art and life to fit the cultural models of Europe and spoke out vigorously against it.

Still, there is an unease and even indecision in Benson's treatment of American life. He seems to be characterizing his own position in speaking of the "sincere but cultivated man" who "finds it difficult which he must prefer -- the heartless culture of the critic who follows the lead of the foreign review, or the raw and local barbarisms of the untravelled American mind." Perhaps nothing better expresses both how close Benson as a writer came to the American civilization and yet how far he remained from it than his statement that the writer, "to serve the people," need not go "down to the level of their common life" but should instead appeal "to their consciousness of the highest life. As literary men we must share their ideas; as literary men we must correct and advance their ideal.";15 As reflected in his eventual expatriation, Benson experienced a sense of separation and distance not present in Whitman's more radical formulation of the problem, both as creative artist and theorist of culture.

Benson's fourth essay, "Solitude and Democracy," corresponds roughly to Whitman's "Personalism." Both essays formulate strategies for the maintenance and development of personal identity in the modern world. Like Whitman, Benson places the highest possible value on individualism. For Whitman, the "only large and satisfactory justification" for democracy is the "copious production" of "rich, luxuriant, varied personalism" (p. 392). Both writers recognize that solitude is absolutely essential. To use Benson's terms, it provides a "centre of resistance" to the familiarity and fusion of modern life:

> I know of no condition more foreign to the
> whole spirit of American life than that of
> solitude. And yet solitude, which begets
> contemplation, which begets revery, the two
> essential conditions of philosophy and poetry,
> is the source of all ideas that enoble man and
> address his highest nature.;16

Whitman too spoke of the recourse to solitude in rapturous, religious language: "Only in the perfect uncontamination and solitariness of individuality may the spirituality of religion positively come forth at all. . . . Only here . . . the meditation, the devout ecstasy, the soaring flight" (pp. 398-99). Solitude served Benson, much as Personalism served Whitman, as a vital concept, an essential mediating term, to set beside the levelling, destructive forces of the modern world.

Benson's last two essays in the series, "To-Day" and "Democratic Deities," are slashing attacks, in the spirit of the literary frondeur, on the pervasive corruption, the shameless worship of the material, and

the mindless conformity of the new age. Nowhere does he
approach the inspiring vision of the religious potential
of democracy that Whitman formulates, especially in his
essay "Democracy." Here Whitman approaches democracy
not only as a political system and an idea which
encourages full individual development, but also as a
source of value which brings to the individual a sense
of brotherhood, a vital human "Solidarity." In this, as
throughout the work, Whitman's genius is reflected in
the ability to bring seemingly opposite ideas,
individuality and human brotherhood, the self and the
group, into a vital, creative tension. Democracy, he
writes,

> seeks not only to individualize but to
> universalize. The great word Solidarity has
> arisen. Of all dangers to a nation . . .
> there can be no greater one than having
> certain portions of the people set off from
> the rest by a line drawn. . . . To work in
> . . . and justify God, his divine aggregate,
> the People . . . this, I say, is what
> democracy is for; and this is what our America
> means, and is doing. (P. 382)

As throughout <u>Democratic Vistas</u>, Whitman's vision here
is simply more profound than Benson's.

Still, in a time not especially notable for
self-criticism, both Whitman and Benson consciously
adopt the role of the social critic. Both insist that a
society is to be evaluated by the quality of its life,
not its material achievements, and both, to use
Whitman's terms, find the "spectacle . . . appalling."
Acutely aware of the threat to personal identity in this
world, both celebrate the essential value of solitude as
an antidote to the pressure of the mass. In the absence
of a shared religious faith and with the failure of
other secular guides and teachers, both place great,
perhaps unrealistically great, faith in the writer as a
source both of social criticism and the creation of
larger cultural values. Dealing scornfully with
contemporary writing, both denounce the reliance of the
literary establishment on foreign, particularly British,
literary values. Both redefine accepted notions of
culture, seeing it as, in its deepest sense, the
reflection of the entire life of the people.

<u>Democratic Vistas</u> is ostensibly based on a sure,
three-stage concept of the unfolding of America. The
first two stages, the political and material, have
established the basis for the third, a "sublime and
serious Religious Democracy sternly taking command,
dissolving the old, sloughing off surfaces, and from its
own interior and vital principles, reconstructing and

democratizing society" (p. 410). The prophetic
literature for which Whitman called would serve as the
"support and expression" of this new democracy. Benson,
of course, had no such vision; indeed, far more than
Whitman, he senses the dangers of materialism and the
new mass economy. He puts greater stress than does
Whitman on the writer's role as social critic. Benson's
discussion of the growing importance of a realistic
prose fiction for the new age may suggest a keener
insight into the contemporary literary situation.
Today's reader, however, need not attempt to reconcile
such differences and decide between them. Adopting
something of Whitman's dialectical method, he can see
them as two writers who, in thinking seriously about the
same problem, reached many of the same conclusions, but
whose differences -- the one implicitly pessimistic,
rejecting the emerging material culture, the other
professedly optimistic, accepting the material as the
basis of a higher growth -- may provide the terms for a
productive and continuing inquiry into the meaning of
the American experience.

NOTES

1. Cleanth Brooks, R.W.B. Lewis, and Robert Penn
Warren, <u>American Literature: The Makers and the Making</u>
(New York: St. Martin's Press, 1973), p. 944.
2. Walt Whitman, <u>Prose Works, 1892</u> (New York: New
York University Press, 1964), vol. 2, p. 369. All
quotations from <u>Democratic Vistas</u> are from this edition
and are given in the text.
3. For a complete discussion of these events, see
Edward Grier, "Walt Whitman, <u>The Galaxy</u>, and <u>Democratic
Vistas</u>," <u>American Literature</u>, 23 (Nov. 1951): 332-50.
4. <u>The Correspondence</u>, ed. Edwin Haviland Miller
(New York: New York University Press), vol. 2, p. 338.
5. E. L. Godkin, "Commercial Immorality and
Political Corruption," <u>North American Review</u>, 107 (July
1868).
6. Gay Wilson Allen, <u>The Solitary Singer</u> (New
York: New York University Press, 1967), p. 427.
7. O. B. Frothingham, "Democracy and Moral
Progress," <u>North American Review</u>, 137 (July 1883): 28.
8. Eugene Benson, "To-Day," <u>The Galaxy</u>, 4 (Nov.
1867): 816-817.
9. Eugene Benson, "About the Literary Spirit," <u>The
Galaxy</u>, 1 (July 15, 1866): 492.
10. Eugene Benson, "Literature and the People," <u>The
Galaxy</u>, 3 (April 1867): 874.
11. Ibid., 876.
12. Ibid.
13. Benson, "About the Literary Spirit," p. 487.
14. Benson, "Literature and the People," p. 871.

15.   Ibid., pp. 871, 874.
16.   Eugene Benson, "Solitude and Democracy, The
Galaxy, 4 (June 1867): 166.

17.

Whitman's *Drum-Taps* Reviewed: The Good, Gray, Tender Mother-Man and the Fierce, Red, Convulsive Rhythm of War

WILLIAM BURRISON

Whitman, above all others, emancipated American verse. As far back as 1927, however, Amy Lowell contended otherwise. In an essay entitled "Walt Whitman and the New Poetry," Lowell pointed to the French Symbolists as instrumental to her own Imagist deviations. But too many "free" modern American poets -- from Stephen Crane and Hart Crane to Ezra Pound, Stephen Vincent Benet, Robinson Jeffers, Carl Sandburg, William Carlos Williams, Charles Olson, Gary Snyder, Imamu Baraka, and Allen Ginsberg -- have attested (by confession or craft) to Whitman's influence for us not now to grant it.

He sang of the open road of experience, of sex and the body, of the pulse and heartbeat of an "athletic" democracy, of a great leader's death and the mystery of sea and stars and of a single spear of grass as powerfully and originally as few poets ever have. For this we love him. We also love him because, in his rich, large humanity, as he fostered that intimate personal engagement between the almost ever present "I" and "you" of his poems, Walt Whitman contradicted himself -- with all his multitudes, his questions and exclamations, his widening latitudes and lengthening longitudes -- yet without seeming the hypocrite. He was too frank, too gross with appetite for life, too apparently lacking in guile or venality, and too long-lived and prematurely "wooly white" to be dismissed as a hypocrite. And like the preacher from the Bible one can extract from Whitman citations in support of almost any viewpoint under the "splendid silent" sun.

Militant and pacifist, nationalist and internationalist,
laborer and loafer, mystic and materialist, idealist and
pragmatist, bookworm and anti-intellectual,
individualist and communitarian, scientist and romantic,
master-builder and conservationist, selfish
existentialist and do-good Christian, seafarer and
landlubber, country bumpkin and city slicker,
Southerner, Westerner, and Yankee alike can soothe or
arouse their souls at Whitman's abundant fountain. Yet,
for all this, above the fray rises the voice of the
poet, in "Myself and Mine":

> I charge you forever reject those who would
>   expound me, for I cannot expound myself,
> I charge that there be no theory or school
>   founded out of me,
> I charge you to leave all free, as I have left
>   all free.

While respecting the spirit of our bard's behest,
however, we need not go so far as to assume that there
was no consistent core to Whitman's personality or
meaning in his free-spirited work worth expounding;
otherwise, biographers and critics might as well pack up
their work-kits. Whitman was, after all, knit into the
fabric of the times in which he lived (if fancying
himself a weaver of that fabric), and, like any
thinking, sensitive man (if not more so because of his
experience as a journalist and civil servant), he had
strong opinions or sentiments on important issues of the
day. Whitman's artistic relationship to and
psychological involvement with the Civil War is of
special interest to me in this regard. Although he did
not deem himself among the "fanatics" and in fact was to
have a violent falling out with William O'Connor over
the issue of black enfranchisement after the war, there
has been little mystery or debate as to Whitman's
abolitionist sentiment and loyalty to the Union cause.
But we have somehow tended to underestimate a fierce,
hot-blooded, warlike side of his nature. The lingering
elegaic spell of some of his most popular poetry ("O
Captain My Captain" was his standard on the lecture
circuit), his pantheism and devotion to "adhesive"
camaraderie, and his wartime career as a volunteer nurse
all undoubtedly have had much to do with an almost
feminine, all but vegetarian view of Whitman -- an
inveterate lover of meat (and admirer of flesh), after
all.
But this view of Whitman the "good gray poet," the
gentle giant, the veritable jolly Santa Claus of
American letters -- almost a part of our heritage -- is
also due to the image-making of such contemporary
friends as O'Connor, John Burroughs, and Horace Traubel;

the latter two much younger men for whom Walt was a kind
of benevolent uncle figure. Although D. H. Lawrence,
for one, knew better than to fully accept such imagery,
celebrating Whitman's darker side as a "very great post
mortem poet" after debunking his democratic optimism,;1
so recent and respected a native critic as R.W.B. Lewis,
even while conceding his subject's conscious flirtation
with "wickedness," has given the old sentimental line a
new twist by casting Whitman as an innocent "Adamic
archetype.";2 Burroughs, still defending his long-
departed friend as of 1904 against the charge that he
could and should have served in the Union army, went so
far as to insist: "Whitman was the lover, the healer,
the reconciler. . . . He was not an athlete, or a rough,
but a great tender mother-man, to whom the martial
spirit was utterly foreign.";3

     Walt Whitman was, for certain, a great tender
mother-man. Reading of his efforts to comfort the sick
and wounded (at the possible expense of his own health),
it is hard not to share Gay Wilson Allen's view that it
"would be difficult to imagine a more compassionate
man.";4 And Whitman did choose, for reasons he himself
may not have been fully able to expound, not to fight in
the war. But this is far from the image he cultivated
for himself in his poetry, and, in any case, the martial
spirit was not at all foreign to him. Before discussing
that spirit's place in Drum-Taps we should note that it
resounds in much of his other work.

> My call is the call of battle, I nourish
>   active rebellion,
> He going with me must go well arm'd,

he warns in "Song of the Open Road." In "Song of Joys"
he exclaims:

> O to resume the joys of the soldier! . . .
> To go to battle -- to hear the bugles play and
>   the drums beat!
> To hear the crash of artillery -- to see the
>   glittering of the bayonets and
>   musket-barrels in the sun!
> To see men fall and die and not complain!
> To taste the savage taste of blood -- to be so
>   devilish!
> To gloat so over the wounds and deaths of the
>   enemy.

In "Song of Myself" Whitman delights in telling us the
proud family "yarn" of an "old-time sea-fight" as "my
grandmother's father the sailor told it to me." In
"Starting from Paumanok" Whitman projects himself (among
other past persona) as "a soldier camp'd or carrying my

knapsack and gun." In "Song of the Broad-Axe" Whitman
celebrates, if not without some ambiguity, the
subjugation of the land to "fierce men and women" who
"pour forth as the sea to the whistle of death pours its
sweeping and unript waves," and thus celebrates the
emerging "shapes of turbulent manly cities."
Furthermore, "to take good aim with a gun" is one of the
"gymnastic" virtues Whitman proclaims in "Myself and
Mine," adding, "Let others praise eminent men and hold
up peace, I hold up agitation and conflict." In two
brief consecutive poems appearing early in the
definitive 1891-92 Leaves of Grass, "What Place Is
Besieged?" and "Still Though the One I Sing," Whitman
confers upon his two symbolic subjects an impressive
defensive arsenal on the one hand and the "quenchless,
indispensable fire" of "insurrection" on the other.
"The Dying Veteran" recalls the death-bed nostalgia,
"likely to offend you" amid "these days of order" and
"ease," of a veteran of the Revolution for his "old wild
battle-life again!" And when in "As I Ponder'd in
Silence" (chosen by Whitman as the second poem
introducing his definitive Leaves) a phantom confronts
the poet with the proposition that "there is but one
theme for ever-enduring bards" -- the "theme of War, the
fortune of battle, and the making of perfect soldiers"
-- the poet, while allowing himself some metaphorical
license (his "field" of battle being the "world," / For
life and death, for the Body and the eternal Soul"),
does not hesitate to concur, concluding that

> chanting the chant of battles,
> I above all promote brave soldiers.

In Drum-Taps such images and impulses found their
consummation. A comprehensive analysis of the form,
rhythm, style, themes, imagery, symbols, and overall
narrative method or structure of Drum-Taps (as revised
by 1881) is not feasible here. But we can concentrate
on some important aspects of this work. First, it
should be noted that, as of the first publication in
1865, Whitman viewed his purpose "to express . . . the
pending action of this Time and Land we swim in, with
all their large conflicting fluctuations of despair and
hope." This sense of himself as the "singer of joy and
sorrow," as a kind of bipolar mimetic medium, was
elaborated late in Drum-Taps itself:

> Spirit of hours I knew, all hectic red one
>   day, but pale as death next day,
> Touch my mouth ere you depart, press my lips
>   close,
> Leave me your pulses of rage -- bequeath them
>   to me -- fill me with currents
>   convulsive,

> Let them scorch and blister out of my chants
>   when you are gone,
> Let them identify you to the future in these
>   songs.

Whitman regarded the 1865 edition as free from the "perturbations" and "verbal superfluity" of his earlier Leaves of Grass, more "under control" and "superior" as a "piece of art.";5 Nonetheless, contrasts from poem to poem were too jarring; too many poems (even one fine in and of itself, such as "When I Heard the Learn'd Astronomer") had little or nothing to do with the war, and a continuous, coherent narrative perspective giving one the sense, at least, of a meaningful passage through crisis was sorely lacking. But by 1881, Whitman was able to rectify the worst of this. From the first edition he deleted 22 poems, most of which were either autobiographical and introspective, prior to the war, or symbolic (i.e., "The Torch," "The Ship," "Mother and Babe," "Old Ireland"), with oblique, if any, relevance to the war -- simply reworking these poems into other more appropriate groupings or books of Leaves. He retained 31 poems (making small revisions on a few) and added 12, 9 of which had already been included (along with the 2 Lincoln elegies) in the "Sequel" bound to the original 1865 Drum-Taps text -- now dispensing with the sequel form altogether. Allowing for these changes, Whitman still significantly rearranged the final order (although the last 10 poems included 6 from the sequel and 2 of the 3 full additions). That rearrangement provided much greater continuity and concentration of mood, theme, and narrative perspective, greater dramatic clarity, and more subtle shifts of emotion.
   One revealing, if small, revision made by Whitman concerned the brief "Not Youth Pertains to Me." It concluded the original text, ending:

> I have nourish'd the wounded and sooth'd many
>   a dying soldier;
> And at intervals I have strung together a few
>   songs
> Fit for war, and the life of the camp.

In the final text, however, this poem was followed by 14 others, its last two lines becoming

> And at intervals waiting or in the midst of
>   camp,
> Composed these songs.

Clearly, the later Whitman did not feel the need to end Drum-Taps on a backward-looking, almost apologetic note of self-justification or explanation. The first edition

has, indeed, the almost impromptu, haphazard order of a
few (if too many) songs strung together. Whitman
confided to Traubel that the text, emerging out of
sundry pocket notebooks bound together, was "all put
together by fits and starts, on the field, in the
hospitals, as I worked with the soldier boys.";6 But,
given time, a mostly negative or indifferent critical
reception to his initial effort, and less distracted
objectivity, Whitman was able to impose a more sensible
order on his material and could be content to let the
quality of his revision speak for itself.

The final Drum-Taps (unlike the first) has three
major movements. The first movement is, in effect, a
celebration -- at times not unlike a lover's serenade --
of the Union mobilization and an elaborate invocation of
the spirits of war. Although sounding the war-drums
"lightly" at first, it reaches a quick enough crescendo
with the third of its seven poems, "Beat! Beat!
Drums!" Not only is the outbreak year of 1861 welcomed
and personified as violent (". . . a rifle on your
shoulder . . . a knife in the belt at your side . . ."),
masculine, determined, and Yankee ("in blue clothes") --
it is the height of "robust" health: "a strong man erect
. . . with well-gristled body and sunburnt face and
hands . . . sonorous voice . . . springy gait" and
"sinewy limbs." The instruments of war, before seen by
the poet only as playthings in pageantry, are now to be
"unlimber'd" in healthy, if deadly serious, exercise:
"Put in something now, besides powder and wadding."
Images pour and burst so that one, even if not
psychoanalytically inclined, can sense a great sexual
power being sublimated. But there is something almost
demonic about the role the poet assumes for himself; he
is courting powerful spirits, engaging in a modern rite
of Mars. "I'll pour the verse with streams of blood,
full of volition, full of joy," he resolves in the
curious allegorical dialogue "Song of the Banner at
Daybreak," having been "taught" his true "theme . . . at
last" by a child's infatuation with the Union flag
flapping freely in the wind. "Thunder on! . . .
Democracy! strike with vengeful stroke," he exhorts in
"Rise O Days from Your Fathomless Deeps" and, ending
this movement, he urges Manhattan, his "City of Ships,"
to "be indeed yourself, warlike!" Then, to

> Behold me -- incarnate me as I have incarnated
>   you! . . .
> In peace I changed peace, but now the drum of
>   war is mine,
> War, red war is my song . . .

Lines quicken and expand with enthusiasm in this
movement, pleasing emotions or thoughts are amplified

and explode with exclamation points, rhythms vary
greatly, with crisp consonants and vowels that are not
too soft (creating an alert, electric atmosphere). It
is a dazzling scene: the "silent" cannons are "bright as
gold," the point of the bayonet "flashing." Even that
which does not dazzle by nature is lit up by the poet's
elated state of mind. Of his soldiers in "First O Songs
for a Prelude":

> How good they look as they tramp down to the
>   river, sweaty, with their guns on their
>   shoulders!
> How I love them! How I could hug them, with
>   their brown faces and their clothes and
>   knapsacks cover'd with dust!

But now Whitman has struck up his bargain, has
appropriated the drum of war for himself. No naive or
angry young man, however, even in this first movement he
has admitted (if only in passing) that war is a "red
business," that the hollow drums can be "terrible," that
the flag can "undulate like a snake hissing" or give off
an "ironical call," and that the beautiful ships at
harbor are ominous and black. Now a deft transition
occurs. Whitman gives us six poems that detach us,
through time and space, from the overwhelming sweep and
urgency of the mobilization movement. "The
Centenarian's Story" is told through the perspective of
a "volunteer" -- also self-deemed "connecter" of the
past and present and "chansonnier of a great future" --
who accompanies an aged veteran at a commemorative
ceremony in Washington Park, Brooklyn. Although
invoking the patriotic precedent of the Revolution and
the inspirational leadership of Washington, this
minisaga takes us through the veteran's memory back to
Washington's first battle, a "slaughter" ending with the
night-time retreat of "my General." The tone and rhythm
of that trip, then, are sombre and weary; pale as death
rather than hectic red. "Nobody clapp'd hands here
then," the veteran recalls.
    Tale told, the volunteer having returned,
contemplatively, to the same "hills and slopes" of the
present, now four imagistic vignettes actually take us
far out into the war wilderness, the age of the poet (no
longer medium or invoker, but distant observer) all but
lost. "Cavalry Crossing a Ford" and "Bivouac on a
Mountain Side," while close to the slow, deliberate
rhythm of "The Centenarian's Story," retain some of the
romance and heroic dazzle of the initial war venture
expressed in the first movement. The cavalry's arms
"flash in the sun," there is a "musical clank," a
"silvery river." The "brown-faced" men are each a
"picture" (of health, presumably) -- the "guidon flags

flutter gayly in the wind." On the mountainside the "shadowy forms of men and horses" loom "large-sized, flickering" -- with, "over all . . . studded, breaking out, the eternal stars." There is a strange, dreamlike quality to these two poems. The insouciance of the first cannot quite be trusted because so dreamlike, entrapped in a rhythm more tired, or ominous, than gay. The grandeur of the second, while embracing the resting soldiers, also dwarfs them -- the stars "far, far out of reach" -- reminding us of the now puny mortality of those shadowy, flickering forms.

"An Army Corps on the March" brings us down to harsh reality. The soldiers "advance," but barely, to the cut of a retreating, receding syntax. Whitman makes us feel their laborious, oppressive progress. Whatever romance may once have lingered now is surely worn away -- with the "cloud of skirmishers," the shot "snapping like a whip" followed by an "irregular volley," the "swarming ranks" and "dense brigades" that "press on and on,/ Glittering dimly, toiling under the sun . . . dust-cover'd" as wheels "rumble" and horses "sweat." What was once happiness and righteous adhesiveness in numbers has now become abject misery.

"By the Bivouac's Fitful Flame," with its sleepy or sinister "s" and lulling "l" sounds, culminates the transition in terms of mood and tone. Whitman makes his melancholy campfire image capture both the desolate forlornness of homesickness young soldiers can feel and the terrible fickleness of chance, the danger of death in battle. "Come Up from the Fields Father" initially materializes, as if by magic, the bucolic kind of home scene vaguely evoked in the mind of the poet sitting at night by the campfire. Then, with cruel irony, it plunges us down into the land of sorrows, introducing us to the tragic reality of personal loss through the grief of a mother over her slain son. The mother (wife of a prosperous Ohio farmer) intuits that the boy is already dead despite an official Army letter assuring her that he "will soon be better." She awakens late in the night "longing with one deep longing" to "withdraw unnoticed" and be with him. This introduction to sorrow is no accident. For as Whitman saw it the story of the "real" war would "never get into the books" because it featured the unspectacular, prolonged suffering of the wounded and sick in the hospitals and of the families of the combatants,;7 families often (as Whitman's was concerning his captured brother George) so uncertain as to the condition of their loved ones.

But it is in the seven poems that follow -- what one can consider the second movement -- that the full horror of the war hits home. Whereas before Whitman's narrative persona was an empathetic civilian or a rather detached observer, now he becomes a participant and eyewitness, a weary marcher in the ranks, paternal grave-digger, and "old" wound-dresser. Indeed, we can sense him aging. Whereas early in Drum-Taps we were bombarded by exclamations, now we find questions: "Who are you sweet boy with cheeks yet blooming?"; "Must I learn to chant the cold dirges of the baffled? / And sullen hymns of defeat?"; "(was one side so brave? the other was equally brave;)." Whereas in the first movement images, sounds, or simple denotative units featured joy, excitement, relief, eagerness, heat, energy, electricity, appetite, attraction, health, the light of day, and life itself, now we turn fully round the axis from the pole of joy to sorrow -- engulfed in a region of sickness, pain, dread, repugnance, prolonged tension and uncertainty, weariness, listlessness, numbness, coldness, night, and death. Instead of the gold and silver of a glorious war, in this region, upon entering an "impromptu" hospital, we encounter the insidious "glisten of the little steel instruments catching the glint of the torches." This region is saved from total desolation only by the narrator's resolve to yet "compose a march for these states," and by his tenderness.

Then, with "Long, Too Long America" and "Give Me the Splendid Silent Sun" (expressing a sort of stock-taking and second wind), Drum-Taps enters its final movement: in part, a synthesis intermingling many of the contrasting elements of the two preceding movements. Here, we are, at times, projected prophetically or literally into the future. Faith is declared in America's capacity to recover and learn from the War and in the existence of "kindred souls" that cannot be annihilated by bullets, and notes of reconciliation are sounded. The poet, in fact, ends Drum-Taps pointing to the "hot sun of the South" as the one thing, above all, "to fully ripen my songs."

But, beyond the accomplishment of "The Artilleryman's Vision," the thing most striking about this movement is Whitman's deliberate juxtaposition of peaceful and pugnacious sentiments. "Beautiful that was and all its deeds of carnage must in time be utterly lost," he muses in "Reconciliation." But, shortly thereafter, addressing what would seem to be his sleepy fancy or soul, he confesses:

> I know I am restless and make others so,
> I know my words are weapons full of danger,
> > full of death,
> For I confront peace, security, and all the
> > settled laws, to unsettle them, . . .
> I have urged you onward with me, and still
> > urge you, without the least idea of what
> > is our destination,

> Or whether we shall be victorious or utterly
>   quell'd and defeated.

Shortly thereafter he challenges his "certain civilian"
(some genteel monster of a critic, certainly):

> Did you ask dulcet rhymes from me?
> Did you seek the civilian's peaceful and
>   languishing rhymes? . . .
> (I have been born of the same as the war was
>   born,
> The drum-corps' rattle is ever to me sweet
>   music, I love well the martial
>   dirge. . .)

Then briefly, conciliatory again, to the "Victress on
the peak":

> No poem proud, I changing bring to thee, nor
>   mastery's rapturous verse,
> But a cluster containing night's darkness and
>   blood-dripping wounds,
> And psalms of the dead.

Finally, after "Spirit Whose Work Is Done," the old hot
blood rises up again, if on a tender note, as he bids
"Adieu to a Soldier":

> Your mission is fulfill'd -- but I, more
>   warlike,
> Myself and this contentious soul of mine,
> Still on our campaigning bound. . . .
> Here marching, ever marching on, a war fight
>   out -- aye here,

To fiercer, weightier battles give expression.
Whitman looked forward, then, to the full ripening of
his song -- but not to a peaceful life. How much of the
volume of these battle-cries was poetic posturing or
overly zealous mediumship, and how much the true
expression of temperament or inner conflict, we cannot
resolve here. Certainly, however, the war did not
create Whitman's style. But, with its convulsive
rhythms and harsh discordances, its shrieks and sighs
and stops and starts, long marches and thinning ranks,
it did reaffirm and refine it. Certainly, the war's
reality lives more vividly through that style than
through the strained meters and rhymes of Melville or
the conventional artifice of other less interesting
poets. Hence Whitman has given us an invaluable
artifact -- not so much about the war (for topical
references to battles and generals, which abound in
Melville's Battle-Pieces, are rare) as of it, out of it.

As for Whitman himself, his "real" attitude toward the war was somewhat ambivalent, like his convulsive book. A lifelong lover of Homer, of the Greek tragedies, and of Shakespeare's histories, Whitman was artistically ripe for the war, challenged and invigorated by it to the point not only of taking great initiative to publish Drum-Taps (under the mistaken hope of pecuniary success) but also of thinking in terms of a prose book, first proposed to a publisher in 1863 and published as Memoranda during the War little more than a decade later. From an intellectual standpoint, Whitman regarded the Civil War as the "boil," not "root," of the problem.;8 Inevitable and unavoidable, he argued, it was both a necessary catharsis and a long overdue test, a crucible, of the national character. Unable to violate the spirit of the "idea of all" that he so fervently sang, however, and genuinely fond of the South and its people (especially the "poor white, so-called," whom he considered much neglected and maligned),;9 Whitman blamed the institution of slavery and the "Secesh Government," whose "tyranny" he became convinced of as he watched the arrival of boatloads of Confederate "escapees" and became acquainted with the prison system that held his brother captive.;10 Not only that, Whitman was disturbed by official Northern actions, bewailing, for instance, the execution of an 18-year-old deserter: "O the horrid contrast and the sarcasm of this life -- to know who they really are that sit on judges benches, & who they perched on the criminal's box.";11

It did not take Whitman long to know firsthand what war in general really was.

> The wounded -- the surgeons and ambulances --
> O the hideous hell, the damned hell of war
> Were the preachers preaching of hell?
> O there is no hell more damned than this hell
>   of war,

he wrote in an 1862 draft of what was later to become "The Artilleryman's Vision" and, to a lesser extent, "A March in the Ranks Hard-Prest, and the Road Unknown.";12 Artist that he was and made himself better become, however, Whitman was able to depict this hell in varicolored shades through Drum-Taps, without preaching about it. Then, in a letter of September 8, 1863, reiterating that sense of convulsiveness that he was so conscious of:

> Mother, one's heart grows sick of war, after
> all, when you see what it really is; every
> once in a while I feel so horrified and
> disgusted it seems to me like a great

    slaughterhouse and the men mutually butchering
    each other -- then I feel how impossible it
    appears, again, to retire from this contest,
    until we have carried our points (it is cruel
    to be so tossed from pillar to post in one's
    judgment).;13

Finally, much later in life, when delivering his
standard lecture, "Death of Abraham Lincoln," he would
refer, in a sentence without need of a predicate, to
"Four years of lurid, bleeding, murky, murderous
war.";14
    I mention all this lest you should think that I
have been trying to vilify the good gray poet or, at
least, detenderize him. I hope you will agree with me
now, though, that, in fancy and song at least, the
mother-man and the warrior were one, and that struggle
may well have constituted as critical an aspect of
Whitman's pantheon as sex, love, or "adhesiveness."
After all, a man -- a self-professed Darwinian who could
so flout convention, dare ridicule, and blaze
pioneering trails for those free poets of the future
that he himself challenged in "Poets to Come," must
indeed have had great fight in him -- and the spirit of
the soldier.

Notes

1. D. H. Lawrence, Studies in Classic American
Literature, 14th ed. (New York: Viking Press, 1975),
pp. 163-77.
    2. R.W.B. Lewis, The American Adam (Chicago:
University of Chicago Press, 1955), pp. 41-53.
    3. F. DeWolfe Miller, ed., Walt Whitman's
Drum-Taps (1865) and Sequel to Drum-Taps (1865-6), a
Facsimile Reproduction (Gainesville, Fla.: Scholars'
Facsimiles and Reprints, 1959), p. xiv.
    4. Gay Wilson Allen, The Solitary Singer (New
York: Grove Press, 1960), p. 280.
    5. Miller, p. xxix, from a January 6, 1865 letter
to O'Connor.
    6. Ibid., p. xxiii; citing with Walt Whitman in
Camden (New York: D. Appleton and Co., 1908), vol. 2,
p. 137.
    7. Walt Whitman, Specimen Days (Boston: David R.
Godine, 1971), pp. 58-60.
    8. Walt Whitman's Civil War, Compiled and Edited
from Published and Unpublished Sources, ed. Walter
Lowenfels (New York: Knopf, 1960), p. 234.
    9. Ibid., p. 235.
    10. Walt Whitman's Memoranda during the War (&)
Death of Abraham Lincoln (reproduced in facsimile),
ed. Roy P. Basler (Bloomington: Indiana University
Press, 1962), pp. 40-41, 50.

11.   Walt Whitman and the Civil War, a Collection of
Original Articles and Manuscripts, ed. Charles I.
Glicksberg (Philadelphia: University of Pennsylvania
Press, 1933), p. 127.   This case concerned William
Glover and was well publicized.   Other than for his
desertion because of exhaustion and homesickness for his
mother, Glover was alleged to have served bravely in
previous battles.
12.   "A Battle (Scenes, Sounds &c.)," in ibid., p.
123.
13.   Walt Whitman, The Wound Dresser, ed. Richard
M. Bucke (New York: Bodley Press, 1949), p. 112.
14.   Walt Whitman's Memoranda, p. 5 (of Lincoln
lecture sequel transcribed from Whitman's reading copy).

Part V

Whitman and the World of Literature

18.
Whitman's Re-Vision of Emersonian Ecstasy in "Song of Myself"

JOHN GATTA, JR.

In retrospect, one is struck by a delicious irony -- maybe intentional -- in Emerson's mention of a "long foreground" to Whitman's genius in the famous letter of 1855. For today it is hard to doubt what some reviewers guessed from the first: that Emerson was himself a central figure in that obscure gestation, perhaps even the final catalyst who brought Whitman to creative self-awareness. Despite the confused disclaimers with which the younger writer tried to cover his debt later on, he had evidently read, marked, and inwardly digested his transcendental precursor well before the annus mirabilis of 1855.;1 He had surely heard Emerson lecture in New York. It was scarcely from feigned deference, then, that Whitman addressed his fathering shadow as "Master" in 1856. Behind the miracle, if miracle it was, that turned an insipid versifier into the potent author of Leaves of Grass stood America's most eloquent spokesman for spiritual self-reliance. As Whitman almost confessed to John Trowbridge, he might have sat simmering into oblivion had not Emerson brought him "to a boil" at that crucial time.;2

But what precisely did Whitman get from Emerson? Scholarship has already pointed out a good deal. Whitman must have seized eagerly upon Emerson's conception of the poet as set forth in the essay by that name. He also seems to have responded to Emerson's theory of language and to the chief transcendental doctrines of Nature, Self-Reliance, and the Over-Soul -- however modified by private temper and the countervailing force of his New York rowdyism. Meanwhile, Whitman's personal relation to Emerson, troubled at times by displays of Harold Bloom's defensive "anxiety of influence," has been traced into periods long after the first edition of Leaves of Grass.

Yet beyond the undoubted influence of Emerson's person, his memorable words, and his philosophic theory, another facet of his impact on Whitman remains to be explored. I refer to those rare but all-important revelations of the holy sublime, those palpable "announcements of the soul," described in Emersonian essays like "The Over-Soul," "The Transcendentalist," and "Experience.";3 All such descriptions in the early essayist lead inevitably to his focal dramatization of a privileged moment of influx in chapter 1 of his first book, Nature. And can one doubt, given Whitman's disposition, that this first-person testimony of ecstatic self-discovery would have struck even deeper chords in the incipient writer than any abstract exposition of transcendental theory?

To narrow my argument for the present case to a fine point, I believe that Emerson's account of enthusiastic transport as a "transparent eyeball" in chapter 1 of Nature has been dramatically reimagined in Whitman's equally famous record of sublime self-realization in section 5 of "Song of Myself." Whitman's re-vision of the transcendental moment indicates how much Emerson had helped him recognize what an "original relation to the universe" must look and feel like, experientially. A passage like the one in Nature might indeed turn Whitman's "world to glass," was a gift of transparency wherein Whitman saw what it would mean to behold his "aboriginal Self" in its occult unity with the world.;4 But if Whitman shaped his section 5 chant in mainly sympathetic accord with Emerson's visionary precedent, he also left signs here of dialectical resistance. So far Bloom's general theories will hold: Whitman's unusually forceful revisionary response, which Bloom associates with a distinctively American brand of poetic repression, shows more inclination to "complete" and even to absorb the parent-precursor than it does to "swerve" away in the manner of most British responses.;5

That Whitman had read Emerson's Nature before 1855 seems more than likely, based on a wealth of internal evidence beyond the passages at issue here;6 and on the work's fame by the time it appeared in the 1849 Nature; Addresses, and Lectures. No doubt Whitman would have encountered Nature in this collected format rather than in the separate issue of 1836. External evidence that he saw the 1849 volume is at least tentatively available in disclosures he passed on to John Burroughs for the 1867 Notes on Walt Whitman as Poet and Person. Burroughs records first that Whitman had never read Emerson prior to the first Leaves of Grass. So far, from other evidence, we know the statement to be an outright lie. Yet the rest of Burroughs' story, which has Whitman carrying a volume of Emerson to the beach in a dinner basket the summer just after publishing <u>Leaves of Grass</u>, may present a glimmer of truth. For certain of Burroughs' details do repeat themselves curiously in Trowbridge's later and more reliable narration of how and when Whitman encountered the essays. According to Trowbridge, Whitman was indeed reading Emerson before 1855 -- and while at work building houses rather than while lounging at the beach. Still, Trowbridge's version agrees that at some point Whitman found himself carrying a single volume of Emerson in his dinner pail. If the odd congruence points to a residue of honesty in the Burroughs-Whitman fable, that fable just might be fact when it goes on to mention, with almost gratuitous specificity, that the name of the Emerson volume Whitman first carried was "'Nature,' &c." -- that is, <u>Nature; Addresses, and Lectures</u>.;7

More assuredly, readers, have long found the transparent eyeball sequence in chapter 1 of <u>Nature</u> occupying a crucial position in that work. Here is the compelling experience, the action, the proof, to support the essay's parallel line of discursive argument. Here Emerson gives direct, intuitive validation for his philosophic case that the ME and NOT ME may join in rapturous relation, that the transcendental Self enjoys immediate access to infinitude. In religious terms, the free influx of life so evidenced might be called a mystical experience; in more naturalistic terms, described simply as a "sudden and irreducible sense of being alive.";8 To cite Emerson's familiar words is in any case to see one man's original relation to the universe realized concretely as personal testimony:

> Crossing a bare common, in snow puddles, at
> twilight, under a clouded sky, without having
> in my thoughts any occurrence of special good
> fortune, I have enjoyed a perfect
> exhilaration. I am glad to the brink of fear.
> . . . In the woods we return to reason
> and faith. . . . Standing on the bare ground,
> -- my head bathed by the blithe air and
> uplifted into infinite space, -- all mean
> egotism vanishes. I become a transparent
> eyeball; I am nothing; I see all; the currents
> of the Universal Being circulate through me; I
> am part or parcel of God. The name of the
> nearest friend sounds then foreign and
> accidental: to be brothers, to be
> acquaintances, master or servant, is then a
> trifle and a disturbance. I am the lover of
> uncontained and immortal beauty. In the

> wilderness, I find something more dear and
> connate than in streets or villages.;9

Whitman's chief relation to transcendental ecstasy, in what came to be divided as section 5 of "Song of Myself," can likewise be read as the mystical and experiential "root-centre" of the work in which it appears:

> I mind how we lay in June, such a transparent
>   summer morning;
> You settled your head athwart my hips and
>   gently turned over upon me,
> And parted the shirt from my bosom-bone, and
>   plunged your tongue to my barestript
>   heart,
> And reached till you felt my beard, and
>   reached till you held my feet.
> Swiftly arose and spread around me the peace
>   and joy and knowledge that pass all the
>   art and argument of the earth;
> And I know that the hand of God is the
>   elderhand of my own,
> And I know that the spirit of God is the
>   eldest brother of my own,
> And that all the men ever born are also my
>   brothers . . . and the women my sisters
>   and lovers,
> And that a kelson of the creation is love;
> And limitless are leaves stiff or drooping in
>   the fields,
> And brown ants in the little wells beneath
>   them,
> And mossy scabs of the wormfence, and heaped
>   stones, and elder and mullen and
>   pokeweed.;10

No one can presume to know whether Whitman is recounting here an actual mystical experience, as early readers like R. M. Bucke and William James believed, or a "dramatic representation . . . conceived in the imagination," as James E. Miller would have it.;11 Generations of readers have yet confirmed the chant's motivating centrality of "Song of Myself." But while this section has occasionally been discussed in loose connection with Emerson's testimony on the soul,;12 it may also be approached as a direct response to the first-person testimony in Nature, a considered re-vision of Emerson's illumination on the bare common. Whatever Whitman was representing in section 5 from his own experiences of "devout ecstasy";13 he had already filtered through his recollections of Emerson's prototypic experience. In this light the two epiphanies

present several telling points of comparison having to
do, first, with the circumstances and setting of the
action; second, with the exact nature of the experience
described; and finally, with the credal consequences or
conclusions inspired by the event.

The preliminary circumstances for each happening
are unpromising, distinctly ordinary. Whitman's speaker
is loafing on a level expanse of grass, seeming to
expect nothing; Emerson's, in the first of two moments
conflated within the other passage, is "crossing a bare
common, in snow puddles, at twilight, under a clouded
sky," with no anticipation of "special good fortune."
As the ancient masters of contemplation would attest,
the aspiring self must at some point give over
exertions, waiting in that mood of receptive leisure,
that active passivity, which alone permits the influx of
revealing grace. But clearly our locus is the natural
world, and a particular scene of encounter within that
world. Nowhere else does Emerson's essay confront
Nature so directly in its concretized body rather than
in its abstracted, philosophic identity as the NOT ME.
In section 5 Whitman likewise draws the reader more than
usual toward a specific time and event. With his
allusion to a particular summer morning in June, he does
so even more in 1855 than in subsequent versions, where
he omits the exact month.

What is probably most essential about the
predisposing topography of these two settings is the
open, unfenced condition of the landscape. Though
lacking the breathtaking grandeur of the Alps, the
settings of Emerson and Whitman are reduced beyond
distraction, spread open to the dynamic influences of
nature. Emerson stands first on a "bare common," later
on the "bare ground" directly beneath the moving spaces
of heaven. No wonder, then, that "transparency" is a
key Emersonian term all through this essay, and not
simply in the "transparent eyeball" reference. To see
the world as open and "transparent" rather than "opaque"
is to restore its original beauty and unity. So
Emerson's poet turns "the world to glass.";14 For
Whitman, the "transparent summer morning" is a necessary
con ition for that universal seeing into the life of
things that flows from his initial meditation on a blade
of grass. Whitman likewise re-creates the transparent
atmosphere of Emerson's Nature when he boasts of his
lucid apprehension of the ME and NOT ME back in section
3: "Clear and sweet is my soul . . . and clear and sweet
is all that is not my soul."

Into this prepared atmosphere breaks the experience
itself, whose first characteristic for both writers is
the typical romantic shock of joy. Even more than
Emerson, Whitman in his erotic ecstasy confirms that one
cannot only "have" an original relation to the universe,

but can quite literally "enjoy" one! Yet tender
gladness blends at once with another sensation, that
precipitated by the awesome force of the _mysterium
tremendum_. Emerson is exhilarated, "glad" -- but "to
the brink of fear." Whitman experiences his joy as a
piercing gift, mixed with something of physical violence
as he feels a tongue "plunged . . . to [his] barestript
heart."

     This purgative violence destroys "all mean
egotism," releasing the hidden power of Emerson's
Over-Soul -- or Whitman's "Me myself." The "original"
relation so enacted is not to be confused with mere
novelty in experience. Instead Emerson's originality,
as in his allusion elsewhere to the "aboriginal Self,"
has first to do with first principles, primal origins
and the organic connection. In this context we can
appreciate Whitman's fascination with the hum of his own
"valved voice" as a delving after the instinctive
vibrations of the "aboriginal Self." We can understand
why he promises earlier that by his revelations "you
shall possess the origin of all poems" and why, in later
versions of this poem, he declares himself the speaker
of "Nature without check with original energy.";15

     But while Whitman celebrates the equivalent of
Emerson's wedding between the ME and the soul of Nature,
between the particular and the universal, aboriginal
Self, he makes some notable changes in the ceremony.
The most prominent difference, of course, lies in the
sexual and bodily accents of Whitman's drama, his
arresting literalization of the usual marriage metaphor.
Whitman declares his body, his "other I am," to be no
less god-bearing than the soul. And in section 5 their
union as equals gives birth to the transcendental Self
celebrated in the poem's opening lines. By contrast,
Whitman could scarcely miss noticing how thoroughly
Emerson's epiphany reduces to a cerebral event -- an
uplifting of the head away and apart from the body.
Instead of Whitman's orgasmic, interpenetrative union
with the body, a plunging downward from tongue to heart,
Emerson records his bodily evaporation. Of his body
nothing remains at last but a naked eye -- or indeed
"nothing" at all. While Emerson enjoys transparent
commerce with "currents of the Universal Being"
circulating through "the blithe air" above, Whitman
thrills to an immediate touch of Nature's procreative
rhythms surging beneath.

     Yet the dissenting re-vision of Emerson in "Song of
Myself" goes beyond Whitman's obvious redefinition of
"soul" as a self-realized body. Against his master's
insistence that "the soul knows no persons," Whitman
typically posed a belief in personality and "the
identified soul.";16 Nor does the disciple hesitate to
recast Emerson's impersonal deity, the Universal Being,

into "a loving bedfellow" whose hand dispenses letters,
grassy handkerchiefs, and plentiful baskets. Resisting
what he could feel to be Emerson's absorption of fleshy
particulars into universal anonymity, Whitman also
resisted his precursor's tendency in Nature to
assimilate the NOT ME into the ME, favoring a more
cyclic exchange and erotic polarity between the two.
Indeed, the credal conclusions Whitman pronounces
after his epiphany converge toward a doctrine of love:

> And I know that the spirit of God is the
>   eldest brother of my own,
> And that all the men ever born are also my
>   brothers . . . and the women my sisters
>   and lovers,
> And that a kelson of the creation is love;
> And limitless are leaves stiff or drooping in
>   the fields, . . .
> . . . mossy scabs of the wormfence . . . elder
>   and mullen and pokeweed.

Set this beside the parallel yet rhetorically
inverse unfolding of Emerson's post-illuminative credo:
"The name of the nearest friend sounds then foreign and
accidental: to be brothers, to be acquaintances, master
or servant, is then a trifle and a disturbance. I am
the lover of uncontained and immortal beauty." Emerson
calls himself a lover. But idealizing Platonist that he
is, he loves "uncontained and immortal beauty" -- not
people, to say nothing of pokeweed. His experience of
transport seems to cancel rather than extend brotherly
and sisterly affection toward his fellows.
I say "seems" because a fair rendering of Emerson
would grant that he intends here no absolute
disparagement of human love. His severe expressions
make sense, after all, when recognized as traditional
language of the negative way mystic. Emerson only wants
to say, not so differently from Whitman along the
affirmative way, that his ecstasy dissolves ego
attachments within a broader spirit of cosmic
benevolence. I expect Whitman perceived as much. But
where Whitman sensed the rhetorical and imagistic
current of the Emerson text running counter to his
master's best intent, he would have to clarify and
correct. If in theory Emerson's definition of the soul
gave full play to faculties like physical instinct and
emotion, Whitman was not alone in sensing a practical
stress on cold, impersonal intellect at the expense of
warm-blooded affection. In Emerson's essay on 'love,
which together with that on friendship Whitman once
called the "least good" piece in the whole of Essays:
First Series, Emerson admits that some believe his
"reverence for the intellect has made . . . [him]

unjustly cold to the personal relations." And the
charge appeared commonly in critical reviews.;17

     What Emerson provides in chapter 1 of Nature is an
exalted image of Man Thinking, not yet of Man Loving.
The two are finally as distinct as Emerson's transparent
eyeball and Whitman's barestript heart. Emerson's
spheric emblem of the Central Man is almost always the
eye. Often it is for Whitman, too. But in "Song of
Myself," section 5, the double-protagonist's gestures
suggest another circular image -- a sphere of flesh
stretching from beard to feet, from tongue to heart.
This heart-centered sphere of married flesh at once
extends and corrects Emerson's warning in "Experience"
that "the universe is the bride of the soul. All
private sympathy is partial. Two human beings are like
globes, which can touch only in a point.";18

     Finally, then, what does this restricted analysis
of two texts reveal about Whitman's fundamental use of
Emerson? For one thing, it indicates how distinctive
Whitman's relation to Emerson was against Harold Bloom's
primary model of warring competition among strong poets.
Though Whitman clearly betrayed something of Bloom's
resisting "anxiety" toward the precursor, and though
Emerson clearly played some fathering role, conditions
peculiar to the case served to reduce certain of the
otherwise predictable tensions. Thus Emerson was for
Whitman a Master Seer whose words "shed light to the
best souls," but not a Master Poet as such.;19 Far from
leaving Whitman a potentially overwhelming poetic
inheritance, he all but commissioned Whitman's
appearance as the long-awaited American bard. And as
Bloom recognizes, the ironic peculiarity of a
transcendental legacy lies in its being "the only poetic
influence that counsels against itself, and against the
idea of influence"; or, as Whitman himself put the point
in later life, "The best part of Emersonianism is, it
breeds the giant that destroys itself.";20

     Whitman's discovery of this fact allowed him to
reach behind his specific literary parent toward that
original relation to the universe constituting "the
origin of all poems." It left him free to "correct"
Emerson not only in Bloom's primary sense of combative
misreading, but also at times in the more benign and
common sense of clarifying his master's best intent.
Perhaps, therefore, a better term than "father" to
express the essential role of Emerson in Whitman's early
achievement would be "midwife." It is as midwife above
all that the Concord sage figures into the action of
"Song of Myself," section 5, for here Emerson is invoked
to preside at the younger poet's procreation and birth
of himself.

NOTES

1.   Though there is still no full-length publication on the Emerson-Whitman nexus, the main import of several shorter studies affirming Whitman's early and substantial debt to Emerson is summed up in Floyd Stovall's "Emerson and Whitman," chapter 17 in The Foreground of "Leaves of Grass" (Charlottesville: University Press of Virginia, 1974), pp. 282-305. See also Hyatt Waggoner, American Poets from the Puritans to the Present (Boston: Houghton Mifflin, 1968), pp. 150-80, 637-56; and Roger Asselineau, The Evolution of Walt Whitman. Vol. 1, The Creation of a Personality (Cambridge, Mass.: Harvard University Press, 1960), pp. 52-57. The most thorough and judicious account of the personal relationship is in Alvin H. Rosenfeld's unpublished study, "Emerson and Whitman: Their Personal and Literary Relationships," Ph.D. dissertation, Brown University, 1968. In his New Walt Whitman Handbook (New York: New York University Press, 1975), Gay Wilson Allen declares flatly, "Nearly all scholars now agree that Emerson himself was the one single greatest influence on Whitman during the years when he was planning and writing the first two or three editions of Leaves of Grass" (p. 256).

2.   John T. Trowbridge, "Reminiscences of Walt Whitman," Atlantic Monthly, 89 (Feb. 1902): 163-75, esp. 166.

3.   See The Complete Works of Ralph Waldo Emerson, ed. E. W. Emerson, 12 vols. (Boston: Houghton Mifflin, 1903-4), vol. 1, pp. 334-35, 351-53; vol. 2, pp. 267, 273-74, 280-84; vol. 3, p. 71; vol. 4, pp. 96-97.

4.   Emerson, Works, vol. 1, p. 334; vol. 3, p. 20; vol. 2, p. 63.

5.   Harold Bloom sets forth his theory of influence and its preliminary application to the Emerson-Whitman nexus in several studies from which I draw this statement: The Anxiety of Influence (New York and London: Oxford University Press, 1973), esp. p. 68; A Map of Misreading (New York: Oxford University Press, 1975); The Ringers in the Tower (Chicago: University of Chicago Press, 1971), pp. 217-34; Figures of Capable Imagination (New York: Seabury Press, 1976); and Poetry and Repression (New Haven: Yale University Press, 1976), pp. 235-66, esp. pp. 265-66. I had already completed the main text of this essay before encountering Bloom's most extensive treatment of Whitman and Emerson in Poetry and Repression. Though I find useful insights scattered through Bloom's work I do not share all his theoretical assumptions nor endorse all his readings. As the student of Bloom will notice, my handling of terms like "ecstasy" and "the sublime" does not always correspond to the complicated usage specified within his scheme.

6.   For discussion of this evidence, see Rosenfeld, pp. 154-57 and 160-63, and F. O. Matthiessen, _American Renaissance_ (New York: Oxford University Press, 1941), p. 520.   The only specific comparisons I have seen of the two passages in question are in Leon Howard, "For a Critique of Whitman's Transcendentalism," _Modern Language Notes_, 17 (Jan. 1932): 79-85; and one sentence in Albert Gelpi, "Emerson: The Paradox of Organic Form," in _Emerson: Prophecy, Metamorphosis, and Influence_, ed. David Levin (New York: Columbia University Press, 1975), pp. 151-52.   Neither Howard nor Gelpi makes a case for direct literary influence.

7.   John Burroughs, _Notes on Walt Whitman as Poet and Person_ (1867; repr. New York: Haskell House Ltd., 1971), pp. 16-17.   In "Reminiscences," Trowbridge mentions "the words that burn in the prose-poem Nature" (p. 165) as part of Whitman's general legacy from Emerson; but whether this statement draws on Whitman's direct testimony is unclear.

8.   Jonathan Bishop, _Emerson on the Soul_ (Cambridge, Mass.:   Harvard University Press, 1964), p. 26.

9.   Emerson, _Works_, vol. 1, pp. 9-10.   My sense of the position occupied by this section of _Nature_ matches that of Lawrence Buell in _Literary Transcendentalism_ (Ithaca, N.Y.: Cornell University Press, 1973), pp. 286-87.

10.   Cited from the 1855 version of _Leaves of Grass_ (facsimile repr., New York: Eakins Press, 1966), pp. 15-16.

11.   William James, _The Varieties of Religious Experience_ (1902; repr. New York: New American Library, 1958), p. 304; James E. Miller, Jr., _A Critical Guide to Leaves of Grass_ (Chicago: University of Chicago Press, 1957), pp. 6-7.

12.   As by Emory Holloway, _Whitman: An Interpretation in Narrative_ (New York: Alfred A. Knopf, 1926), pp. 105-7.

13.   _Prose Works 1892_, ed. Floyd Stovall, in _Collected Writings of Walt Whitman_ (New York: New York University Press, 1963-64), vol. 2, p. 398.   Other notable cases where Whitman writes of mystical states include his "root-centre" reference in _Prose Works_, vol. 1, p. 258; and his self-description as a "mystic," _Leaves of Grass: Comprehensive Reader's Edition_, ed. Harold Blodgett and Sculley Bradley (New York: New York University Press), p. 164.

14.   "The Poet," in Emerson, _Works_, vol. 3, p. 20. Besides Harold Bloom, at least two critics -- Kenneth Burke and Merton Sealts, Jr. -- have expounded on the transparency motif in _Nature_.

15.   _Leaves of Grass: Comprehensive Reader's Edition_, p. 29.

16. Emerson, _Works_, vol. 1, p. 130; Whitman, _Prose Works_, vol. 2, p. 398.

17. Manuscript cited in Stovall's _Foreground_, p. 290; Emerson's _Works_, vol. 2, p. 174. Cf. _Uncollected Poetry and Prose of Walt Whitman_, ed. Emory Holloway (New York: Doubleday Page, 1921), vol. 2, p. 81; Clarence Gohdes and Rollo Silver eds., _Faint Clues & Indirections_ (Durham, N.C.: Duke University Press, 1949), pp. 28-29; and the remarks on Emerson in _The American Phrenological Journal_, 19 (March 1854): 55.

18. Emerson, _Works_, vol. 3, p. 77.

19. _Notes and Fragments_, ed. R. M. Bucke, in _The Complete Prose Works of Walt Whitman_ (New York: G. P. Putnam's Sons, 1902), vol. 9, p. 163. Whitman nonetheless expressed a relatively high estimation of Emerson's poetry.

20. Bloom, _Map of Misreading_, p. 163; Whitman, _Prose Works_, vol. 2, pp. 517-18. To a point, Bloom's theoretical categories of Daemonization and the Romantic Counter-Sublime parallel my view of Whitman's reach toward an "original relation" behind the Emersonian shadow.

19.
Lear and the
Leaves of Grass Poet

DENNIS K. RENNER

I sometimes teach both <u>King Lear</u> and Whitman's poems to students perplexed because the texts do not yield gracefully to their assumptions about human behavior. They seem embarrassed by the easily flattered old king and the grandstanding young rough: such diplays of passion do not seem appropriately "cool." Looking for a way to deal with this embarrassment, I discovered Maynard Mack's small book on "the problematic Lear," which offers surprising help for <u>Leaves of Grass</u> in addition to Shakespeare's tragedy, suggesting another way to appreciate Whitman's contribution to world literature. I am accepting the general sense of the term <u>tragedy</u> as a serious story about a protagonist who yearns for self-respect and fulfillment but suffers a defeat of great consequence for which he shares responsibility as the result of a weakness of character.

What Professor Mack seeks to recover in his book, <u>King Lear in Our Time</u>, is "tragic heroic" content that still appeals to an audience. After two world wars and Auschwitz, we are "better qualified to communicate and respond to the full range of experience in <u>King Lear</u> than any previous time, save possibly Shakespeare's own," Mack concludes.;1 Perhaps now we are also in a better position to recognize the tragic vision in <u>Leaves of Grass</u>, one of the literary achievements of the world's first new nation. We have witnessed the formation of more than 60 new nations when colonial regimes crumbled in the aftermath of World War II.

What has happened in these new nations too often has paralleled the history of the United States, with its successful independence movement, then disillusionment and bitter civil war. Anthropologist

Clifford Geertz has said about revolutions in the Third World: "It is not that nothing has happened, that a new era has not been entered. Rather, that era having been entered, it is necessary now to live in it rather than merely imagine it, and that is inevitably a deflating experience." After "the heroic excitements of the political revolutions have passed," the "questions 'What is it all for?' 'What's the use?' and 'Why go on?' arise in the context of mass poverty," corruption, and violence. Insofar as hope can be sustained it is by "images of a heritage worth preserving, a promise worth pursuing," the anthropologist explains.;2

The full cycle from exuberant hope to defeat and despair had appeared in Walt Whitman's poetry by 1860. Most of the poems in the first two editions of Leaves of Grass nurture the heroic excitements of the political revolution as Whitman understood it, but by the end of the crisis decade leading to civil war, major poems deal with the questions "What was it for?" and "Why go on?" However, despite the prospect that the Union would be torn apart, the 1860 edition of Leaves of Grass sustains hope by its devotion to a revolutionary heritage worth preserving, a promise worth pursuing.

Professor Mack blames interpretive problems of the tragedy on recent "tides of psychological realism" that stress interior motives of characters at the expense of their external significance, whereas Shakespeare's characters are emblematic, his scenes exemplary. The dialogue, although "often highly individualized, is always yet more fully in the service of the vision of the play as a whole than true to a consistent interior reality," Mack notes. Like a morality play, King Lear presents "a vision acted upon a platform whereby the invisible" becomes "visible and man's terrestrial pilgrimage" is "glimpsed whole in its entire arc of pride and innocence, temptation and fall, regeneration and salvation or ruin and damnation.";3 The reverberations of Professor Mack's remarks for Whitman's poems are substantial, since the most influential recent Whitman criticism also has stressed the interior motives of the character who speaks, presuming that Whitman's poetry is in the private, rather than the public mode.;4 We have admired individual poems as symbolist lyrics more than we have explored public meanings of the volume of poetry as a whole, excluding the tragic dimension of Leaves of Grass and obscuring the fullness of Whitman's vision.;5

By noting several analogies between the two protagonists, Lear and the Leaves poet-figure, I propose to examine the implications of Professor Mack's book for Leaves of Grass in our time. Along the way I hope to demonstrate the usefulness of the analogies by discussing the rarely explicated poem "Faces," which

first appeared in the 1855 edition of <u>Leaves of Grass</u>.
I will assume, as Floyd Stovall has suggested, that the
poet-figure of <u>Leaves of Grass</u> is "the product of
Whitman's imagination as Hamlet was a product of
Shakespeare's and as Satan of <u>Paradise Lost</u> was a
product of Milton's.";6 As the <u>Leaves</u> poet himself
declares, "Outlining a history yet to be, I project the
ideal man, the American of the future.";7

As a heroic embodiment of New World hopes, the
protagonist of <u>Leaves of Grass</u> graces a poetic drama
presented in spatial rather than narrative form,
following the precedent of Hebrew scripture.;8 The
reader is given the responsibility of reading and
rereading until the story is completed by innumerable
references and cross-references that are relational
apart from any sequence in time. Just as the legacy of
medieval culture contributes an emblematic dimension to
characters, scenes, and action in morality plays, the
legacy of the American Revolution contributes the
central meaning to the parables, anecdotes, historical
accounts, vignettes, proclamations, laments,
celebrations, and reminiscences in <u>Leaves of Grass</u>.
Flashes of lyric brilliance appear, also, because
Whitman intermingles autobiographical and historical
materials freely, as befits the American conflation of
individual and national identities described by Sacvan
Bercovitch.;9

Professor Mack notes that Lear enacts his tragic
role in what is "in some sort an emblematic kingdom
. . . almost a paradigm of hierarchy and rule.";10
Whitman's protagonist graces an emblematic Republic, a
paradigm of democracy and moral consensus, rather than
hierarchy and rule. In <u>King Lear</u> the protagonist's
identity is distinguished by the office of king, whereas
the identity of the poet-protagonist of <u>Leaves of Grass</u>
is defined by the tenets of American civil religion
rooted in the American Revolution.;11 Professor Mack
observes that tragic drama provides an archetypal act of
choosing for the protagonist. Lear, of course,
preciptates tragic consequences by choosing to abandon
his divine role in a hierarchical political order and
betray his faith in the love object, Cordelia. For the
<u>Leaves</u> poet the archetypal choice is between the
unifying beliefs of American civil religion and
disruption of the Union in civil war.

The love object for the <u>Leaves</u> poet,
cross-referenced in the spatial form of the book, is the
Union, which represents ameliorative or eschatological
hopes for the shaping of democracy against the
degradations of social injustice -- the coming of the
Kingdom on Earth. The Union celebrated by many of
Whitman's poems represents assent and dedication to the
abstract faith of the Declaration of Independence that

"the Laws of Nature and Nature's God" hold the state and its people under judgement of these "truths": "all men are created equal," "they are endowed by their creator with certain inalienable rights," and "among these are life, liberty and the pursuit of happiness." This was the convenant between Providence and the American people, in Whitman's understanding.;12 In reality, of course, the covenant was broken from the start by the accommodation of slavery. Yet, while the Union survived, the promises of the covenant seemed plausible. Cross-references in Leaves of Grass present the requisite antecedent action -- the opening of a bountiful continent for the salvation of mankind from the specters of Old World evils, subservience, poverty, and war.

From this perspective, a rarely explicated Whitman poem, "Faces," seems to portray the fruition of the American Revolution as it was imagined, not the tragic resolution which was experienced. At first, faces of disease and suffering dominate the procession moving through time. Then republican countenances -- "faces of friendship," the "grand faces of natural lawyers and judges," and the like -- are followed by images of the antagonists, the self-aggrandizing connivers who threaten the Union, a face whispering a snakelike "sibilant threat" and a "dough-faced" Northerner "more chill than the artic sea.";13 The stage has been set to include the decisive characters in the cast, the faces of empty, listless "orthodox" citizens who seem univolved in the drama. In this poem the resolution is triumphant rather than tragic, however, because the procession concludes with images of "banners and horses," "pioneer-caps," "victorious drums," a face "commanding and bearded," and a "life-boat." Even Whitman's incarnation figure, the procreative sexual rendezvous of a man and woman out-of-doors, appears prominently at the point of reversal, followed by the figure for the American Republic, which springs "in crimson youth from the white froth and water blue," Whitman's symbol for the Soul. Finally, Whitman's customary figure for democracy, the Quaker "mother of men," concludes the poem.;14

But this poem, like "Song of Myself" in the 1855 edition, is the celebrative, affirmative part of the tragedy of Leaves of Grass -- the exposition and complication. It evokes the dream of the protagonist-people to incarnate the creative potential of American civil religion in a better society. The rest of the story -- crisis, reversal, and resolution -- appears in new poems of the 1860 edition of Leaves of Grass, proofread and arranged in Boston by Whitman while newspapers reported disturbing speeches that included such remarks as one by a senator that "no two nations on

earth are or ever were more distinctly separated and
hostile!";15 New poems of the 1860 edition include
strident passages about the politics of disunion which
intensify the conflict from antagonistic forces, a
Calamus section of poems that displays the protagonist's
continued will to triumph by legitimating the solidarity
of free men in defiance of the slavocracy, and the most
admired new poems of the 1860 edition of Leaves of
Grass, "A Word Out of the Sea" ("Out of the Cradle
Endlessly Rocking") and "Leaves of Grass 1" ("As I Ebb'd
with the Ocean of Life"), poems of recognition and
defeat.

     "A Word Out of the Sea," for example, is an
expressionistic monologue displaying the consciousness
of a protagonist moving toward dramatic resignation and
resolution. What we hear is the poetic translation of
the song of the bird as it glimpses first a dark speck
on the distant sea, then a "dusky spot" on the
"low-hanging moon" -- the "shape of his mate!" From the
bird come "carols of lonesome love! Death carols!"
while the shape and the moon drop "almost down into the
Sea!" (273). In the same way, the protagonist has been
a solitary singer, having yearned and sung while his
lost mate -- democracy -- dropped from sight in the
crisis decade leading to civil war in America.;16

     Returning to our comparison of tragic protagonists,
in Shakespeare's tragic vision Lear's moral principles
live on in the hopes for restored order Kent brings to
the kingdom in the resolution. Like Shakespeare,
Whitman opts for order and engagement, rather than
despair. In "So Long!" his poet-protagonist departs the
stage affirming moral principles that could anchor the
self for new resolution, despite the coming debacle of
civil war that could destroy the Union:

     I announce natural persons to arise,
     I announce justice triumphant,
     I announce uncompromising liberty and equality
          . . .

                                             (453)

"Remember my words," the Leaves poet says:

     I love you -- I depart from materials,
     I am as one disembodied, triumphant, dead.
                                             (15-17)

     Sidney Mead has said of mid-nineteenth-century
American history as tragic drama that it was not in the
"simple fact that the actuality of America appeared more
and more ugly and less and less the progressive
incarnation of the ideal. Rather it [the tragedy] lay
in the fading from the mind of the artist-people of the

creative idea -- the evaporation of their dream.";17
The _Leaves_ protagonist displays his recognition of such
a failure of vision, suffers and dies, but not without
offering earned insight to his audience. Recognizing
tragic elements in _Leaves of Grass_ has not been common
in Whitman criticism, yet the _Leaves_ poet and
Shakespeare's King Lear hold much in common. The tragic
elements discernible in Whitman's work may also appear
in the literature of Third World nations homogeneous
enough to sustain a literary culture.

NOTES

1. Maynard Mack, _King Lear in Our Time_ (Berkeley:
University of California Press, 1965), pp. 68-79.
2. Clifford Geertz, "After the Revolution: The
Fate of Nationalism in the New States," in _The
Interpretation of Cultures: Selected Essays_ (New York:
Basic Books, 1973), pp. 234, 253.
3. Mack, p. 94.
4. Earl Miner offers a convincing case for
distinguishing public from private modes in literary
history in "Problems and Possibilities of Literary
History Today," _CLIO_, 2 (June 1973): 232-33.
5. I discuss Whitman's tragic vision in more
detail in "Tradition for a Time of Crisis: Whitman's
Prophetic Stance," _Poetic Prophecy in Western
Literature_, ed. Raymond Jean-Frontain (Madison, N.J.:
Fairleigh Dickinson University Press, 1984).
6. Floyd Stovall, "Walt Whitman: The Man and the
Myth," _South Atlantic Quarterly_, 54 (October 1955): 542;
"Whitman and the Poet in _Leaves of Grass_," in _Essays
Mostly on Periodical Publishing in America: A Collection
in Honor of Clarence Gohdes_, ed. James Woodress (Durham,
N.C.: Duke University Press, 1973), pp. 3-21.
7. _Leaves of Grass: Facsimile Edition of the 1860
Text_, ed. Roy Harvey Pearce (Ithaca, N.Y.: Cornell
University Press, 1961), p. 181. Subsequent
documentation from this source will be by parenthesis
within the text with later titles for 1860 poems
included.
8. Joseph Frank discusses spatial form in _The
Widening Gyre: Crisis and Mastery in Modern Literature_
(New Brunswick, N.J.: Rutgers University Press, 1963),
pp. 17-19. In his earliest Whitman scholarship, Gay
Wilson Allen explored Biblical "analogies" and "echoes"
in Whitman's works. For a recent survey of Whitman's
formative contact with Biblical precedent, see Floyd
Stovall, _The Foreground of Leaves of Grass_
(Charlottesville, Va.: University of Virginia Press,
1974), pp. 56, 184-88.

9. Sacvan Bercovitch, The Puritan Origins of the American Self (New Haven, Conn.: Yale University Press, 1975), pp. 70-76.

10. Mack, p. 25.

11. "By civil religion, I refer to that religious dimension, found I think in the life of every people, through which it interprets its historical experience in the light of transcendent reality," Robert N. Bellah explains in The Broken Covenant: American Civil Religion in Time of Trial (New York: Seabury Press, Inc., 1975), p. 3. Sidney Mead explores the religion or theology of the Republic in The Lively Experiment: The Shaping of Christianity in America (New York: Harper and Row, 1963), The Nation with the Soul of a Church (New York: Harper and Row, 1975), and The Old Religion in the Brave New World: Reflections on the Relation between Christendom and the Republic (Berkeley: University of California Press, 1977).

12. I explore the Revolutionary legacy in Whitman's thought in "Walt Whitman's Religion of the Republic," Ph.D. dissertation, University of Iowa, 1975. For a reading of "the twenty-eight young men" section of "Song of Myself" as a celebration of the Union, see "The Conscious Whitman: Allegorical Manifest Destiny in "Song of Myself," Walt Whitman Review, 24 (Dec. 1978): 149-55, a revision of my paper for a Special Session, "Walt Whitman's Poetry," held at the 1977 Convention of the Modern Language Association in Chicago.

13. The association of the North with arctic chill in relation to the political situation appears also in a poem written in 1857: "What a filthy Presidentiad! (O south, your torrid suns! O north, your arctic freezings!)" (Pearce, p. 401). For sources of the face imagery in phrenology, see Harold Aspiz, "A Reading of Whitman's 'Faces,'" Walt Whitman Review, 19 (June 1973): 37-48. Aspiz notes that the poem has rarely been explicated, "possibly because its meanings are obscured by a seemingly unintelligible jargon derived from phrenology and physiognomy."

14. The Quaker mother, seated, is Whitman's poetic rendition of a symbol he believed sculptors and painters should immortalize. In notes he enjoined them to

> make a Picture of America as an IMMORTAL
> MOTHER, surrounded by all her children young
> and old. . . . Make her seated. . . . around
> her are none of the emblems of the classic
> gooddess -- nor any feudal emblem. . . . For
> as to sons and daughters the perfect mother is
> the one where all meet and [who] binds them
> all together as long as she lives, so The
> Mother of These States binds them all together
> as long as she lives.

See Walt Whitman's Workshop, ed. Clifton J. Furness
(1928; repr. New York: Russell and Russell, 1964), p.
60. Also see the poem, "Thou Mother with Thy Equal
Brood," in Harold W. Blodgett and Sculley Bradley, eds.,
Leaves of Grass: Comprehensive Reader's Edition (New
York: New York University Press, 1965), p. 455.
Benjamin T. Spencer discusses Whitman's use of the
"federal Mother" as a "unifying political symbol" in The
Quest for Nationality: An American Literary Campaign
(Syracuse, N.Y.: Syracuse University Press, 1957), p.
234.
      15. Fredson Bowers' study of Whitman's manuscripts
for the 1860 edition and the identification and
publication of journalistic items by William White have
opened the way for examination of those previously
mysterious Whitman years, 1857-60. I examine the
evidence in "Walt Whitman's Religion of the Republic,"
pp. 201-7, 249-52.
      16. I present extended allegorical readings of "A
Word Out of the Sea" and "As I Ebb'd with the Ocean of
Life" in "Tradition for a Time of Crisis: Whitman's
Prophetic Stance," following Sholom J. Kahn's suggestion
that "a category of 'allegorical lyricism'" is
applicable to Whitman in "Whitman's Allegorical
Lyricism," in Studies in English Language and
Literature, ed. Alice Shalvi and A. A. Mendilow
(Jerusalem: Magnes Press, Hebrew University, 1966), pp.
209-25.
      17. Sidney Mead, "American History as Tragic
Drama," The Journal of Religion, 52 (Oct. 1972): 336-60.

20.
Kingdom of This World:
Whitman and Nietzsche
Compared

ADRIAN DEL CARO

That study on Whitman and Nietzsche which seeks only to
uncover parallels and similarities does injustice to
both thinkers. The easy juxtaposition of superficial
points is tempting but not productive, yet underlying
the respective views of these writers is a common
appreciation for the transforming social life of the
latter half of the nineteenth century. No amount of
scholarship on the topic of Whitman and Nietzsche will
ever reconcile their differences. In the case of
Whitman, who represents that peculiar brand of American
democracy, the writer still serves as a spokesman for
his nation. With Nietzsche, however, who considered
himself the aristocrat par excellence, there is no
nation or people which he represents. But as disparate
as their respective backgrounds and goals may have been,
it is yet clear that Whitman and Nietzsche stand out as
two prolific individuals whose thoughts contribute to
the intellectual environment of the twentieth century.
    It is no secret that Nietzsche was radically
anti-democratic, while Whitman literally sings of
democracy. Behind Nietzsche's aversion to this
political or sociological form was his firm belief that
people are not equal, and this condition, rather than
contributing to the sublimation of our race, would
merely arrest the evolutionary progress of humanity.
What appalled Nietzsche was the democratic consequence,
namely, the proliferation of mediocre standards, rather
than the upward self-overcoming which the race can
achieve only by trying to follow its highest
representatives. In an article on Thomas Mann and Walt
Whitman, Vincent Cosentino describes how the

anti-democratic Mann became sold on Whitman's concept of
democracy when he realized that "what Whitman calls
democracy is nothing other than what we [Germans], in a
more oldfashioned way, call 'humanitarianism.'";1 It is
true that Whitman's concept of democracy transcends the
purely political, and it is also true that Mann had a
notable change of heart vis-a-vis Nietzsche and his
other heroes after he recanted on his nonpolitical
stand. But Nietzsche, had he been exposed to the works
of Whitman, would have recanted nothing. As eclectic as
Whitman's notions about democracy may be, they are still
opposed on principle to Nietzsche's views about culture
and the proper governing of the race.

Constantine Stavrou, in the book Whitman and
Nietzsche, finds all too many parallels between the two
thinkers. With regard to their respective readers,
Stavrou writes:

> Anxious for an audience, and convinced, with
> the cocksureness of genius, of their right,
> nay, of the world's danger should it fail to
> grant them an audience, it is understandable
> that Whitman and Nietzsche should, when
> refused the ears of the many, seek, if only in
> reverie, for the select few who might
> appreciate them.;2

Perhaps it is true that for a time Whitman was unheard,
and that his readers were a select few, but was this
ever the aim of Walt Whitman? Could the poet who wrote
"To a Common Prostitute," who counted every man and
woman among his friends, who spoke of "camerados" and
universal brotherhood -- in short, could the poet of the
people in the highest sense of the word truly write for
a select few? The iconoclasm of Whitman resides
precisely in his having written for everyone, whereas
Nietzsche's iconoclasm resides in his having written not
for the herd, which he despised, but for the "free
spirits," the few kindred souls of Europe whom he
regarded, like himself, as "good Europeans." The
following excerpt from The Gay Science unequivocally
states Nietzsche's purpose and projected readership:

> One does not merely want to be understood when
> one writes, but just as surely one wants not
> to be understood. . . . Each more refined mind
> and taste selects his listeners when he shares
> himself; in selecting them, he simultaneously
> draws a line against "the others.";3

Toward the end of his life, and in our time, Whitman's
acceptance among the people became a reality. But to
this day Nietzsche has not been accepted on the popular

level, and sympathy for his ideas is limited to certain members of the intellectual community.

The core of Nietzsche's philosophy is the individual, the core of Whitman's is the en masse. In The Gay Science Nietzsche refers to individuals as "the seeds of the future, the founders of intellectual colonization" (vol. 2, p. 57). The name which Nietzsche has earned for himself, first given to him by Georg Brandes in 1887, is that of the aristocratic individualist. Nietzsche is a radical philosopher not in a political sense from right to left, but according to the vehemence with which he opposed anything related to the collective spirit of the times. Whitman himself was no stranger to individualism, but in a more qualified sense. In Democratic Vistas this point is made:

> For a democracy, the leveler, the unyielding
> principle of the average, is surely joined
> another principle, equally unyielding, closely
> tracking the first, indispensable to it,
> opposite (as the sexes are opposite) . . .
> this second principle is individuality, the
> pride and centripetal isolation of a human
> being in himself -- identity -- personalism.;4

These words, in the mouth of an earnest democrat, are high praise for the individual, and they show a mature understanding of the dialectics of history. Yet in Whitman's view, individuality is the second principle behind the "leveling one." The indication is that individuality serves "the unyielding principle of the average," by stirring up a dialectic tension conducive to sublimation en masse. Hence progress, in Whitman's sense, must be a slow lateral movement en masse, with the masses eventually absorbing the individuals. The cultural priority of Nietzsche is opposite. In the Untimely Meditation entitled "On the Use and Disadvantage of History," he writes: "The goal of humanity cannot lie in its end, but only in its highest representatives" (vol. 2, p. 270). Nietzsche's so-called "highest representatives" do not contribute to a better mass, but are the raison d'etre of the masses.

Although it is said that both Nietzsche and Whitman were iconoclastic, there is much to distinguish in the use of this term. Whitman was iconoclastic when he spoke out against the stilted, when he spoke out in favor of the common. Because he believed in a universal brotherhood and progress, his voice could be directed against the establishment. Whitman earned the reputation of a libertarian, but Nietzsche detested the notion. Stavrou focusses on what he calls the common romanticism of the two thinkers:

> Although it might be said, in one sense,
> Whitman and Nietzsche were anti-romantic in
> refusing to confound the real with the ideal
> of life with dream, they displayed many of the
> romanticist's traits: through their faith in
> the vital instincts; through their iconoclasm;
> through their delirious eulogies and renitent
> denunciations: through their rampant egoism;
> through their libertarianism.;5

Most of these traits, in one degree or another, are shared, but one fails to heed the aristocratic side of Nietzsche if one insists on casting him as a libertarian. In Beyond Good and Evil, Nietzsche is adamant about drawing a distinction between his "free spirit" (Freigeist) and the free thinker or libertarian: "We are something different than 'libres-penseurs,' 'liberi pensatori,' 'Freidenker' and whatever else these good spokesmen of 'modern ideas' like to call themselves" (vol. 2, p. 607). The difference Nietzsche wishes to emphasize is one which removes the free spirit from the broad social plane of ameliorization. For example, Whitman could well champion the cause of equal rights for women, while Nietzsche not only rejected the idea of equal rights for women, but equal rights for any. The general rule of thumb for Nietzsche is, if the idea is modern, if it represents the belief in progress and is even remotely related to democratic optimism, then Nietzsche is the opponent. Whitman the iconoclast does not easily compare with Nietzsche the active nihilist, whose mission it was to annihilate existing values in the transvaluation of all values. Similarly, Whitman's iconoclasm in the sphere of religion centers on his natural religion, and perhaps his belief in the transmigration of the soul. But whether he saw God in every living thing or not, Whitman still maintained a belief in a divine power. Nietzsche, on the other hand, set about to destroy the foundations of faith in God in such works as The Antichrist. Both Whitman and Nietzsche tried to retain some form of afterlife, possibly as a result of their hyper-awareness of transitoriness and their suffering from it. But one gets an idea how radically nihilistic Nietzsche was when one considers the eternal recurrence of the same, which Nietzsche himself called "the most nihilistic thought." Not a better life, not a different life with the hope of variety and perhaps deliverance, but the same life lived without variation; this is a telling difference in the thoughts of two thinkers whose religious backgrounds may have been quite similar. Whitman's love of life and his amor fati were not as radical as Nietzsche's, for in the case of the latter, there is only one chance to live and affirm the goodness of earthly existence.

Before moving to a closer textual juxtaposition of
Nietzsche and Whitman, which will surely uncover a few
things in common, one final difference should be noted.
Although critical of his nation and not blind to its
shortcomings, Whitman was still an extremely vocal
patriot. The form of Whitman's patriotism is not
narrowly nationalistic, for he believed that the true
seeds of American democracy would scatter, as indeed
the States themselves were expanding. In the Vistas he
writes:

> Political democracy, as it exists and
> practically works in America, with all its
> threatening evils, supplies a training-school
> for making first-class men. It is life's
> gymnasium, not of good only, but of all.
> . . . Vive, the attack -- the perennial
> assault! Vive, the unpopular cause -- the
> spirit that audaciously aims -- the never
> abandoned efforts, pursued amid opposing
> proofs and precedents.;6

But for the name "America," this exhortation, this bold
and affirmative cry, is extremely reminiscent of
Nietzsche's attitude and mentality. The all-important
difference, however, resides in the naming of America as
the "gymnasium" of these positive new people. Nietzsche
could not speak for his native country or any country at
all. He despised nationalism and would not compromise
his principles to adopt the saber-rattling, anti-semitic
haughtiness of mainstream Germany after the victory in
the Franco-Prussian War. In short, whether he spoke
critically of it or not, Whitman had a country and
appointed himself its spokesman. For all intents and
purposes, Nietzsche did not have a country, although he
wrote for "free spirits" and "good Europeans." Of his
native Germany, Nietzsche would say in Ecce homo: "As
far as Germany extends, it ruins culture" (vol. 2, p.
1088).
     In an article on Whitman and the language of the
romantics, V. K. Chari observes that "in his insistence
on the values of sanity and normality, in his dislike of
Romantic sensationalism and metaphysics of night . . .
Whitman reflected the essential classicism of an age
which preferred . . . objectivity.";7 The same dislike
is shared by Nietzsche, and for this reason Zarathustra
proclaims the high noon of mankind, that ultimate moment
of brightness, when the transition from all-too-human to
overhuman or superhuman shall take place. And like the
sun, which is the highest symbol of consciousness,
according to C. G. Jung, Zarathustra "goes down"
(untergehen) to illuminate the dealings of men.
Nietzsche and Whitman shared an aversion for the dark,

the obscured, and the effeminate, all of which are
staple romantic traits. In the Vistas Whitman speaks
out with perfect Nietzschean candor, when he maintains:

> In our times, refinement and delicatesse are
> not only attended to sufficiently, but
> threaten to eat us up, like a cancer. Already
> the democratic genius watches, ill-pleased,
> these tendencies. Provision for a little
> healthy rudeness, savage virtue, justification
> of what one has in one's self, whatever it is,
> is demanded. Negative qualities, even
> deficiencies, would be a relief.;8

Overrefinement and delicatesse are decadent signs, and
both Whitman and Nietzsche equate strength with
virility. In the Zarathustra chapter entitled "On the
Diminishing Virtues," Zarathustra exclaims, "There is
little here which is manly; therefore their women
masculinize themselves" (vol. 2, p. 419). When Whitman
speaks of the "negative" qualities which would come as a
relief to him, he grows closer to Nietzsche in spirit.
Strength and austerity are required for the battle
against decadent values and baroque conventions. Again
in the Vistas Whitman writes that as

> a basic model or portrait of the personality
> for general use for manliness of the States
> . . . a clear-blooded, strong-fibered
> physique, is indispensable; the questions of
> food, drink, air, exercise, assimilation,
> digestion, can never be intermitted.;9

This curious statement, with its equivocal term
"clear-blooded," has a companion passage in Ecce homo,
where Nietzsche discusses his aversion to alcohol and
the dangers of German cuisine. Among other tips,
Nietzsche gives us to understand that "one must know the
size of one's stomach" and that "all prejudices derive
from the intestines." With regard to exercise,
Nietzsche warns: "Do not trust a thought which is not
born out in the open and during free movement. . . . the
behind [is] the actual sin against the holy ghost"
(vol. 2, pp. 1084-85). Hence in this appreciation for
robustness, for manly as opposed to effeminate virtues,
Nietzsche and Whitman are much in agreement. But a word
of caution must be inserted: in Nietzsche's thinking,
democracy was an effeminate and modern idea, whereas for
Whitman, democracy is the manly "democratic genius."
     Three attitudes or moods stand out as distinct
markers of what Nietzsche called amor fati. These are
aggressiveness, respect for the here and now, and
affirmation. The best of both Whitman and Nietzsche is

to be sought among these positive moods. Zarathustra
does not see man as a victim of nature, nor does he see
nature as a part of some grander divine scheme: "Where
I found life," explains Nietzsche's prophet, "there I
found the will to power; and even in the will of the
servant I found the will to be master" (vol. 2, p. 371).
Whitman's mood toward all things living is remarkably
similar and expresses the same love for life. Malcolm
Cowley discusses Whitman's picture of life in connection
with the dithyrambic "Song of Myself": "In 'Song of
Myself' as originally written, God is neither a person
nor, in the strict sense, even a being; God is an
abstract principle of energy that is manifested in every
living creature.";10 Even though Whitman does not speak
of a "will to power," yet he is extremely generous in
recognizing the autonomy and <u>diffusio sui</u> of all living
things. In the final analysis, this constitutes a sort
of will to power in which no form of life is to be
robbed of its intrinsic energy principle, or its
"godliness." The immediate consequence of the
heightened love for life shared by Whitman and
Nietzsche is a deeper understanding of, and appreciation
for, <u>things in the world</u>, as opposed to those things
projected into the beyond.
     With the affirmation of life reduced to the world
of experience, of actual as opposed to hypothetical
living, it stands to reason that Whitman and Nietzsche
glorify the human body as the ultimate measure of life.
In "Starting from Paumanok," chant 13 closes with this
important and recurring word:

          Behold, the body includes and is the meaning,
               the main concern, and includes and is the
               soul;
          Whoever you are, how superb and how divine is
               your body, or any part of it!

And now the words of Zarathustra on the body:

          Behind your thoughts and feelings, my brother,
          stands a powerful master, an unknown sage --
          he is called Self. He resides in your body,
          he is your body.
               There is more reason in your body, than
          in your best wisdom. (Vol. 2, pp. 300-301)

Only those whose hopes for life transcend the sensual
and empirical try to deny the body and view it as the
Platonic prison of the soul.
     A further example of affirmation is expressed in
the love for the earth. In chant 3 of "A Song of the
Rolling Earth," another dithyrambic poem reminiscent of
the style of <u>Zarathustra</u>, Whitman exclaims:

> I swear the earth shall surely be complete to
>   him or her who shall be complete,
> The earth remains jagged and broken only to
>   him or her who remains jagged and broken.
> I swear there is no greatness or power that
>   does not emulate those of the earth,
> There can be no theory of any account unless
>   it corroborate the theory of the earth.

The earth is not the prison, not the madhouse or
purgatory in the mind of the affirmative thinker, rather
it is a playground and, in a sense, a field of battle.
Nietzsche's exhortation, through the mouth of
Zarathustra, is not only similar in content but in
delivery -- for there can be no casual, intellectual
delivery of one's pledge to the earth:

> The overman is the purpose of the earth. Your
> will should say: the overman <u>shall be</u> the
> purpose of the earth!
>   I entreat you, my brothers, <u>remain true
> to the earth</u> and do not believe those who
> speak to you of extraterrestrial hopes!
>   They are despisers of the body, moribund
> and self-poisoned ones who are weary of the
> earth: may they depart! (Vol. 2, p. 280)

The dithyrambic, primordial calling which is evident in
the words of Whitman and Nietzsche, when they speak for
the earth and therefore speak for the here and now, is
not a mere poetic device; herein lies the truest and
most far-reaching affinity between the two. This manner
of calling is an honest enthusiasm deriving from the
inspiration of a heightened experience in living, or
what I have elsewhere called "lifing." From the acutely
vital affirmation of all living forms, both poets
proceed to the unmitigated affirmation of the earth as
the home of life. Mankind, however, is the living
promise of life, the ultimate synthesis of conscious and
unconscious, so that Whitman and Nietzsche envision a
stronger, heartier, and healthier human being, not
through the intervention of metaphysical teachings, but
through the affirmation of life which must originate in
the respect for one's body.
      "Song of Myself" is the poem which best exemplifies
the kindred thought of Whitman and Nietzsche. This is
so, once again, not merely because of content, but also
because of the manner of delivery. Cowley writes that
Whitman "tramps a perpetual journey and longs for
companions, to whom he will reveal a new world by
washing the gum from their eyes -- but each must then
continue the journey alone" (LC, xx). It will surprise
no one, by now, to learn that Zarathustra also tramps a

lonely journey and has a strong sense of mission,
namely, to announce overman and the transvaluation of
all values, and to be the teacher who rejects his
disciples and sends them forth. In "Song of Myself"
Whitman addresses his anonymous audience:

> Not I, not any one else can travel that road
>   for you,
> You must travel it yourself,
>
> (LC, 80)

while Zarathustra says: "That -- is now my way -- where
is your way? . . . For the way -- there is no such
thing!" (vol. 2, p. 443). When Whitman wants to express
that he is there to assist, but not to carry anyone
along, he writes:

> Here are biscuits to eat and here is milk to
>   drink,
> But as soon as you sleep and renew yourself in
>   sweet clothes I will certainly kiss you
>   with my goodbye kiss and open the gate
>   for your egress hence.
>
> (LC, 81)

Zarathustra desires to maintain the same existential
freedom, for he asserts: "I am a railing along the
stream: hold on to me, whoever can! But I am not your
crutch" (vol. 2, p. 305). On teaching and the teacher's
role, Whitman writes in chant 47:

> I am the teacher of athletes,
> He that by me spreads a wider breast than my
>   own proves the width of my own,
> He most honors my style who learns under it to
>   destroy the teacher.
>
> (LC, 81)

When Zarathustra bids farewell to his disciples, he has
a very similar message:

> Verily, I advise you: go forth from me and
> protect yourselves against Zarathustra! And
> better yet: be ashamed of him! Perhaps he
> has deceived you.
>   One repays a teacher badly if one always
> remains only a disciple. (Vol. 2, p. 339)

At the end of "Song of Myself," Whitman offers hope for
a reunion with his disciples:

> Failing to fetch me at first keep encouraged
> Missing me one place search another,
> I stop some where waiting for you.
>
> (LC, 86)

But to stop and wait is not to set out on the same path
with those who catch up, the indication is; and Whitman
is a forerunner of the twentieth-century existentialists
because he encourages others to follow him only insofar
as it serves to lead one to one's self. Zarathustra
also hints at a possible reunion in symbolic terms:

> Now I bid you lose me and find yourselves; and
> only when you have all denied me shall I
> return to you. (Vol. 2, p. 340)

These words and Whitman's are reminiscent of the Bible,
Matthew 10, wherein is written, "It is enough for a
pupil to be like his teacher, and for the servant to be
like his master." Both Whitman and Nietzsche were
familiar with the Bible, and, like their apostolic
predecessors, they were inspired with the wisdom of what
they expressed. Yet the words of Whitman and Nietzsche
are a transvaluation of the Bible message, rejoicing
more in striking out on new ways than in following the
old. More will be said concerning the manner of
inspiration of these two thinkers toward the conclusion
of this paper.;11
     A well-known Nietzschean tenet is found in an
aphorism of The Gay Science entitled "People in
Preparation":

> The secret which enables the greatest
> fruitfulness and the greatest pleasure to be
> harvested from Dasein is: Live dangerously!
> Build your cities on Vesuvius! Send your
> ships onto uncharted seas! Live at war with
> your neighbors and with yourself! (Vol. 2, p.
> 166)

This exhortation is not romantic bravado, but the
logical consequence of living according to the motto
amor fati. Whitman was no stranger to this manner of
thinking himself, as witnessed once again in his
inspiring and inspired "Song of Myself":

> Long have you timidly waded, holding a plank
>   by the shore,
> Now I will you to be a bold swimmer,
> To jump off in the midst of the sea, and rise
>   again and nod to me and shout, and
>   laughingly dash with your hair.
>
> (LC, 81)

Not only do Whitman and Nietzsche encourage dangerous
living, but they themselves tried to embody this ideal
in their writings, that is, they considered themselves,
in varying degrees, as dangerous and therefore
beneficial to the race. Zarathustra comes down from his
mountain to awaken mankind from the slumber of
inauthentic existence, and he cries out to the masses:

> Where is the lightning which would lick you
> with its tongue? Where is the madness with
> which you must be injected?
> Behold, I teach you the overman: he is
> this lightning, he is this madness! (Vol. 2,
> p. 281)

The sense of power and prophetic energy which Whitman
felt is evident in these lines from "Starting from
Paumanok":

> No dainty dolce affetuoso I,
> Bearded, sun-burnt, gray-neck'd, forbidding, I
>   have arrived . . .
> These, my voice announcing -- I will sleep no
>   more but arise,
> You oceans that have been calm within me! how
>   I feel you, fathomless, stirring,
>   preparing unprecedented waves and storms.

In other words, that which is offered by Whitman and
Nietzsche is no piece of cake; even to follow in their
footsteps requires a sincere reappraisal of one's
comfortable habits and the courage to face the human
abyss. The realm within which the initiate must work is
also conducive to living dangerously, for Whitman and
Nietzsche were adorers of the sun, so much so, in fact,
that their teachings and encounters almost always take
place out in the open, in the wind and the sunshine. It
has already been mentioned that C. G. Jung refers to the
sun as the highest symbol of consciousness; if the work
of Whitman and Nietzsche can be interpreted as bringing
a new gospel of affirmation and _amor fati_ to humanity,
it is important to strip away any background and
traditional underbrush that might be a refuge for those
who prefer to sleep in the darkness. Nietzsche's high
noon, the decisive brightness of which marks the
transition of man to overman, is basically a confession
of his Enlightenment sympathies. Whitman, too, is an
enlightener, and he preferred "scars and faces pitted
with smallpox over all latherers and those that keep out
of the sun" (LC, 81). And if this is not suggestive
enough of Whitman's Enlightenment sympathy, another
passage from the 46th chant of "Song" shows the
correspondence to Nietzsche's Enlightenment task:

> Long enough have you dreamed contemptible
>   dreams,
> Now I wash the gum from your eyes,
> You must habit yourself to the dazzle of the
>   light and of every moment of your life.
>
> (LC, 81)

These words succinctly express what the great 20th
century philosopher Martin Heidegger developed into a
theory of "authentic existence" (<u>eigentliches Dasein</u>);
one is also reminded of Soren Kierkegaard's living in
the faith, which requires a manner of "fear and
trembling" before one's existence in the world with
God. When Whitman speaks of "washing the gum" from our
eyes, he is making a seemingly inflated statement; the
topic of megalomania in Whitman and Nietzsche will be
discussed later, though only briefly.
     Behind the affirmation of life is courage in the
face of change. Change here is not meant in a strictly
social or political sense, but ontologically and
psychologically, in the sense which equates change with
transitoriness and death. There is little in Whitman
that suggests finality or dogma, or the philosophical
system that pretends to be the dictionary of living.
Like Nietzsche, Whitman was a man who worked on an
effect, who desired not disciples, but readers who would
be led to themselves by means of provocative and
essential, as opposed to exhaustively analytical,
observation. And again like Nietzsche, this makes
Whitman vulnerable to that eternal cluster of
unimaginative souls who measure human greatness only in
accordance with the yardstick of convention and baroque
propriety. I submit that when a person, regardless of
the century and place, feels the primordial calling of
life, or participates in the worlding of the world, now
sadly despiritualized and reified as a laboratory
specimen -- such a person does not think or deal in
terms of being, but in terms of <u>becoming</u>, just as the
world which he feels "worlding," or coming into being
within him is constantly transforming. Cowley addresses
this rare and admirable trait in Whitman when he writes
that "the universe was an eternal becoming for Whitman,
a process not a structure, and it had to be judged from
the standpoint of eternity" (LC, xxiv). In "Song of
Myself" Whitman writes:

> And as to you, life, I reckon you are the
>   leavings of many deaths,
> No doubt I have died myself ten thousand times
>   before. . . .
> I depart as air. . . . I shake my white locks
>   at the runaway sun,

          I effuse my flesh in eddies and drift it in
               lacy jags.
          I bequeath myself to the dirt to grow from the
               grass I love,
          If you want me again look for me under your
               bootsoles.
                                        (LC, 4984-86)

Nietzsche's entire philosophical outlook is based, or
rather, deliberately "not based upon" but woven into,
the concept of change and becoming. My dissertation on
the Dionysian aesthetic of Nietzsche addresses the
Dionysian affirmation of becoming and how it governs
Nietzsche's thought. Although to cite scores of
passages would be possible, one insightful observation
from Human, All-too-Human is sufficient to demonstrate
how Nietzsche conceived of becoming:

          Everything which is finished, perfected, is
          held in awe, while everything which is
          becoming is underestimated. In the work of an
          artist no one can watch how the work became
          such; this is to his advantage, for whoever
          sees becoming grows somewhat standoffish. The
          perfected art of representation banishes all
          thought of becoming; it tyrannizes as present
          perfection. For this reason, representational
          artists are chiefly viewed as genial, but not
          so the scientific people. In truth the
          estimation of the former and underestimation
          of the latter is a mere childishness of
          reason. (Vol. 2, p. 554)

Nietzsche's preference for becoming extended into all
areas of his thought, including the moral philosophy.
Two thinkers who were at the same time doers, two
observers who were at the same time participants,
Whitman and Nietzsche found a more fertile ground for
cultivating the Voltairian garden in the soil of
becoming than in retilling the arid soils of the status
quo. Writes Whitman:

          A child said, What is the grass? fetching it
               to me with full hands,
          How could I answer the child? I do not know
               what it is any more than he.
          I guess it must be the flag of my disposition,
               out of hopeful green stuff woven.
                                        (LC, 29)

          In his introduction to the death-bed edition of
Leaves of Grass, Gay Wilson Allen touches upon a central
aspect of Whitman's amor fati, suggesting that

> Whitman worships the human body not only
> because every man or woman is the son or
> daughter of God (a basic tenet of his "new
> religion") but also because it ferries the
> seeds of life, so that each person bridges
> (potentially at least) past and future
> generations.";12

This comment is insightful because Whitman not only glorified man in the present, but spoke often of the coming man, the future person. In the poem entitled "So Long!" Whitman makes a Zarathustrian announcement:

> I announce an end that shall lightly and
>   joyfully meet its translation.
> I announce myriads of youths, beautiful,
>   gigantic sweet-blooded,
> I announce a race of splendid and savage old
>   men.

Clearly Whitman was no longer a young man at the writing of this poem. But the meaning of his words is quite suggestive: man is not "man," as Bertolt Brecht would insist, but man becomes man. Thus far we have seen how certain patterns of affirmation and exuberance in living contribute to an entire semantic field originating with the individual and later encompassing all of humanity and the earth. Nietzsche's conception of man could easily have been uttered by Whitman:

> Man is a rope fastened between beast and
> overman -- a rope over an abyss. . . .
>   The greatness of man is that he is not a
> purpose but a bridge; that which can be loved
> in man is that he is a crossing-over and a
> falling-down (<u>Ubergang und Untergang</u>). (Vol.
> 2, p. 282)

Nietzsche's meaning in this passage, with its typical play on words, is that not all of humanity will negotiate the bridge leading to overman, that is, Nietzsche, like Whitman, foresees sublimation for mankind, when the all-too-human traits are left behind, supposedly in the abyss which only those people are able to cross who have experience in living dangerously.
    It is but a small step from <u>amor fati</u> to <u>amor omnium</u>, and thence to an attitude beyond good and evil. In "Starting from Paumanok" Whitman reveals how he has passed the Nietzschean test of affirmation:

> Omnes! Omnes! let others ignore what they
>   may,

> I make the poem of evil also, I commemorate
>   that part also,
> I am myself just as much evil as good, and my
>   nation is -- and I say there is in fact
>   no evil.

Nietzsche's final word on good and evil is to be found
in the work bearing the title Beyond Good and Evil, but
Zarathustra has an appropriate summary in the form of
his beloved paradox:

> And whosoever must be a creator in things good
> and evil: verily, he must first be an
> annihilator and break values.
>   Hence the highest evil belongs to the
> highest good: but the latter is the creative
> one. (Vol. 2, p. 372)

There can be no real affirmation and love for life, in
the unqualified sense of Whitman and Nietzsche, without
this sovereign attitude toward that which is evil by
tradition or definition.
     One of the dangers of being a spokesman for life,
for humanity and a future humanity, is that the
spokesman runs the risk of indulging in what often
appears to be megalomania. For one thing, a reader's
reaction might be: Who asked you? Who appointed you to
pontificate on our future?, and so on. My feeling on
megalomania is that the term is extremely relative and
that it exemplifies a certain double standard. Divine
megalomania, for example, as it is rendered by Christ
and the Apostles and various religious and political
figures, does not necessarily constitute a breach in the
etiquette of humility, while Nietzsche's megalomania in
Ecce homo, which is actually more subtle and humorous
than most would suspect, is branded as the mark of a
disintegrating personality. The philosophical systems
of Aristotle and Hegel may appear perfectly legitimate
to the professional philosopher, but what of the layman,
and what of the average person who does not wrestle with
omniscience? In short, anyone who speaks out for
humanity, whether directly, as is the case with Whitman
and Nietzsche, or indirectly, as in the case of
philosophers, runs the risk of acquiring a reputation
for delusions and illusions of grandeur. Cowley writes
that Whitman was for a time working "on the Great
Construction of the New Bible," and Cowley continues:
"During those years before the Civil War, Whitman was
afflicted with megalomania to such an extent that he was
losing touch with the realities of American life" (LC,
xxviii). Whitman was restored to reality, apparently,
by the war; it is somewhat ironic that a person should
be restored to sanity by the insanity of warfare.

Nietzsche was not so fortunate, for in his case,
megalomania set in after his experience as an ambulance
orderly in the Franco-Prussian War. Karl Marx, Whitman,
Nietzsche -- to an extent all of these great
nineteenth-century thinkers were megalomaniacs, but it
can be safely concluded that a bit of megalomania is
usually constructive in connection with real thinkers,
but always destructive in connection with dictators.

The question of megalomania raised further
questions on the manner of inspiration peculiar to
certain thinkers. What is the impetus for inflated
proclamations and announcements? Precisely who is
speaking during moments of inflation, and are there any
patterns in the works of those poets who are known to
have written under overpowering inspiration? In the
consideration of these questions the archetypal
psychology of C. G. Jung is invaluable, especially when
differentiating between what is known as megalomania and
what we call the creative urge. Commenting on the
distinct "Eastern quality" of "Song of Myself," Cowley
suggests that Whitman had a mystical experience which
provided him with an ecstasy:

> Such ecstasies consist in a rapt feeling of
> union or identity with God (or the Soul, or
> Mankind, or the Cosmos), a sense of ineffable
> joy leading to the conviction that the seer
> has been released from the limitations of
> space and time and has been granted a direct
> vision of truths impossible to express. (LC,
> xii-xiii)

There are various explanations for this _unio mystica_ of
which Cowley speaks, and none of them is really very
mystical: Jung gives us the theory of archetypes,
Nietzsche would relate the inspiration to the breakdown
of the _principium indivuationis_ as represented by the
Dionysian, and Heidegger, strongly influenced by
Nietzsche, might refer to the experience as a primordial
"worlding" with the world. In _Ecce homo_ Nietzsche
described the inspiration the result of which was _Thus
Spoke Zarathustra_: "One listens, one does not search;
one takes, one does not ask who gives; a thought kindles
like lightning, with necessity, formulated without
hesitation -- I never had a choice" (vol. 2, p. 1131).
The condition of inspiration under which Nietzsche had
written Zarathustra, and Whitman the "Song of Myself,"
was not peculiar to them only. Kierkegaard was also
vulnerable to overpowering inspirations, so that Walter
Lowrie writes in the introduction to _Fear and Trembling_
how Kierkegaard boasted of having written the entire
work _Either/Or_ in only eight months.;13 In addition to
writing under strong pressure from within, Kierkegaard

also suffered from the dubious illness of megalomania,
as witnessed in this entry from his <u>Journal</u>:

> Oh when once I am dead -- then <u>Fear and
> Trembling</u> alone will be enough to give me the
> name of an immortal author. Then it will be
> read, then too it will be translated into
> foreign tongues. People will shudder at the
> frightful pathos of the book.;14

An interesting comparative study might be done on
Kierkegaard and Walt Whitman, beginning with the premise
that both are assertive spokesmen for a heightened
experience in living.

In the case of Whitman, Nietzsche, and Kierkegaard,
it is as if some other were in command during the
writing process -- in terms of Jungian theory, this
"some other" is not one, but a collective of voices, or
the archetype. The individual is not necessarily
speaking in such moments, at least not as the individual
per se; rather, a direct link with the collective
ancestry of humanity is opened up by the unconscious,
wherein the individual submerges, losing his identity
for the duration of the archetypal manifestation. In
Jung's own words:

> The primordial image or archetype is a figure,
> whether it be a daemon, man, or process, that
> repeats itself in the course of history
> wherever creative phantasy is freely
> manifested. Essentially, therefore, it is a
> mythological figure. If we subject these
> images to a closer investigation, we discover
> them to be the formulated resultants of
> countless typical experiences of our
> ancestors. They are, as it were, the psychic
> residue of numberless experiences of the same
> type.;15

The often close procedural and contextual parallels in
the works of Whitman and Nietzsche, who appeared to know
nothing of one another, are at once similar and
dissimilar; similar because each spoke out as the voice
of our collective ancestry, calling for a robust and
earthy affirmation of life, dissimilar because after the
archetype abandoned them to their respective
"personalities," the conscious individual viewed the
unconscious production not in a universal, but in a
personal way. To clarify this point, another
observation by Cowley, who hints at but does not
specifically mention archetypes, is of use to us:

> It would have been better for his strictly
> poetic reputation if [Whitman] had allowed the
> early illuminated Whitman to speak for
> himself, the bohemian or inflated Whitman to
> speak for himself, and the good gray poet to
> speak for himself, each in his separate
> fashion. (LC, xxxii)

Cowley suggests that Whitman thought, or worked, on various planes. Often the unconscious, inspired Whitman would tackle a sober philosophical issue, such as democracy, say, while another issue might have demanded the expertise of the good gray poet. This manner of confusion of tasks was also evident in Nietzsche's life and works, so that he earned the reputation of being a "philosopher-poet." Zarathustra itself is a great lyrical dithyramb and a philosophical essay. But in the case of Whitman and Nietzsche, I think the ambivalence in style is a positive, indeed, deliberate trait. Carl Jung refers to extroverted as opposed to introverted types; an example of a consistent introvert is Friedrich Schiller, whose works maintain a careful observance of the subject object relationship and are therefore rather analytical in nature.;16 Whitman and Nietzsche crossed over the lines of introvert versus extrovert with prolific skill, or rather, with natural inclination. Since neither proposed a doctrine or projected a system of thought, since neither desired to use literature as a "moral institution," it is in keeping with their motto of "follow me to follow yourself" that the poet should mingle with the philosopher in an inextricable way.

Addressing the style of "Song of Myself," Cowley writes that the doctrines are not expounded logically, but presented dramatically as the new convictions of the hero, as successive unfoldings of the states of mind (LC, iii). This description pertains to _Zarathustra_ with equal precision. If we consider for a moment the type of inspiration that went into the two great poems, is it not impossible for the result to assume any other form? The wandering of the hero, with its revelation and dramatic presentation of truths or findings, corresponds to the manner of inspiration: Nietzsche tells us that he "had no choice" in the writing of _Zarathustra_, as if the entire drama were simply forced through him. Neither Whitman nor Nietzsche was a firm believer in logic as the summa of human being, so it stands to reason that both preferred to abide by their respective inspirations, rather than to translate the inspired production into grammatic format, thereby destroying its greatness. A testimony on the preference of Whitman is in the poem "When I Heard the Learn'd Astronomer":

When I heard the learn'd astronomer,
When the proofs, the figures, were ranged in
     columns before me,
When I was shown the charts and diagrams, to
     add, divide and measure them,
How soon unaccountable I became tired and
     sick,
Till rising and gliding out I wander'd off by
     myself,
In the mystical moist night-air, and from time
     to time,
Look'd up in perfect silence at the stars.

Hence what the works of Nietzsche and Whitman truly
have in common is the voice of humanity which sings out
and disrupts the principle of individuation, calling
instead with a collective voice to reinforce our faith
in ourselves, in our good Earth as opposed to the land
of the Hyperboreans. Whitman was fond of "singing"
rather than speaking or lecturing, and Zarathustra's
dithyrambs, in the form of the nine poems called the
Dionysus Dithyrambs, are subtitled "the songs of
Zarathustra." It is the dithyrambic love of life which
is behind the "singing" of the respective thinkers. In
chant 33 of "Song of Myself," Whitman exclaims: "I am
the man. . . . I suffered. . . . I was there." In the
place of "the man" one could substitute "man" or even
"mankind," for it is the experience of human being which
Whitman delights in and points out to us. Nietzsche's
word was ecce homo, behold the man, even as it was
uttered by Pilate to designate the godman Jesus. "Song
of Myself" and Ecce homo have this in common: that they
seek not to glorify the self for the purpose of
self-glorification, but to reveal, in so doing, what
there is in each of us, in each human being, waiting to
be realized. "Beyond the man" has that special meaning
attached to it, which focusses on the individual as a
god and a hero unto himself. For although according to
Jungian theory the individual personality succumbs to
the collective unconscious during the inspiration, still
the experience is a temporary one, confined to rare
moments, so that when the personality of a Whitman or a
Nietzsche emerges into the conscious world once again,
it is with a deeper understanding of what lies below the
surface within each of us.
     In his excellent introduction to the first edition
of Leaves, Malcolm Cowley is concerned with the nature
of that work and its manner of delivery. Speaking in
particular of "Song of Myself," Cowley suggests:

     The real nature of the poem becomes clearer
     when it is considered in relation to quite
     another list of works, even though Whitman had

212   Adrian Del Caro

> [probably] read none of them in 1855. . . .
> that list might include Blake's prophetic
> books . . . and Nietzsche's <u>Thus Spake
> Zarathustra</u>. . . . "Song of Myself" should be
> judged, I think, as one of the great inspired
> (and sometimes insane) prophetic works that
> have appeared at intervals in the Western
> world. (LC, xii)

In his preface to the <u>Leaves</u>, Whitman maintains that "the prescient poet projects himself centuries ahead and judges performer or performance after the changes of time. Does it live through them? Does it still hold on untired?" (LC, 21). That which will concern humanity for centuries to come is the nature of the race and the understanding which we try to arrive at concerning our place in the universe. Surely Whitman contributes to such an understanding, and surely, too, he will continue to be read for centuries to come. Nietzsche's was a similar attitude toward change and the future. In <u>Ecce homo</u> he conceded; "It is not yet my time, some people are born posthumously" (vol. 2, p. 1099). And we recall, of course, that during his conscious lifetime, until January 1889, Nietzsche was not known outside of a small circle familiar with the Danish comparatist Georg Brandes. As was the case with Whitman, Nietzsche's works were at first more favorably received outside his native country. But this, too, is a good test of a real poet: Does he flatter and cajole his readers, does he offer <u>divertissement</u> but no criticism? How often must it happen that a country's greatest writers, because they represent humanity and attempt to expose the all-too-human, are first acknowledged in foreign lands, where the message must necessarily fall somewhat short?

When Whitman died in 1892, Nietzsche had already been "dead" for three long years, that is to say, he had been in a condition of madness. He lingered until 1900, possibly choosing the threshold of the twentieth century to die, for his Zarathustra taught that "one must die at the right time" (vol. 2, p. 333). Oblivious to his growing fame, Nietzsche could do nothing to prevent the distortion of his works which was being perpetrated by his audacious sister. Nietzsche's life had been a catastrophe, but who was Walt Whitman? The opening words of chant 24 in "Song" tell us:

> Walt Whitman, an American, one of the roughs,
>   a kosmos,
> Disorderly fleshy and sensual . . . eating,
>   drinking and breeding,

> No sentimentalist . . . no stander above men
> and women or apart from them . . . no
> more modest than immodest.
>
> (LC, 48)

It is hard to picture Nietzsche saying, "Fritz
Nietzsche, a German, a rough, a kosmos. . . ." This
difference is a major one, for it reflects what each
thinker ultimately stood for Whitman stood for his
country, for democracy's greatest experiment, for a
better race through the hearty brand of living he
celebrated in the States. Nietzsche, however, the
voluntary exile, much like his predecessor Heinrich
Heine, was an aristocratic person whose self-imposed
isolation and stringent cultural demands denied him a
place in the nationalistic fervor of Germany. Perhaps
this difference can be expressed in other words; Whitman
represented the hope and wild expansionist dream of a
young nation, while Nietzsche represented the dying
breed of "good Europeans," the type of person who was
everywhere forced into hiding by the nationalistic
movements and doctrines of those European nations
rapidly trying to scratch out their borders in the tired
soil of the Old World. Whitman sings the en masse, and
although his projected new people are liberated, still
they are "a gang of kosmos and prophets en masse" (LC,
22). The very term "en masse" connoted the herd to
Nietzsche, and the herd should exist, according to his
theory, only as the soil for the master. Whereas
Whitman's robust iconoclasm enabled him to laugh at
style and artistic convention, Nietzsche prided himself
on being a stylist. Whereas Whitman was no "stander
above men and women," Nietzsche certainly was,
especially with regard to women. Whoever thinks this
difference is but a small one had better ask a woman.
It even became important to Nietzsche, toward the end of
his conscious life, to maintain that he was not of
German but noble Polish descent. Whitman had honor in
his lifetime, the recognition of the great philosopher
Emerson, whom Nietzsche also admired, while Nietzsche
himself could hardly earn a review of his books, and
during his consciousness never earned a good one.

   Yet that which makes Walt Whitman and Nietzsche
thinkers for our time is a deeper, more underlying
trait. They recognized that religion was on its way out
as the fabric for values. According to Whitman, "It is
. . . inconsistent with the reality of the soul to admit
that there is anything in the known universe more divine
than men and women" (LC, 15). And according to
Nietzsche's alter ego Zarathustra: "Dead are all gods,
now we want that the overman should live" (vol. 2, p.
340). When ancient values lose their power, when the
ancien regime crumbles and various splinter factions war

among themselves for political leverage, those who see
beyond the politics of their contemporaries stand the
greatest chance for surviving into the future and
maintaining their healthy, sane, and down-to-earth
standards for future generations. Herein lies the
importance of Whitman and Nietzsche for our time.

NOTES

1. Vincent Cosentino, "Walt Whitman's Influence on
Thomas Mann, the 'Non-Political' Writer," in _Vergleichen
und Verändern_: Festschrift für Helmut Motekat, ed.
Albrecht Goetze and Günther Pflaum (Hueber: Munich,
1970), p. 232.

2. Constantine M. Stavrou, _Whitman and Nietzsche_
(Chapel Hill: University of North Carolina Press, 1964),
p. 166. Stavrou presents a somewhat declawed and
Whitmanized picture of Nietzsche. To an extent, this
result of Stavrou's otherwise informative study may rest
on his having falsely read into Nietzsche certain traits
which are not really there. On page 23, for example,
Stavrou writes: "The Superman is best exemplified,
Nietzsche continues, by Zarathustra, an 'idealistic'
type of a higher kind of man, half 'saint,' half
'genius.'" Had Stavrou consulted a correct translation,
or perhaps read the German himself, this unfortunate
error would not have been made. What Nietzsche is
really saying in the respective passage, which is not
easy to translate, is that his Zarathustra and the
overman _do not_ represent some "idealistic" half-saint
and half-genius type. In fact, Nietzsche is adamant
about making this distinction clear. Throughout his
book Stavrou depicts Nietzsche as considerably more
idealistic than he was, and therefore draws free
parallels to Whitman. There is little or no mention of
the Dionysian aesthetic and the role of annihilation in
Nietzsche's philosophy, for example. Walter Kaufmann
offers this translation of the passage in question: "The
word 'overman' . . . has been understood almost
everywhere with the utmost innocence in the sense of
those very values whose opposite Zarathustra was meant
to represent -- that is, as an 'idealistic' type of a
higher kind of man, half 'saint,' half 'genius'"
(Nietzsche, _On the Genealogy of Morals and Ecce homo_,
trans. Walter Kaufmann [New York: Vintage, 1967], p.
261). Had Stavrou consulted the foreword to _Ecce homo_,
he would have discovered the same _denial_ of Zarathustra
and the overman as an idealistic type stressed once
again, inasmuch as Nietzsche often repeated those points
which he felt would be misunderstood or interpreted in a
naive way (vol. 2, p. 1067). Stavrou also makes use of
incorrect translations in citing the titles of
Nietzsche's works, example, _Joyful Wisdom_ instead of the

correct <u>Gay Science</u>, and so on. For the sake of
accuracy and consistency, the translations of Walter
Kaufmann are by a long shot the best available in
English.

     3. Friedrich Nietzsche, <u>Die Frohliche Wissenshaft</u>,
in <u>Nietzsche Werke in drei Banden</u>, ed. Karl Schlechta
(Munich: Hanser, 1966), vol. 2, p. 256. Further
reference to this three-volume collection of Nietzsche's
works will be made parenthetically within text. All
translations from the German are my own, unless
otherwise indicated.

     4. Walt Whitman, <u>Democratic Vistas</u>, in <u>The
Complete Prose of Walt Whitman</u> (New York: Pellegrini and
Cudahy, 1948), vol. 2, p. 231.

     5. Stavrou, p. 36.

     6. Whitman, <u>Democratic Vistas</u>, p. 226.

     7. V. K. Chari, "Whitman and the Language of the
Romantics," <u>Etudes Anglaises</u>, 30, No. 3 (1977): 314-28.

     8. Whitman, <u>Democratic Vistas</u>, p. 233.

     9. Ibid., p. 235.

     10. Walt Whitman, <u>Leaves of Grass</u>, ed. Malcolm
Cowley (Harmondworth: Penguin, 1978), p. xiv. Further
reference to this "original edition" of <u>Leaves</u> will be
made parenthetically in text as (LC, xiv), etc.

     11. In the poem "Myself and Mine," Whitman makes
another statement to this effect: "I charge you forever
reject those who would expound me, for I cannot expound
myself."

     12. Walt Whitman, <u>Leaves of Grass</u>, ed. Gay Wilson
Allen (New York: New American Library, 1958), p. xiii.

     13. Soren Kierkegaard, <u>Fear and Trembling</u> and <u>The
Sickness unto Death</u>, trans. Walter Lowrie (New York:
Doubleday, 1954), p. 14.

     14. Ibid., p. 18.

     15. C. G. Jung, <u>Contributions to Analytical
Psychology</u>, trans. H. G. and Cary F. Baynes, 4th ed.
(London: Routledge & Kegan Paul, 1948), p. 246.

     16. Ibid., p. 236.

21.
Whitman in the Eighties:
A Bibliographical Essay

WILLIAM WHITE

Finding the right words to sum up Walt Whitman
scholarship in the years 1980 to 1984, the period of
time that has elapsed between the conference on "Walt
Whitman, Here and Now," and the time of this essay, is
not just difficult, it's all but impossible. Merely to
cite the statistics makes one gasp, and they are not
even complete: 373 articles about the poet and his
works, 144 book reviews, 59 chapters in books, 23 books,
29 doctoral dissertations, and 9 "new" editions of
Whitman writings. To call the poet of <u>Leaves of Grass</u> a
man for all seasons is accurate enough, except that the
seasons go on and on and on. There is no end to the
research and the critical and scholarly production of
Whitmaniana.
   In a review essay of "The Whitman Project," <u>The
Collected Writings of Walt Whitman</u>, being published by
the New York University Press, Ed Folsom of the
University of Iowa wrote in the <u>Philological Quarterly</u>,
61 (Fall 1982), 393:

> The abundance of important work -- textual,
> bibliographical, biographical and critical --
> done on Whitman in the last couple of years is
> a testament of his largeness, his multitudes.
> The project to understand Whitman is -- like
> <u>Leaves of Grass</u> was -- an ongoing process:
> Whitman's message continues to grow as it is
> read in new lights. Everything about Whitman
> scholarship right now is in flux,
> half-evolved, incomplete, yet energetic, at
> moments brashly confident, future-oriented.
> What could be more appropriate?

If this was true in 1982, it is equally true in 1984.

However, since one must choose the most important publications of the 1980-84 period, the place to begin is with the newly edited additions to Whitman's Collected Writings, especially the three volumes of Leaves of Grass: A Textual Variorum of the Printed Poems, edited by Sculley Bradley, Harold W. Blodgett, Arthur Golden, and William White, which was issued late in 1980. If, as is the case, the Complete Writings of Walt Whitman (which, by the way, were not truly complete) published in 1902 by G. P. Putnam's Sons is still in use 82 years later, then one may well expect the NYU Press Collected Writings to be the standard Whitman text in the year 2084. Next in importance is the six volume edition of Whitman's Notebooks and Uncollected Prose Manuscripts, edited by Edward F. Grier of the University of Kansas, which appeared in August 1984.

Still to be added to the 21 volumes of the Collected Writings currently in print are 5 volumes of Journalism, now in the hands of the printers, Arthur Golden's edition of Leaves of Grass: A Textual Variorum of the Manuscript Poems; and finally, the fully descriptive Whitman Bibliography. As unpublished letters continue to turn up at a rate of one or two a month, a seventh volume of Correspondence is likely, plus a comprehensive index to all the Collected Writings.

Enumerative bibliographies of Whitman go back many years and are still issued regularly in the Walt Whitman Quarterly Review, but we presently have two monuments of this kind of useful and valuable research, Scott Giantvalley's Walt Whitman, 1838-1939: A Reference Guide (Boston: G. K. Hall, 1981), and Donald D. Kummings' Walt Whitman, 1940-1975: A Reference Guide (Boston: G. K. Hall, 1982). Giantvalley has an annotated chronological list of 4,879 items, and Kummings 3,172 annotated items, and anyone working seriously on Whitman from now on must first consult these two highly satisfactory volumes. Unfortunately, they are already ten years out of date, but that situation will surely be remedied in the not too distant future.

Among the editions of Whitman's poetry and prose produced in the last four years, two are worth singling out. William Everson, a printer and a poet once known as Brother Antoninus, has taken the Preface to the first (1855) Leaves of Grass, which is set in long lines of prose and is typographically very unattractive, and rearranged the entire text into verse form, calling the volume American Bard: The Original Preface to Leaves of Grass (New York: The Viking Press, 1982). The spelling is modernized and punctuation added, but the order of Whitman's words is left unchanged. The result, says

poet Karl Shapiro, "is electrifying. What Everson has
done is one of those simple acts of perception which
changes everything." What we now have is a poem that
has been masquerading as prose for years.

The second noteworthy edition is Justin Kaplan's
selection of Walt Whitman: Complete Poetry and Collected
Prose (New York: The Library of America, 1982), which
includes in its 1,380 pages the 1855 Leaves of Grass,
the complete 1891-92 "death-bed edition," the Complete
Prose Works, 1892 (Specimen Days, Collect, Notes Left
Over, Pieces in Early Youth, November Boughs, Good-Bye
My Fancy, and Memoranda), and "Supplementary Prose,"
consisting of "The Eighteenth Presidency!," Emerson's
1855 letter and Whitman's reply, and Whitman's notes to
various editions of Leaves. There is also a chronology
of the poet's life, ending with a few brief notes on the
text. The general reader could hardly ask for more than
this handsomely printed volume, which is well edited and
produced on acid-free paper to guarantee a long life.
Whitman, along with Hawthorne, Melville, and Stowe, has
been honored in the inaugural volumes of the highly
acclaimed and widely reviewed Library of America Series.
Indeed, Whitman has come a long way since he paid to
have the first Leaves printed in Brooklyn in 1855.

Another edited volume is Walt Whitman: The Measure
of His Song (Minneapolis: Holy Cow! Press, 1981),
compiled by James M. Perlman, Ed Folsom, and Dan
Campion. This compilation is not of Whitman's writings,
but of writings about Whitman, or more precisely,
responses to Whitman, 33 prose commentaries and 67
poems, written between 1855 and 1981. Beginning with
Emerson's famous letter, the attractively designed
book contains responses to Whitman from Henry David
Thoreau, Harrison Blake, Ezra Pound, D. H. Lawrence,
Allen Ginsberg, Louis Simpson, Theodore Roethke, and
Robert Creeley among others, plus an engaging
introduction by Ed Folsom, "Talking Back to Whitman,"
and a bibliography of about 300 poems and more than 125
essays along with eighteen photographs. Not only is it
a delightful book to handle and read, it gives one
important and joyful glimpses into the manner in which
sensitive readers and writers have "absorbed" Whitman as
he asked America to do 130 years ago.

Recognized from the time of the appearance of the
very first volume in 1906 as a very important and
absolutely indispensable source of intimate details,
Horace Traubel's With Walt Whitman in Camden never sold
well, hence the many changes in publishers. Volume 2
came out in 1908, Volume 3 in 1914, Volume 4 not until
1953, Volume 5 in 1964, and now Volume 6, edited by
Traubel's daughter Gertrude Traubel and William White
(Carbondale: Southern Illinois University Press, 1982).
It is far more than an account of Whitman's last four

years, spent in declining health; Whitman's
conversations with his young disciple give us the raw
material for biography to be found in illuminating and
touching moments as the poet recalls friends, foes, and
countless incidents among all the talk, talk, and
endless talk.

Of all the books and studies of Whitman in the four
years being surveyed, the most widely and
enthusiastically reviewed, distributed, and read was
Justin Kaplan's Walt Whitman: A Life (New York: Simon
and Schuster, 1980). It certainly was not meant to be a
study of the poetry, but a readable biography, and even
at that Kaplan had no intention of replacing Gay Wilson
Allen's 1955 life, The Solitary Singer, which remains by
far the fullest and best biography we have of the poet.
The Kaplan life of Whitman does fill in a number of
gaps, however, work that comes out of 30 years of
scholarship, and as a result we have more details of the
poet's later life, some of them gleaned from Traubel.
These years are somewhat neglected by Allen, largely
because he had to trim his biography at the publisher's
request and felt it best to make the cuts after
Whitman's productive years had been recounted. If one
reports that Kaplan is sometimes more readable than
Allen it in no way diminishes Allen's major contribution
to Whitman biography, though it does explain why
Kaplan's life of America's greatest poet has made him
come alive for countless readers who might otherwise
only remember Whitman from a high school or college
literary history or anthology.

The same can be said about another commercial -- as
distinct from academic -- publication Paul Zweig's Walt
Whitman: The Making of the Poet (New York: Basic Books,
1984). Most interesting to me is the fact that this
"study" of a poet by a poet (for that is what it is)
should be published by Basic Books for general
distribution rather than by a university press for
scholars and critics. One can only conclude from this
that Whitman has become a much more popular figure in
America. Restricting his view to Whitman's formative
years, when he was a newspaperman and editor and author
of very mediocre short stories and derivative verses,
Zweig hopes to tell us how such an individual became,
with Leaves of Grass, our most original and authentic
poet. Not all poets write a readable prose, but Zweig
has written clearly (though, regrettably, with numerous
gaffes) and with some insight about Whitman's family,
his jobs, his reading, and his literary relationships.
We also get some perception of the relationship between
the poet's developing personality and his highly
original art. But the myth, if not the miracle, of how
this unexciting and almost drab hack journalist became
at the age of 35 the Walt Whitman of Leaves of Grass is

left unexplained by Zweig, just as it was left
unexplained by the last full attempt, made ten years ago
in Floyd Stovall's excellent The Foreground of Leaves of
Grass (Charlottesville: University Press of Virginia,
1974).

Without meaning at all to do so, Jerome Loving, in
his Emerson, Whitman, and the American Muse (Chapel Hill
and London: The University of North Carolina Press,
1982), by tracing the close relationship between the two
great figures of the American nineteenth century,
furnishes us with more possibilities for why Whitman
became Walt Whitman the poet than either Zweig or
Stovall. It was Emerson who turned the trick, as we
have more than suspected all along, and brought Whitman
from simmering to a poetic boiling point. Meant for
specialists, this fresh and thoughtful study could only
be written in the light of previous research, especially
the more recent psychological studies that have been
done of Whitman and of Emerson.

Other important studies, representing foremost
scholars at work in the 1980s, are seen in Harold
Aspiz's Walt Whitman and the Body Beautiful (Urbana and
London: University of Illinois Press, 1980), which
offers a wide-ranging investigation of the relationship
between literature and nineteenth-century scientific and
pseudoscientific treatises to support the claim that
Leaves of Grass may be "read as a guidebook to the
secrets of health, social justice, and spiritual
advancement," and in C. Carroll Hollis' Language and
Style in Leaves of Grass (Baton Rouge and London:
Louisiana State University Press, 1983), which looks in
great detail at the stylistic changes between the early
and later editions of Leaves, as well as at Whitman's
uncollected poetry and prose, for the use made of speech
acts, such as negation, metonymy, and metaphor.

Two slighter works, more of a gathering together of
previously discovered material, are Walter H. Eitner's
Walt Whitman's Western Jaunt (Lawrence: Regent's Press
of Kansas, 1981), a well-illustrated collection of
anecdotes and particulars of the poet's 1879 trip to the
Colorado Rockies, to show how Whitman "reordered his
experiences" for the pose he maintained in Specimen
Days; and James Woodresses' edition of Critical Writings
on Walt Whitman (Boston: G. K. Hall, 1983), a collection
of 57 early reviews and reactions by Whitman's
contemporaries in essays, articles, letters, poems, and
two original pieces (by Jerome Loving and Roger
Asselineau), which give us an overview of the reception
of Whitman and his writings from 1855 and the Emerson
letter to the present time. Included are the reactions
of Thoreau, Edward Everett Hale, Anne Gilchrist, John
Burroughs, R. M. Bucke, Sidney Lanier, Swinburne, and,
more lately, Roger Asselineau, Richard Chase, James E.

Miller, Jr., Floyd Stovall, Edwin Haviland Miller, and
Gay Wilson Allen. One might, nevertheless, have wished
for more recent essays since there are only eight from
after 1955. For a view of Whitman here and now, one
must look elsewhere.

The learned journals paid rather wide attention,
usually favorable, to Betsy Erkkila's Walt Whitman among
the French: Poet and Myth (Princeton: Princeton
University Press, 1980), in which she suggests that all
French movements that influenced twentieth-century
American writers actually came in large part from
Whitman. Of considerably less importance and wholly
different in style -- really more of a tribute -- is a
long poem by Philip Dacey, Gerard Manley Hopkins Meets
Walt Whitman in Heaven and Other Poems (Great
Barrington, Mass.: Penmaen Press, 1982).

Among the more recent books, two are worth
commenting on. The first, Stephen Tapscott's American
Beauty: William Carlos Williams and the Tradition of
Modernist Whitman (New York: Columbia University Press,
1984), is directed to those involved in modernist
criticism and approaches esoterica in its specialist
jargon. On balance, the work is of more interest to
Williams' admirers than to Whitman readers. The second,
Dear Brother Walt: The Letters of Thomas Jefferson
Whitman, edited by Dennis Berthold and Kenneth M. Price
(Kent, Ohio: The Kent State University Press, 1984), is
much more wide-ranging, not only giving us an intimate
view of Whitman family life as seen through the eyes of
Jeff, the poet's favorite brother, but a look at social
history in America in the Civil War period and after.
Jeff Whitman was a highly successful civil engineer in
St. Louis and elsewhere who rose from the poet's "divine
average" and may very well have served, in his close
early relationship with Walt, as the stimulus for his
brother's Calamus emotion, as Horace Traubel suggested.

Among the doctoral dissertations on Whitman written
in the past few years, there is no discernable trend;
their topics vary enormously, as can be seen from the
following titles: "Collage Techniques and Epic Traits
in Modernist Poems by Walt Whitman, Guillaume
Apollinaire, and T. S. Eliot," "Walt Whitman and the
American Estimate of Nature: A Study in the Rhetoric of
Environmental Reform," "Apocalyptic Motif in Selected
Poems of Walt Whitman," "A Study of the Two Complete
Translations of Walt Whitman's Leaves of Grass into
Italian," "Lists in Literature: Homer, Whitman, Joyce,
Borges," "Melville's Battle-Pieces and Whitman's
Drum-Taps: Two Northern Poets Interpret the Civil War,"
"Our Muse in a Golden Frame: A Study of Whitman, Money,
and Language," and "Walt Whitman's Language and Style,"
among others. Variety is the spice of living Whitman
studies in academia.

The same variety exists on the learned periodical front. There are still four Whitman magazines: <u>The West Hills Review: A Walt Whitman Journal</u> (Huntington, N.Y.: Walt Whitman Birthplace Association), <u>The Mickle Street Review</u> (Camden, N.J.: Walt Whitman House Association), <u>Calamus: Walt Whitman Quarterly, International</u> (Tokyo: Taibundo Ltd.), and <u>Walt Whitman Quarterly Review</u> (Iowa City: The University of Iowa). WWQR has replaced the <u>Walt Whitman Review</u>, which was discontinued by the Wayne State University Press in 1982, and although Charles E. Feinberg has relinquished his co-editorship, he remains its "angel" in more ways than one. The <u>Review</u> is still edited by William White, with Ed Folsom of the University of Iowa as co-editor and James M. Perlman as assistant editor.

It is impossible to generalize about what Whitman specialists, be they critics, scholars, or students, are commenting on in these organs. Occasionally there will be an article or two, or a chapter in a book, on the subject of Whitman's homosexuality, with Justin Kaplan, Paul Zweig, Gay Wilson Allen, and most of the other biographers not sidestepping the "issue" (though for some of us it is simply not an issue since there is still no real evidence that Whitman was a practicing homosexual, though he had many young male friends), and the writers in the gay magazines feeling that Whitman was one of them because his <u>Calamus</u> and <u>Children of Adam</u> poems are full of homoerotic imagery. In the main, contributors to the periodicals prefer dealing with other subjects, as the table of one issue of <u>WWQR</u> demonstrates: "Dating Whitman's Language Studies," "Uroboric Incest in Whitman's 'The Sleepers,'" "On Whitman, Dickinson, and Readers," "The Case of Dr. Bowen: An Unknown Whitman Letter Recommending an Army Doctor," "Whitman and Spenser's 'E. K.,'" "Richard Selzer: Poet of the Body and Poet of the Soul," and "Whitman in China," plus three reviews of Whitman books, the usual current bibliography, and an unpublished letter (to Jeanette Gilder) on the back cover.

If one wishes to get a picture of Whitman in the here and now, a fleeting glance can be seen in what may seem an unlikely place, the Walt Whitman Supplement to <u>The Long-Islander</u> of May 31, 1984. Here, in the four pages headed "Walt Whitman and 1984," 12 professors each tried to sum up the poet of <u>Leaves of Grass</u> in about 350 words or so. R. W. French finds Whitman where he was in 1855: "still out ahead of us, a lonely figure down the road, looking back to see if we are following. We are, but at a distance." Robert E. Morsberger feels that Whitman would have been appalled at the "me" generation of today, while Florence B. Freedman asks, "Is Whitman with us in this year of ominous prophecy?" and finds that there is evidence of his presence. Ed Folsom

believes in <u>Leaves of Grass</u> as an on-going answer to
Orwell's "newspeak," and C. Carroll Hollis believes that
Whitman's day "was no lighter, no darker than our own,"
and that "clearly '1984' is not inevitable while Whitman
lives." Melvin Cherno discovered that his first-year
University of Virginia students did not respond at all
to "As I Ebb'd with the Ocean of Life," but he himself,
a professor of history who had felt no prior admiration
for Whitman, was "extraordinarily impressed and moved by
it." Harold Aspiz's statement was that "perhaps our
need in 1984 is not so much for politicians as it is for
national poets -- and for Whitman, too -- to awaken us
to our democratic destinies and to a respect for the
sacredness of all life." Gay Wilson Allen, for his
part, saw Whitman's current stature as on the rise, with
Paul Zweig's study, Edward F. Grier's edition of
<u>Notebooks and Unpublished Prose Manuscripts</u>, and
Whitman, along with Emily Dickinson, being enshrined in
May 1984 in The Poets' Corner of the Cathedral Church of
St. John the Divine in New York City, the first poets so
honored. Whitman, like George Orwell, says Jerome
Loving, "knew that democracy was often down but never
out in such 'imperfect' societies as Paris and London"
(and America, I might add). While Whitman would be
unhappy with today's "Star of France," now headed by a
Marxist regime, reports Roger Asselineau, "despite our
politicians, grass still grows in France. Long live
<u>Leaves of Grass</u>." Milton Hindus, recalling President
Ronald Reagan's conferring of the Medal of Freedom
posthumously on Whittaker Chambers in March 1984,
reminds us that Chambers, as a young Communist, had "a
particular affinity to Walt Whitman" and that this
enthusiasm survived Chambers' conversion "and may even
have contributed to it -- another instance of the
mysterious love for one's native land" which Whitman
inspired in many. Finally, James Perrin Warren likens
Orwell's and Whitman's "free and intelligent command of
the 'expression-spirit' of [the English] language, which
was necessarily connected to the political and moral
regeneration the post-war world required." In sum,
cautious optimism seems to be the attitude adopted by
these commentators on the creators of <u>1984</u> and <u>Leaves of</u>
<u>Grass</u>.

     As for the current field of Whitman scholarship in
general, the word seems to be diversity and again,
diversity. And that is as it should be, for the man and
his writings are as diverse as are "These States," as
Whitman called America, and within that diversity <u>Leaves</u>
<u>of Grass</u> lives long and tall.

WALT WHITMAN
HERE AND NOW

APRIL 25 - 26, 1980

A Conference *in* Celebration *of the* 125th
Anniversary *of the* Publication of

Leaves *of* Grass

Hofstra University

CONFERENCES AT HOFSTRA UNIVERSITY

Publication Dates:

George Sand Centennial - November 1976   Vol. I - Spring 1980

Heinrich von Kleist Bicentennial - November 1977   Vol. II - Spring 1980

The Chinese Woman - December 1977

George Sand: Her Life, Her Works, Her Influence -   Vol. III - Fall 1980
     April 1978

William Cullen Bryant and His America - October 1978   Vol. IV - 1980

The Trotsky-Stalin Conflict and Russia in the 1920's -   Vol. V - 1980
     March 1979

Albert Einstein Centennial - November 1979   Vol. VI - 1981

Renaissance Venice Symposium - March 1980   Vol. VII - 1981

Sean O'Casey - March 1980   Spring 1981

Walt Whitman - April 1980   Vol. VIII - 1981

Nineteenth Century Women Writers - November 1980   Vol. IX - 1982

Fedor Dostoevski - April 1981   Vol. X - 1983

Gotthold Ephraim Lessing - November 1981   Vol. XI

Johann Wolfgang von Goethe - April 1982   Vol. XII

Twentieth Century Women Writers - November 1982   Vol. XIII

Jose Ortega y Gasset, 1883-1983 - Centennial Celebration   Vol. XIV
     Spring 1983

Romanticism in the Old and the New World - Celebrating the Vol. XV
     Bi-Centennials of Washington Irving, Stendhal, and
     Vasilii Andreevich Zhukovskii -- 1783-1983 - Fall 1983

WALT WHITMAN CONFERENCE

PROGRAM

CONFERENCE DIRECTOR: Robert N. Keane
                                 Chair, Dept. of English

CONFERENCE COORDINATORS: Natalie Datlof
                                 Alexej Ugrinsky

CONFERENCE COMMITTEE:

                                 Joseph G. Astman
                                 Stanley Brodwin
                                 Edward Chalfant
                                 Arthur Gregor
                                 Rhoda Nathan
                                 Ruth Prigozy

COOPERATING INSTITUTIONS:

                                 Hempstead Public Library
                                     Irene Duszkiewicz, Director
                                 Huntington Historical Society
                                     Marian Adams, President
                                 Nassau County Office of Cultural Development
                                     Marcia E. O'Brien, Director
                                 Smithtown Historical Society
                                     Edward Hayden, President
                                 Walt Whitman Birthplace Association
                                     William T. Walter, President

<u>Thursday, April 24, 1980</u>

<u>Pre-Conference Events</u>

4:00 P.M.

Hofstra University Library, David Filderman Gallery
Department of Special Collections - 9th Floor

William Heyen - Poetry Readings

Author of four volumes of poems, grew up on Long
Island, and his volume, <u>Long Island Light</u>, contains
many poems set on the Island.

7:00

Hempstead Public Library
115 Nichols Court at Washington St.
(2 blocks from Holiday Inn Motel)
Hempstead, NY

<u>Greetings from Hofstra University</u>

James M. Shuart, President

Concert by Jeff Warner and Jeff Davis featuring
music of the Whitman era.

Exhibition - Books from the Walt Whitman Collection
on loan from Walt Whitman Birthplace.

Wine and cheese Reception.

<u>Friday, April 25, 1980</u>

9:00 - 10:00 A.M.

<u>Registration</u>   David Filderman Gallery
Dept. of Special Collections
Hofstra University Library - 9th Floor

<u>Reception</u>

10:00

Opening of conference and Walt Whitman Exhibition

<u>Greetings from the Hofstra University Community</u>

Joseph G. Astman, Director
University Center for Cultural & Intercultural Studies

Robert C. Vogt, Dean, HCLAS

Walter Fillin, President, Hofstra Library Associates

Marguerite Regan, Director, Dept. of Special Collections

<u>Friday, April 25, 1980 (cont'd.)</u>

10:30   <u>Opening Address</u>:

                               William White, Editor, <u>Walt Whitman Review</u>
                                        Oakland University, Rochester, MI

                               "The Current State of Whitman Studies."

                               Greetings from Charles E. Feinberg

11:00 A.M. - 12:30 P.M.   <u>PANEL I: THE WORLD OF WALT WHITMAN</u>

                               Chair: Rhoda Nathan
                                       Dept. of English, Hofstra University

                               "Whitman's World View: A Contemporaneous Message."
                               Howard L. Parsons, University of Bridgeport
                               Bridgeport, CT

                               "Walt Whitman and New York."
                               Paul Alan Marx, Harvard University
                               Cambridge, MA

                               "Whitman's Attitude Toward the Civil War."
                               William Burrison, Philadelphia, PA

                               "Walt Whitman: The Critical Heritage."
                               Milton Hindus, Brandeis University
                               Waltham, MA

12:30 - 1:45   <u>Lunch</u> Dining Rooms AB, Student Center, North Campus

                               <u>STUDENT CENTER THEATER, NORTH CAMPUS</u>

2:00 - 3:00   Robert N. Keane, Conference-Director
                               Chair, Dept. of English

                               Introductions

                               Justin Kaplan, Featured Speaker
                               Cambridge, MA

                               "Whitman and the Biographers."

3:00 - 4:30   <u>PANEL II - WHITMAN'S STYLE AND APPROACH</u>

                               Chair: Arthur Gregor
                                       Dept. of English, Hofstra University

                               "Whitman's Body, Whitman's Language."
                               Jon Rosenblatt, Rhode Island College
                               Providence, RI

                               "Running Aground in Barnegat Bay: Whitman's Symbols
                                 and Their Rhetorical Intentionalities."
                               Gregory Haynes, University of Virginia
                               Charlottesville, VA

CONCERT PROGRAM

Friday, April 25
8:30 pm

WALT WHITMAN IN POETRY AND SONG

Elizabeth Watson - Reading and Commentary

The Island Chamber Ensemble

Betsy Vondrasek, Director

Betsy Vondrasek - Soprano
Ann Brickner - Mezzo-Soprano
Donald Dwyer - Baritone

Susanne Butterfield - Flute
Mark Dolliver - Clarinet
Diana Mundy - Cello
William Goldberg - Piano

Hamburg Sonata-- C.P.E. Bach

To You (Stranger)-- Ned Rorem
      Betsy Vondrasek, Ann Brickner, Donald Dwyer

As Adam early in the morning--- Ned Rorem
      Donald Dwyer

A Noiseless patient spider-- Robert Wochinger
      Betsy Vondrasek, Ann Brickner

Sometimes with one I love--- Ned Rorem
      Betsy Vondrasek

Out of the cradle endlessly rocking--------------------------------- Robert Sanders
      Betsy Vondrasek, Ann Brickner, Donald Dwyer, Susanne Butterfield

Shine, shine, shine--- Ben Ludlow
      Betsy Vondrasek, Ann Brickner

I hear bravuras of birds--- Mary Heurtley
      Betsy Vondrasek, Ann Brickner, Susanne Butterfield,
      Diana Mundy, Mark Dolliver

Lo the most excellent sun-- William Goldberg
      Betsy Vondrasek, Ann Brickner

Reconciliation--- Vaughan Williams
      Betsy Vondrasek, Ann Brickner, Donald Dwyer

By the bivouac's fitful flame--- William Goldberg
    Betsy Vondrasek

When lilacs last in the dooryard bloom'd----------------------------- Robert Sanders
    Betsy Vondrasek, Ann Brickner, Donald Dwyer

Sing on in the swamp-- Paul Hindemith
    Ann Brickner

On the distant waves sail countless ships------------------------------ Mary Heurtley
    Donald Dwyer, Mark Dolliver

Thou knowest my years entire-- Mary Heurtley
    Betsy Vondrasek, Ann Brickner, Susanne Butterfield,
    Diana Mundy, Mark Dolliver

The mystic trumpeter--- Ben Ludlow
    Betsy Vondrasek, Mark Dolliver

Sing me the universal--- Vincent Persichetti
    Betsy Vondrasek, Ann Brickner, Donald Dwyer

Elizabeth Watson, former curator of the Walt Whitman Birthplace, is lecturer and writer, author of the newly published Guests of My Life. She is wife of the moderator of Friends World College, Lloyd Harbor.

Betsy Vondrasek and Ann Brickner have sung in churches on Long Island and have given song recitals both in the solo and duet repertoire.

Donald Dwyer of Lloyd Harbor, has sung in churches and in recital on Long Island. He is Professor of Art History at C.W. Post College.

Susanne Butterfield plays in the Huntington Choral Society Orchestra and in small groups. She teaches flute in her home in Huntington.

Mark Dolliver plays clarinet in chamber groups and is Professor of Music at C.W. Post College.

Diana Mundy plays the cello in small groups and in churches in Oyster Bay and Lattingtown.

William Goldberg is a composer, pianist, accompanist for singers, and teaches piano in his home in Northport.

Sponsored by the Nassau County Office of Cultural Development
    Marcia E. O'Brien, Director

Friday, April 25, 1980 (cont'd.)

3:00 - 4:30

"Reading Whitman Psychoanalytically."
Stephen A. Black, Simon Fraser University
Burnaby, B.C. Canada

"Whitman's Vision of Unity: A 'New Physics' Approach."
Jonel C. Sallee, University of Kentucky
Lexington, KY

4:30 - 6:00

PANEL III - WALT WHITMAN AND DEMOCRATIC VISTAS

Chair: Mariabianca Tedeschini Lalli
        University of Rome, Rome, Italy
        Fellow, Society for the Humanities
        Cornell University, Ithaca, NY

"The American Context of Democratic Vistas."
Robert J. Scholnick, College of William and Mary
Williamsburg, VA

"Whitman's Democratic Vista in the Making of the
   First Leaves of Grass."
Jerome Loving, Texas A & M University
College Station, TX

"The Lament in 'Song of the Broad-Axe.'"
David Cavitch, Tufts University
Medford, MA

"'**America always Pictorial!**' Whitman and
   Landscape Painting."
Philip Herzbrun, Georgetown University
Washington, D.C.

6:00

Banquet Multi-Purpose Room, Student Center, South Campus

Cash Bar

Greetings from Hofstra University

Special Addresses:

Walt Whitman Holdings in New York and Washington, D.C.

John C. Broderick, Library of Congress
Washington, D.C.

Francis O. Mattson, Rare Book Division
New York Public Library, New York, NY

Concert

Walt Whitman in Poetry and Song (See page 6)

<u>Saturday, April 26, 1980</u>

8:00 - 9:00 A.M.   Continental Breakfast - Dining Rooms ABC
                                    Student Center, North Campus

9:00 - 10:30   PANEL IV - WALT WHITMAN ON WOMEN

                         Chair: Joann Krieg
                                 Dept. of English, Hofstra University

                         "Walt Whitman and the New Morality."
                         James T. F. Tanner, North Texas State University
                         Long Beach, CA

                         "Walt Whitman's Pose and the Ethics of
                         Sexual Liberation."
                         M. J. Killingsworth, University of Tennessee
                         Knoxville, TN

10:45 - 12:15   PANEL V - WALT WHITMAN AND HOMOSEXUALITY

                         Chair: Hyman Lichtenstein
                                 Dept. of English, Hofstra University

                         "'Drum-Taps' and Nineteenth-Century Male
                         Homosexual Literature."
                         Joseph Cady
                         New York, NY

                         "Whitman's Homosexual Disguises."
                         Alan Helms, University of Massachusetts-Boston
                         Boston, MA

                         "Whitman's 'Here is Adhesiveness': From Friendship
                         to Homosexuality."
                         Michael Lynch, Erindale College, Univ. of Toronto
                         Mississauga, Ontario, Canada

12:15 - 1:15   <u>Lunch</u> Dining Rooms ABC, Student Center, North Campus

1:30 - 3:00   PANEL VI - WALT WHITMAN AND OTHER WRITERS

                         Chair: Stanley Brodwin
                                 Dept. of English, Hofstra University

                         "Kingdom of <u>This</u> World: Whitman and Nietzsche Compared."
                         Adrian Del Caro, University of California
                         Riverside, CA

                         "Whitman's Re-Vision of Emersonian Ecstasy in
                         'Song of Myself.'"
                         John J. Gatta, Jr., The University of Connecticut
                         Storrs, CT

                         "Lear and the <u>Leaves of Grass</u> Poet."
                         Dennis K. Renner, Gannon University
                         Erie, PA

<u>Saturday, April 26, 1980 (cont'd.)</u>

1:30 - 3:00	"'Taking All Hints to Use Them': The Sources of 'Out of the Cradle Endlessly Rocking.'" Michael Vande Berg, University of Illinois at Urbana-Champaign, Urbana, IL
3:30	Bus to Walt Whitman Birthplace
4:00 - 6:00	Visit and Reception - Walt Whitman Birthplace
6:00	Return to Hofstra University

CREDIT for the success of the Conference goes to more people than can be named on this program, but those below deserve a special vote of thanks:

HOFSTRA UNIVERSITY OFFICERS: James M. Shuart, President
Harold E. Yuker, Provost
Robert C. Vogt, Dean, HCLAS

ARA Slater: Bob Meyn

DAVID FILDERMAN GALLERY: Department of Special Collections
Marguerite M. Regan, Director
Nancy Herb
Anne Rubino

ENGLISH DEPARTMENT: Barbara Stroh, Senior Executive Secretary
Nancy Mumolo, Secretary to the Faculty

HOFSTRA LIBRARY ASSOCIATES: Walter Fillin, President

HOFSTRA UNIVERSITY LIBRARY: Charles R. Andrews, Dean

OFFICE OF THE SECRETARY: Robert D. Noble, Secretary
Armand Troncone
Doris Brown and Staff

SCHEDULING OFFICE: Margaret Shields

UCCIS: Marilyn Seidman, Conference Secretary
Liorah Golomb, Student Assistant

UNIVERSITY RELATIONS: Harold Klein, Director
Brian Ballweg, Assistant Director

GREETINGS

I keep thinking of Walt Whitman and what he would say if he knew people like you
are meeting in his month - his April - and in a country-side he once knew, to speak
of him and to let him speak. He wouldn't know his Republic now but he would know you
and you will feel his love.

> Archibald MacLeish
> Uphill Farm
> Conway, MA

With my best wishes for a very successful conference.

> Roger M. Asselineau
> Université de Paris-Sorbonne
> Paris, France

I think it is admirable that Hofstra University under your leadership is undertaking
a Conference on Walt Whitman next Spring in celebration of the 125th anniversary of the
1855 <u>Leaves of Grass</u>.

Good luck in your great venture.

> Harold W. Blodgett
> Schenectady, NY

I think your occasion is a deserving one, and I wish you the best of conferences.

> Leo Marx
> William R. Kenan, Jr., Professor
> of American Cultural History
> Massachusetts Institute of Technology
> Cambridge, MA

All best wishes for a successful conference.

> James E. Miller, Jr.
> Chairman, Department of English
> The University of Chicago
> Chicago, IL

I wish you a successful Conference.

> Floyd Stovall
> University of Virginia
> Charlottesville, VA

Please accept my very best wishes for the success of this venture. I had a late
"conversion" to Whitman and so am glad to see the increasing recognition which is at
last coming to him.

> Willard Thorp
> Princeton University
> Princeton, NJ

NOTES

Index

About the Contributors

HAROLD ASPIZ is Professor of English at California State University, Long Beach. He is the author of *Walt Whitman and the Body Beautiful* and has published many articles on Whitman, Herman Melville, and Mark Twain. His work often focuses on the relations between literature and the physiological and quasi-medical sciences.

STEPHEN A. BLACK is Professor of English at Simon Fraser University and is a graduate of the Seattle Psychoanalytic Institute where he is currently a faculty member. Hs is the author of *Whitman's Journey into Chaos*. His articles have appeared in major scholarly journals. He is presently writing a book about the late plays of Eugene O'Neill.

WILLIAM BURRISON is a playwright, poet, and journalist who has taught American literature at Rutgers University, has an M.S. in secondary education, and has done graduate work in American civilization at the University of Pennsylvania. He is working on a study of images of the American athlete in film.

JOSEPH CADY is an independent scholar, poet, and psychotherapist in New York. Formerly an Assistant Professor of English at Columbia University and Rutgers University, he has also taught creative writing or gay literature at Hofstra University, SUNY at Purchase, the New School for Social Research, and the Colorado College. His poems have appeared in *The American Poetry Review* and other noted poetry journals, and he has been a MacDowell Colony Fellow.

DAVID CAVITCH is Professor of English at Tufts University and formerly has held appointments at other universities. His principal scholarly interest is the reciprocal relation between literary expression and personal experience. He is the author of *D. H. Lawrence and the New World* and, most recently, of *My Soul and I: The Inner LIfe of Walt Whitman*.

ADRIAN DEL CARO is Associate Professor of German at Louisiana State University. He is the author of *Dionysian Aesthetics*, a book on Friedrich Nietzsche, and of several articles dealing with major German thinkers. Some of his literary translations can be read in *The German Mind of the Nineteenth Century*, edited by Hermann Glaser.

JOHN GATTA, Jr., is Associate Professor at the University of Connecticut, Storrs, and has taught at the University of Missouri. A student of early American literature and of the interplay between religious faith and literary imagination, he has published articles on writers such as Nathaniel Hawthorne, Edward Taylor, and T. S. Eliot.

GREGORY HAYNES wrote "Running Aground in Barnegat Bay: Whitman's Symbols and Their Rhetorical Intentionalities" in 1979 at the outset of his work on rhetoric and symbol in English and American romanticism. He published a correspondent essay on interpretation and the poetic act in Whitman, "Reading Whitman's Meanings and 'The Dalliance of the Eagles,' " in *Walt Whitman Review* in 1981. A University of Virginia Ph.D., he lives in Memphis.

ALAN HELMS is Associate Professor of English at the University of Massachusetts at Boston and has taught at Rutgers University and the University of Paris. His principal research interests, besides Whitman, are prosody and the relations between literature and the visual arts. At present he is engaged in a book-length study of Whitman's work.

MILTON HINDUS is now Professor Emeritus of English at Brandeis University where he was formerly Edytha Macy Gross Professor of Humanities. He is the author or editor of twelve books, the latest of which is *Charles Reznikoff: Man and Poet*. He has also published a book of his own poems. His volume *Leaves of Grass: One Hundred Years After* was awarded the Walt Whitman Prize by the Poetry Society of America.

JUSTIN KAPLAN, of Cambridge, Massachusetts, is the author of *Walt Whitman: A Life*, published in 1980. Among his other books are *Lincoln Steffens* and *Mr. Clemens and Mark Twain*, which won the Pulitzer Prize for Biography and the National Book Award in Arts and Letters. He is currently at work on a biography of Charlie Chaplin.

M. J. KILLINGSWORTH is an Associate Professor of English at New Mexico Institute of Mining and Technology. He has published articles on

American literature and intellectual history in such journals as *American Literature*, *ESQ: A Journal of the American Renaissance*, and *Walt Whitman Review*.

JOANN P. KRIEG is Assistant Professor in the American Studies Program of the Department of English at Hofstra University, Hempstead, New York. She has contributed articles to *Walt Whitman Quarterly Review*, *British Journal of American Studies*, *American Transcendentalist Quarterly*, and *New York State Folklore Journal*.

JEROME LOVING is Professor of English at Texas A&M University and was previously Visiting Professor of American Literature at the Université de Paris, Sorbonne. His books include *Emerson, Whitman, and the American Muse*.

HOWARD L. PARSONS is Professor and Chairman of the Department of Philosophy, University of Bridgeport. He has taught at the University of Southern California, University of Illinois, University of Tennessee, Teachers College of Columbia University, Coe College, Idaho State College, and Victoria College (British Columbia), and he has been a lecturer at Moscow State University. Among his works are *Humanism and Marx's Thought, Man East and West, Marx and Engels on Ecology* (Greenwood Press, 1977). With John Somerville, he co-edited *Dialogues on the Philosophy of Marxism* (Greenwood Press, 1974).

DENNIS K. RENNER is Associate Professor of English at Gannon University where he teaches a graduate seminar on the American Renaissance. He has published several Whitman essays, the most recent of which, "Tradition for a Time of Crisis: Whitman's Prophetic Stance," appears in *Poetic Prophecy in Western Literature*, edited by Raymond Jean-Frontain.

JON ROSENBLATT is Associate Professor of English at Rhode Island College. He has written *Sylvia Plath: The Poetry of Initiation* and edited a book of essays on symbolist aesthetics. His essay on Whitman forms part of an ongoing study of modernist poetry and its uneasy relationship with its nineteenth-century sources in Whitman and symbolism.

ROBERT J. SCHOLNICK is Professor of English and Director of the American Studies Program at the College of William and Mary. He is the author of *Edmund Clarence Stedman* and counts four articles on Whitman among his shorter studies of nineteenth-century American literature and culture.

JAMES T. F. TANNER is Associate Professor of English at North Texas State University and has had a sustained interest in Walt Whitman scholarship. He is the author of *Walt Whitman: A Supplementary Bibliography, 1961-1967*, as well as several articles on Whitman.

WILLIAM WHITE is Visiting Professor of English at University of Southern California, after having taught for 30 years at Wayne State University and seven at Oakland University. He has held numerous visiting posts at universities here and abroad and has been a Fulbright lecturer in Korea. Since 1955 he has been co-editor of the *Walt Whitman Quarterly Review*. He is one of eight editors of *The Collected Writings of Walt Whitman* and has written or edited 39 books and 2500 articles and reviews.

Hofstra University's
Cultural and Intercultural Studies
Coordinating Editor, Alexej Ugrinsky

George Sand Papers: Conference Proceedings, 1976
(Editorial Board: Natalie Datlof, Edwin L. Dunbaugh, Frank S. Lambasa, Gabrielle Savet, William S. Shiver, Alex Szogyi)

George Sand Papers: Conference Proceedings, 1978
(Editorial Board: Natalie Datlof, Edwin L. Dunbaugh, Frank S. Lambasa, Gabrielle Savet, William S. Shiver, Alex Szogyi)

George Sand Papers: Conference Proceedings, 1978
(Editorial Board: Natalie Datlof, Edwin L. Dunbaugh, Frank S. Lambasa, Gabrielle Savet, William S. Shiver, Alex Szogyi)

Heinrich von Kleist Studies
(Editorial Board: Alexej Ugrinsky, Frederick J. Churchill, Frank S. Lambasa, Robert F. von Berg)

William Cullen Bryant Studies
(Editors: Stanley Brodwin, Michael D'Innocenzo)

*Walt Whitman: Here and Now
(Editor: Joann P. Krieg)

---

*Available from Greenwood Press